S0-FCB-591

What's Ethical in Business?

Verne E. Henderson

McGraw-Hill, Inc.

New York   St. Louis   San Francisco   Auckland   Bogotá
Caracas   Lisbon   London   Madrid   Mexico   Milan
Montreal   New Delhi   Paris   San Juan   São Paulo
Singapore   Sydney   Tokyo   Toronto

Library of Congress Cataloging-in-Publication Data

Henderson, Verne.
    What's ethical in business? / Verne Henderson.
        p.   cm.
    Includes index.
    ISBN 0-07-028173-4 — ISBN 0-07-028174-2 (pbk.)
    1. Business ethics. I. Title.
  HF5337.H46 1992
  174'.4—dc20   91-45923
                                                CIP

Copyright © 1992 by McGraw-Hill, Inc. All rights reserved. Printed in the United States of America. Except as permitted under the United States Copyright Act of 1976, no part of this publication may be reproduced or distributed in any form or by any means, or stored in a data base or retrieval system, without the prior written permission of the publisher.

1 2 3 4 5 6 7 8 9 0 DOC/DOC 9 8 7 6 5 4 3 2

ISBN 0-07-028173-4 {HC}
ISBN 0-07-028174-2 {PBK}

The sponsoring editors for this book were Theodore Nardin and Barbara Toniolo, the editing supervisor was Jim Halston, and the production supervisor was Pamela A. Pelton. This book was set in Baskerville. It was composed by McGraw-Hill's Professional Book Group composition unit.

Printed and bound by R. R. Donnelley & Sons Company.

Contents

Preface

People throughout the world are becoming increasingly quick to cry out "That's unethical!" How do they know what's unethical? If you disagree with them, how are you going to decide who's right? And if your business interests are linked with those with whom you disagree, how do you find some common understanding about what's ethical? That prolific playwright George Bernard Shaw cynically remarked, "When you prevent me from doing anything I want to do that is persecution; but when I prevent you from doing anything you want to do, that is law, order, and morals." There is a human tendency, in other words, to label our perspective as ethical and the behavior of others as unethical. As the global economy continues to take shape, we must find ways to accommodate our differences.

This book introduces the Ethical Algorithm as an instrument to help people reason together toward peaceful and ethical ends. It is a product of two underlying assumptions:

1. What's ethical can no longer be determined by your conscience, by gut feelings. Like guilty feelings, these intuitions may tell us that something is wrong but not necessarily what's right.

2. What's ethical cannot be brought down from a mountaintop carved in tablets of stone. Who would write them? Who would obey them? Who would accept them without criticism, comment, or correction?

It is necessary to take a situational approach to business ethics, as the word *algorithm* implies. What's ethical in business depends on a lot of variables. The book identifies those variables, largely the various constituents of business whose expectations must be satisfied. Not only are the expectations of business constituents changing rapidly, but business also faces a measurably different set of constituents and different industries face different kinds of dilemmas. Thus, what's ethical depends on the situation: We live in a new age.

The Ethical Algorithm provides the analytical framework for actual case studies and concrete examples of corporations and executives caught up in ethical dilemmas. Specific suggestions for implementing ethical action plans emerge from the analysts. Readers will have a chance to test their ethical IQ in Chapter 2 and learn how to get a higher grade the second time around. Executives and board members will gain new insights on how to cultivate an ethical climate in the later chapters.

What's ethical in business in this new age will have to be heated in the crucible of controversy and hammered out on the anvil of compromise. Business leaders must devote more time and develop new skills to match this challenge. This book will help each reader take up that challenge.

Acknowledgments

Life is a process of accumulating and discharging debts. Not all of those debts are measured in dollars. Authors, for instance, often discover only in the act of writing just how huge their debts truly are. That is true in my case. I cannot hope to discharge them with simple words of thanks. But I can acknowledge them. I am indebted to many relatives, friends, and professional colleagues over the years who have given or stimulated one or more of the ideas in this book. I must specifically mention parishioners in churches I have served, numerous business executives, present and former professors at the Sloan School of Management at M.I.T., and that marvelous mixture of people at the Arthur D. Little Management Education Institute—the support staff, my professional colleagues, and students over twelve years from more than 40 countries around the world. I am indebted to Dr. Robert B. McKerzie, Dean of Research at the Sloan School at M.I.T., for his help on selected chapters, and to Barbara Toniolo of McGraw-Hill for help on every chapter. My greatest debt is to my wife who has helped me shape my entire life.

Verne E. Henderson
Brookline, Massachusetts

Introduction: The Past Is Prologue

"Frankly, I think we'll regret introducing these organisms into the environment."

Drawing by Lorenz; © 1987 The New Yorker Magazine, Inc.

What's Happened to Business Ethics?

Standards Are Up

Ethical standards, whether formal or informal, have changed tremendously in the last century. Boldly stated, no one can make the case that ethical standards have fallen in the latter decades of the twentieth century. The reverse is true. Standards are considerably higher. Businesspeople themselves, as well as the public, expect more sensitive behavior in the conduct of economic enterprise. The issue is not just having the standards, however. It is living up to them. Determining the degree to which business has complied with established standards presents a real problem. Compliance by itself is difficult to quantify. Comparing ethical compliance between widely separated decades is virtually impossible. In any event, whether compliance has *verifiably* fallen appears to be of less concern than the judgment that a sizable number of citizens *feel* as if it has fallen. How easily we forget.

An Unsavory Past

To the ethical purist, big business in America has an odious past. Even the most myopic magnates cannot read some of the more sordid stories of the industrial development of the United States over the last hundred years and find ethical justification for the destruction of people, natural resources, public trust, and the hopes and dreams of millions of impoverished immigrants to the promised land. Thomas Carlyle opined that "history...is but the biography of great men." The unsavory exploitations of the previous century are largely the biographies of prominent businesspeople. Many of them were not simply greedy; they were mean. They were not simply competitive; their aggression was unbridled. Some of these tales are vicious. There are chapters in the exuberant saga of our industrial development that embarrass even the hardened cynic.

Cornelius Vanderbilt was variously viewed as a pirate, unpredictably generous, viciously competitive, totally unforgiving, unremittingly selfish. His competitors were his enemies. He stopped short only of killing them. Near death and with little to gain financially, he directed a fierce pricing battle on his New York Central railroad, believing, apparently, that his honor was at stake. Competition was his life's blood.

Jim Fisk and Jay Gould, both railroad men, were rogues in the eyes of their contemporaries. Double-dealing, watered stock, and goon squads were tactics they used more than once. The war of the Erie railroad was just that, with corresponding generals, foot soldiers, and casualties in the thousands. Considering the sordid birth of this industry, personified by these two men, it is little wonder that railroads spawned the most vicious, self-serving unions in our nation's history. Their bitterly acquired stranglehold on wages and job descriptions continues to haunt the industry today.

John D. Rockefeller, founder of Standard Oil, was said to regularly use underhanded and sometimes illegal high-pressure tactics in his relentless drive to monopolize the oil industry. Tales are spun wherein he took unfair advantage of widows and children, rarely told all the truth, and consistently "persuaded" public officials to switch their votes in his favor. Like the railroads, the oil industry continues to be plagued by problems from its past: a deep public distrust and easily awakened anger.

Philip D. Armour, founder of the company which still bears his name, also created among the slaughterhouses of Chicago one of the most successful industrial pools of his era. A *pool* was the nineteenth-century version of price collusion. It was technically legal but hardly ethical. Victims of the Big Four slaughterhouses included just about everybody: the ranchers and farmers, railroads, employees, consumers, and competitors. Upton Sinclair turned the inside story of this industry into a popular and polarizing novel, *The Jungle*. Consider the impact upon the reader of this single incident in his book: because of poor safety measures on the part of a greedy employer, one of the young meat cutters falls into a vat and is turned into calf's jelly, which is presumedly packaged and sent to market.

John Pierpont Morgan, one of the more respected names of his time, was not above a personal, destructive bidding war with Edward Harriman over the Northern Pacific railroad. J. P. was one of the few early capitalists who both inherited money and received a college education. Nevertheless, his financial prowess rather than his business ethics distinguished him from his colleagues. He was a very complex man who simultaneously dared to appear in public with his mistress as well as cultivate a role as the nation's leading Episcopalian benefactor, giving generously of his time, treasury, and talented baritone voice.

Andrew Carnegie, whom Mark Twain dubbed "Saint Andrew," died with lingering regret over the labor uprising at one of his steel plants. As he put it in his own autobiography: "No pangs remain of any wound received in my business career save that of Homestead."[1] At his beloved Homestead plant, his first and finest Bessemer steel factory, built as a showcase for the entire world, Carnegie failed to live up to his own high

ethical standards. Workers were brutalized. Nevertheless, Carnegie continued to be viewed as an apostle of "sweetness and light" in American labor-
management relations. Carnegie also confessed to using borrowed money
and insider information to assemble his first pile of capital. This was considered exceedingly clever, rather than unethical, in that era.

Changing Expectations

Neither ethical standards nor compliance has fallen in recent decades.
Our expectations have risen. Hopes have run ahead of deeds. The distinguishing characteristic of the late twentieth century is the gargantuan
growth in our ethical expectations. In the United States these rising aspirations are largely by-products of our affluence and idealistic propen-
sities. Environmentalism, for example, can be viewed as just the newest
item on that list of rising expectations. Lester Thurow, noted economist
and Dean of the Sloan School of Management at MIT, cynically observed that "a developer is someone who wants to build a cabin in the
woods this year. A conservationist is someone who built one there last
year."[2] He formalized this perspective in his book.

> Environmentalism is a demand for more goods and services (clean
> air, water, and so forth) that does not differ from other consumption
> demands except that it can only be achieved collectively....
> environmentalism is a natural product of a rising real standard of
> living. We have simply reached the point where, for many Ameri-
> cans, the next item on their acquisitive agenda is a cleaner
> environment.[3]

Competition for these latest acquisitions is intense. Since our political
mechanisms for allocating these fashionable goodies are imperfect, the
ethics of acquisition is equally blurred.

Ethics Is Process

Not only are today's ethical expectations higher, some are in conflict or
mutually exclusive. Some are simply impossible. Moreover, as we review
the tales of corporate crime and ethical malfeasance, one conclusion is
inescapable. Many managers and executives were simply unclear about
their ethical standards. They were unprepared. What's ethical in business is a never-ending process of clarifying, resolving, and stimulating a
nobler vision of the common good. It is a process. Given the present
state of the world, that process will never be completed. Perhaps this is
what it means to have been kicked out of the Garden of Eden. We have

lost our innocence. We now have full control of and responsibility for our own behavior and that of our societies.

Putting our past into proper ethical perspective requires that we concentrate rather exclusively on the unsavory and unethical. We need to understand the past in order to learn from it. We will try to avoid unwarranted praise, pie-eyed optimism, or unexamined condemnation in subsequent chapters.

It is simply not true, for instance, that the early tycoons were out-and-out robber barons with no social sensitivities whatsoever. Even in his penny-pinching days, John D. Rockefeller contributed regularly and generously to various charities, including his church. Hard-nosed J. P. Morgan was undoubtedly the source of the cliché "staunch supporter of the church." He was an active Episcopalian all his life, so fond of singing hymns that he often arranged a late afternoon songfest with only the church organist and himself present. Jim Hill, backsliding Protestant and builder of the Northern Pacific railroad, whose personal life and business dealings were scandalous beyond measure, gave $1 million to establish a Roman Catholic theological seminary in St. Paul, Minnesota. His reasoning: "No nation can exist without a true religious spirit behind it. Laws that forbid teaching Christianity are the weakest thing in our government."[4] Unfortunately, these nobler sensibilities from deep within the capitalists' hearts were markedly restrained in their business dealings. It eventually fell to the state and federal governments to regulate and legislate the standards business failed to create for itself.

Let the Government Do It

Politicians as Ethicists

Free enterprise rests on the assumption that the role of government in business should be limited so that markets are free to respond to natural fluctuations in supply and demand. Defining that limit has proved to be an inexact science over the past century. Business misconduct has pressured federal and state governments to expand their powers over business. These efforts have been ambiguous and ambivalent, vacillating with the political climate and fortunes of the nation. Following the Civil War, governments tended to be supportive to a fault. Public officials were certainly no more reliable than the industrialists in upholding high ethical standards. In the minds of some, government officials served the public very poorly.

> Government has been the indispensable handmaiden of private wealth since the origin of society....It is a challenging fact that most

of the natural resources owned today by the United States Steel Corporation, the Aluminum Company, the Standard Oil Company, the railroads, and, in fact, nearly all private corporations, were in 1860 communally owned under political auspices.[5]

The transfer of those resources to private industry was ethically defended in the halls of Congress by considerations of "the good of the country." There were few guarantees, however, that the private hands which grasped the government's gratuity fully embraced the public responsibility it carried. Few were as bold and straightforward as William Vanderbilt when he was confronted on his point. He stormed, "The public be damned.... I am working for my stockholders." It evidently never occurred to him that he was indebted to the public coffers. The entrepreneurial emphasis fell on getting rather than giving.

State and federal officials were often accused of colluding rather than clashing with business leaders. Alas, elected officials by the score have accepted bribes and "rebates" for favors bestowed upon enterprising colleagues. In some cases, as with former California governor and later Senator Leland Stanford, the lines separating conflict of interest and obligation were blurred altogether.

Legislating Ethics

The passage of the Sherman Antitrust Act in 1890 served as an early watershed in defining the government's role in regulating business. The federal government openly and successfully challenged the power of big business. The impact of this legislation began to be felt in the early years of the next century. Interestingly enough, it led to legislative reform. Prior to 1910, national senators had been chosen by state legislatures. So many rich businessmen were appointed to the Senate that it was called the "Millionaires Club." Naturally, it was pro-business. The adoption of the Seventeenth Amendment in 1913, providing for the popular election of senators, reduced the power of the states and business interests somewhat. These were crude measures, however, and left the fundamental questions of what's ethical in business unanswered. It was a time of economic expansion. Neither business nor governments wished to slow the engines of industry.

The Pressures for Change Grow

Calvin Coolidge remarked that "the business of America is business." "Cool Cal" delivered his presidential benediction during a decade of unprecedented prosperity. The catastrophic stock market crash of 1929 ended that era. Government during the Roaring Twenties contributed little to better business ethics. The depression years of the 1930s introduced a profound sobriety into conversations about business conduct. Legislation during the first two terms of President Roosevelt created substantial changes in business behavior and feeling. Federal and state authorities flexed their muscles. An adversarial attitude emerged. World War II placed the controversy in limbo for half a decade. But after the war, business again resumed its dominant position in American society under the patriotic umbrella of "life, liberty, and the pursuit of happiness." Doing well received a higher priority than doing good.

World War II had planted deep seeds of change, however. These new expectations came to full bloom in the 1960s. The material well-being of our citizens, measured relative to each other and the rest of the world, supplanted weather as a favorite topic of conversation. Leaders at state and federal levels spawned a raft of new social legislation that again radically challenged the ethics of business. Some of the legislation, however well intended, was provincial in the extreme, poorly written or ill-conceived. Nevertheless, government emerged as a serious contender for the role of business ethicist. From an ethical perspective, government has become the most powerful critic and rectifier of business misconduct — not because politicians are ethically superior or government is uniquely equipped to undertake this task, but unfortunately because corporations, large corporations in particular, have not demonstrated to the satisfaction of their various constituents that they can respond to the changing ethical expectations in the marketplace. They are inviting the dissociation of the word *free* from *enterprise*. If business leaders begin to respond to the heightened hopes of employees and customers, government might not be forced to legislate their ethics.

Business Leaders Can Take Charge

This book will focus on what business leaders can do to retain some autonomy and discretionary control of the ethical side of enterprise. More specifically, what kind of leadership and action are required of business if it aspires to use its power and freedom responsibly? What can we learn from past mistakes? What insights can we gain for the future? What visions of a better world emerge from a candid view of what has gone before?

The ethics of business in the United States has come a long way in the last century. Standards and expectations have indeed risen. The voices of the multitudes have been unleashed. There can be no turning back on these heightened ethical expectations, no matter how difficult or irreconcilable they may appear. Even President Bush expressed the hope that we might become a "gentler and kinder nation." Why not?

Our forebears faced a similar challenge. An analogy from frontier days frames the dilemma very well. The men and women who tamed the west first had to tame the horses which played a major role in their conquest. Contrary to Hollywood portrayals, breaking a horse to ride or use as a draft animal is a delicate chore. You can go too far. You can break a horse's spirit instead of just gain essential control. The hardest-working horses had the most spirit. You wanted to retain as much of the animal's spirit as possible. Consequently, the struggle for control with the best horses was never over. Shaping the ethics of business requires the same delicate handling. We want to awaken and cultivate the gentleness in the hearts of businesspeople without breaking their spirits.

Footnotes

1. John Brooks, *The Autobiography of American Business*, Doubleday, Garden City, N.Y., 1974.
2. Lester C. Thurow, class lecture, Massachusetts Institute of Technology, Cambridge, Mass. The concept is developed at some length in the book cited in note 3, pp. 16–19.
3. Lester C. Thurow, *The Zero-Sum Society: Distribution and the Possibilities for Economic Change*, Basic Books, New York, 1980, pp. 104–105.
4. Matthew Josephson, *The Robber Barons: The Great American Capitalists*, Harcourt Brace Jovanovich, New York, 1934, p. 320.
5. Ferdinand Lundberg, *America's 60 Families*, Vanguard Press, New York, 1937, pp. 50, 53.

1
It's a New Age

"IF WE RUN INTO ANY TRICKY PROBLEMS, WE CAN NOW TURN TO YOUNG MITCHELL, HERE. HE GOT AN A' IN BUSINESS ETHICS."

© 1991 by Sidney Harris—*The Wall Street Journal.*

You're the Boss: What Would You Do?

Imagine that you are the chief executive officer (CEO) of a century-old creator and manufacturer of popular children's games and toys located in staid New England. One of your company's newest sensations is a kit of plastic and rubber rivets with a riveting tool to build lots of different kinds of magical playthings. Nearly half a million young children already use your product. Sales are rising. It's possible that Riviton, presently racking up gross sales of about $8 million, might eventually outsell your more famous product, Monopoly. Then it happens. An eight-year-old boy in Wisconsin has been playing with your toy pleasurably and safely for weeks. For reasons even his parents can't explain, he stuck one of the tiny rivets into his mouth and choked to death. Unfortunately, this is a true story. The company was Parker Brothers of Salem, Massachusetts.

The Wall Street Journal quoted then-company president Randolph G. Barton: "It was a freak accident. After all, peanuts are the greatest cause of strangulation among children, and nobody advocates banning the peanut."[1]

How would you handle this problem product if you were CEO? Would you ignore this isolated incident? Remember that this is the late 1970s. Earlier in the decade Congress created the Consumer Product Safety Commission (CPSC). Broad powers were bestowed upon this controversial federal agency to set design standards, stimulate safe product usage, demand recalls, and sue manufacturers in both state and federal courts. This new law does not preclude the exercise of your own conscience, of course. It does suggest that customers' ethical expectations are rising. Fair or not, many buyers expect considerably more product safety and quality for the same price from sellers today. What would you do about Riviton? Wait? Undertake additional research of either your product or ones similar to it? Put bold warnings on the package: "This product in intended for boys and girls 10 years of age and older"? Add disclaimers such as "Not responsible for accidental deaths due to..."? How would you decide? On what would you base your decision? Would you act alone? Take it to the board of directors? Call a high-level staff meeting? Create a special committee?

To Sell Is to Kill

Parker Brothers crossed its corporate fingers and continued manufacturing and marketing Riviton. Less than a year later a second child strangled on a rivet. Immediately, Parker Brothers halted production and recalled all toys. President Barton said, "The decision was very simple. Were we supposed to sit back and wait for death number 3?"[2] Sales were approaching the $10 million mark. They were perfectly within their legal rights to continue selling Riviton. Their decision not to exercise that legal right was based on ethical considerations, which in this case were a mixture of conscience and fear of negative publicity, or personal values and unacceptable consequences. Let's look at another corporate story.

To Love Is to Lose

Fewer cases convey the multidimensional hazards of chemical waste disposal more dramatically than Love Canal at Niagara Falls, New York. The horror story began to unfold in the mid-1970s as some suspicious statistics on miscarriages and deformed births piled up among pregnant women who lived in Love Canal, an emerging new community of modest homes. Clearly, something was medically amiss. Gradually, some scary facts came to light. The Hooker Chemical Company had used the canal for disposal of chemical waste 30 years earlier. A decade later town leaders decided to develop the old disposal site for a grade school. Hooker company officials warned the school board in memo and public meeting that the area had been used for chemical disposal. Nevertheless, the school board started condemnation proceedings, and Hooker was under threat of losing the land by right of eminent domain. They signed the deed of sale. The price was $1. Despite a warning that Hooker attached regarding future use of the land, an elementary school and tract of houses were soon built next to the contaminated canal.

It is now 1978. Love Canal is still growing with new first-owner homes and new families. The school playground is filled with children. Word spreads that there is some kind of dangerous oozing in one far corner. Whatever the facts, fear is soon rampant. Homeowners and other citizens demand action. State and federal authorities file a lawsuit claiming more than $600 million in damages for failure to prevent the migration of chemicals out of the canal and to warn residents of any danger. The state has already spent nearly $100 million on emergency programs, temporary relocation of residents, and purchase of approximately 200 homes. This figure is included in the $600 million total. Hooker Chemical is dragged into court.

Suppose you are the president of Hooker Chemical Company. What would you do? In addition to the lawsuit, your other sites and situations are being investigated and publicized. You are looking worse and worse in the media. Records clearly indicate that your predecessors sold the land in good faith. You warned the public officials at the time. You gave away the property. Your company executives denied responsibility and mounted a public campaign to state their case. Your company colleagues maintain that the proper procedures had been followed in disposing of the chemicals, but the construction of sewer lines by the town had disturbed the clay linings protecting the waste. You also question the evidence that the chemicals have harmed anyone's health.

There are some additional internal factors you have to consider. Four years ago Hooker Chemical was bought out by Occidental Petroleum Corporation, a multinational conglomerate founded and run by the world-minded Armand Hammer. How will your new bosses react? What do they expect you to do? In the minds of the public you have already been proved unethical. If the case goes to court, there's a good chance you'll be proved illegal as well. You stand to lose both reputation and money. What would you do? Let your conscience be your guide? Has your conscience been schooled in the complexities of the new age? Probably not, but it will get there.

Bad Things Happen to Good Corporations

Parker Brothers and Hooker Chemical share some peculiar ethical attributes:

- Their decisions were undertaken with the best of intentions.
- Their dilemmas were difficult but not impossible to anticipate.
- Their situations arose from something they didn't do rather than did do (omission rather than commission).
- The number of constituents involved relative to their total consumer base was very small.
- The consequences (death or serious illness) were irreversible and no amount of money could fully compensate the victims.
- The cost to the firms, whether measured in time, money, or managerial agony, was very substantial.

On the basis of that list, both companies could justifiably describe themselves as victims. Little wonder if executives involved in ethical dilemmas of this sort feel unjustifiably criticized and misunderstood by the general public. In this new age, bad things do happen to good corporations. Justified or not, the public demands good results as well as good intentions. Ethical expectations are changing.

Threats to the environment and the food supply moved to center stage in the 1980s. There had been a number of major corporate stories arising from pesticide development, manufacture, or usage which reached back a decade or more: Dow Chemical, Allied-Signal, Monsanto, du Pont. A strident tone of alarm entered the conversation as the 1980s wore on. Perhaps the 1983 Union Carbide tragedy in Bhopal, India, triggered the hysteria. That too would be understandable. More than 8000 people died, many as they slept, victims of a poisonous gas seeping through the night air. An Edgar Allan Poe nightmare had come to life. Media coverage of this and other events permitted speedy public reaction to a variety of calamities. For example, at about the same time that actress Meryl Streep was drawing the nation's attention to the dangers of the pesticide Alar, the U.S. embassy in Chile received an anonymous telephone call warning that grapes tainted with cyanide were being shipped to America. The word spread quickly. Imports were embargoed and supplies boycotted. The cost to the Chilean growers was estimated at approximately $250 million. The loss to American retailers was another $750 million. Worse yet, there was still no solid proof that the Chilean grapes were poisonous. Produce importer David Oppenheimer called it "assassination by insinuation."[3]

Good intentions counted for very little in these corporate stories of Parker Brothers, Hooker Chemical, Union Carbide, and the Chilean growers. Such episodes fan the flames of moral indignation. Consumers are confused, frightened, angry. The question of what's ethical in business arises with pressing urgency and growing impatience. When bad things do happen, victims are increasingly inclined to think nobody cares about them, that someone was deliberately careless, that someone ought to pay for their mistakes. Sometimes the victims are right. Sometimes the bad things that happen are followed by lawsuits or legislation. It's a costly process that diminishes the free in enterprise.

What about the corporations? The Parker Brothers story is just one about management which did the right thing. Are the managers always wrong, the ones expected to make amends and adjustments, just because they're big and rich? Unfortunately, a vociferous portion of the populace seems to take this view. It's difficult to know how powerfully it influences others. The news media often appear to be part of a supporting cast of critics. Senior executives are discovering that they not only have to manage the bad thing that happens, they have to manage the public reaction as well. It may seem unfair, but that's the way it is. The senior executive officer is still called the CEO, but it often means "chief ethical officer." An academic field of business ethics has emerged. Not everyone is happy with these various developments. There have been some interesting responses.

The Critics Respond

Management consultant Peter Drucker wonders whether the rising concern about business ethics is just a fad. He is very critical of much of the reasoning and attention given to the subject, referring to it as "ethical chic" rather than real ethics. He even impugns the motives of its devotees.

> Clearly, one major element of the peculiar stew that goes by the name of "business ethics" is plain old-fashioned hostility to business and to economic activity altogether—one of the oldest of American traditions and perhaps the only still-potent ingredient in the Puritan heritage. Otherwise, we would not even talk of "business ethics." There is no warrant in any ethics to consider one major sphere of activity as having its own ethical problems, let alone its own "ethics."[4]

Drucker finds his solution in the Confucian ethics of interdependence. Ethical behavior is to be judged by its "sincerity." Drucker utilizes the oriental understanding of this term: good ethics are "those actions that are appropriate to a specific relationship and make it harmonious and of optimum mutual benefit."[5] That definition invokes the spirit of good old Anglo-Saxon utilitarianism, which asserts that ethical decisions ought to seek the greatest good for the greatest number. Drucker's sincerity appears to divide the burden of ethical proof between the *intentions* of the individual and the *consequences* which ensue. Thus, while Drucker is not sure whether business ethics is little more than a fad, he concludes that greater sincerity is the solution.

Peter Brimelow is also critical of much that passes for business ethics. He notes that "Business school professors, it now appears, have been extracting fees from gullible corporations by hiring themselves out as 'ethics consultants.'"[6] Brimelow cites the case of the traveling salesman who gets a couple of free drink coupons when he checks into his motel. Is it unethical to use them? What if he's offered a $50 "rebate" to stay at that particular motel? Would it be unethical to charge the motel bill to the company and put the $50 in his own pocket? Brimelow avers that "The issue is not remotely 'ethics.' It is economics." While Brimelow remains unclear about his definition of ethics, he worries "that the 'ethics' being imposed are often subtly alien to the free market."

William E. Simon, former U.S. Secretary of the Treasury, is also concerned about ethics and the free market.

> The real question facing the American business community today is not whether it can "afford" stronger ethical standards, but how much longer it can go on without them. Our entire way of life is held together by voluntary, society-wide bonds of mutual trust and respect.[7]

Simon approvingly quotes the former CEO and chairman of the board (COB) of du Pont, Irving Shapiro, in a call for a new, uniform code of ethics to which all large corporations would subscribe. Simon names A. W. Clausen, past president of Bank of America, and former IBM COB Frank T. Carey as supporters of increased attention to business ethics.

Some respondents have implied a solution along with their explanation as to why business ethics suffers. Frank G. Goble, one-time manufacturing executive, cites the decline in the teaching of ethics to our young.

> As long ago as 1966, John Neitz, professor of education at the University of Pittsburgh, found that before 1776 religion and morals accounted for more than 90% of the content of school readers. By 1926 this figure had declined to 6%, and in more recent times had become too small to be measured.[8]

If this is the best explanation and solution, the task of doing something about business ethics falls upon the leaders of our churches, synagogues, temples, and mosques. It certainly wouldn't hurt. But influencing the young is a long-term solution, at best. What should we do now?

J. Irwin Miller was one of the first *Fortune* 500 CEOs to cite the need for better business ethics. A decade before Jimmy Carter launched an attack on the energy crisis by calling for efforts that amounted to the "moral equivalent of war," Miller summoned his colleagues to battle. "Business has a war to win," he argued.

> We are under attack from our workers...our customers...our government...our children...our educators...our church...by the nations we have helped most and that try hardest to imitate us; by racial minorities, who are better off here than in any other nation, and making more rapid progress....I believe that we are truly at a point of crisis...[and]...if we are to control our condition...It could mean going to war, with respect to our domestic problems.[9]

Business did not mount a war on the scale that Miller sought. Now, more than two decades later, some are still wondering whether the war has been won, lost, or proved unnecessary. Does the ethics of business deserve the attention it's receiving?

Have Business Ethics Gotten Worse?

Each day the news media bring us the latest developments in consumer complaints or corporate catastrophe. If they are not of the "continuing saga" type, we get the "it has just been revealed" variety. Unethical business behavior is everywhere, depending on your definition. Federal courts sentence more than 350 companies for criminal violations each year; state courts sentence thousands more.[10] As informal discussions of what's ethical have become more frequent and clamorous, more and more employees at all corporate levels cynically acknowledge that they've known about one or more ethical transgressions all along. Has corporate behavior really gotten worse? Or are we just becoming better informed about it? Let's review some of the facts and factors that make it so difficult to answer that question.

Business Leaders Disagree

"Is the ethics of business changing?" Steven Brenner and Earl Molander addressed this issue in a longitudinal study of approximately 1200 readers of the *Harvard Business Review*. Their comparison of perceptions encompassed the years between 1961 and 1976.[11] The answers they received revealed deep disagreement as to whether business ethics have changed, that is, whether ethics have suffered in practice or whether standards have risen. The authors found that business executives were more cynical in 1976 about their colleagues' behavior, believed that codes were necessary but would not basically improve corporate conduct, and ranked shareholders and employees far below their customers on the constituent priority scale. In comparison with other professions, business executives saw themselves as less ethical than professors and doctors; more ethical than government agency officials, lawyers, elected politicians, and union officials. While the concept of social responsibility has garnered greater acceptance over the years, business executives are not in favor of any rules that curtail their authority. The authors conclude with this observation:

> Business executives and the companies they serve have a personal and vested interest in the resolution of ethical and social responsibility dilemmas. Our respondents recognize these dilemmas and to some extent appear willing to accept generalized guidance for their resolution in the form of general precepts codes and statements from the business media....The manager appears to prefer uncertainty and tension to the loss of freedom and complications that would accompany these more rigorous measures.[12]

The Center for Business Ethics at Bentley College in Waltham, Massachusetts, started up in 1976. According to W. Michael Hoffman, founder and director of the center, that year marks the approximate beginning of a "business ethics boom." Around that time, business ethics emerged as "a defined field of study and social movement" with a "phenomenal growth in research and writing...[that]...enabled the field to carve out fairly well-defined issues and topics for on-going study."[13] Hoffman also notes that more than 30 centers and institutions have been founded or refocused on business ethics. Corporations were suddenly confronting puzzling issues which forced them to reach out and ask how others had handled the problem. Firms without codes of ethics began writing them. Those with a code updated them. The center regularly schedules nationwide conferences on business ethics themes. Naturally, such conferences carry an irresistible appeal to philosophers, ethicists, consumer advocates, and corporate critics. Hoffman managed from the outset to secure significant participation from senior executives in major corporations. These conferences did not produce an ethical consensus on any issue, not that Hoffman nurtured that hope. They did underscore hopeless differences in defining what's ethical.

The ethics of business continued to capture media headlines in the 1980s. Major competitors for news coverage were mergers and acquisitions, a development which in itself many business persons considered unethical. Again, what emerged most clearly was the absence of an ethical consensus on the substantial issues, although what was considered substantial also proved to be controversial. The question of what's ethical matched the frustrating one of what's art — only in the eye of the beholder? If there are no standards, corporations dance at the whim of a fickle public.

Procter & Gamble provides a bizarre example. Their spooky public relations problem developed a quasi-ethical twist. Through word of mouth, evidently, a curiously geographically scattered group of former consumers accused P&G of being in league with Satan. Their logo of seven stars arrayed over a crescent moon formed the basis of this charge. Initially, P&G did not take the charge seriously. Finally, increased media coverage forced them to take action. They investigated, took legal counsel, and scaled down use of the logo. These controversies, ranging from the ethics of mergers and acquisitions to the meaning of corporate logos, suggest how broad and ponderous ethical issues have become.

Have business ethics really gotten worse? It depends on how you measure it. Will you compare the past with the present? Will you contrast actions and expectations? And if so, whose expectations — those of the few or the many, those inside or outside the company? Corporate behavior is certainly the focus of a lot more public attention. Ethical expectations are definitely greater. Many more corporations have become responsive to the public's perceptions of them. They have added departments of corporate responsibility, consumer affairs, stockholder relations, etc. Good ethics may be good public relations. But good public relations are no substitute for good ethics. Isn't there a difference between looking good and doing good? It's going to be difficult to determine to everyone's satisfaction whether business ethics have gotten worse. This difficulty is part of the ethical dilemma. To whom should we listen? A lot of information is being generated. What does it tell us?

The Facts Are Not Good

In December 1980 *Fortune* magazine surveyed over 1000 companies, classifying their crimes into five categories: bribery, fraud, illegal political contributions, tax evasion, and antitrust violations. Mind you, these were not ethical violations or judgment calls about which good friends could differ. These were criminal offenses. Excluded from their list were civil antitrust suits and foreign bribes and kickbacks. *Fortune* found that 11 percent of these major corporations had been involved in at least one major delinquency between 1970 to 1978. The explanation, according to *Fortune,* was as follows:

> Corrupt practices are certainly not endemic to business, but they do seem endemic to certain situations and certain industries. A persuasive explanation for many violations is economic pressure—the "bottom-line philosophy," as Stanley Sporkin, the SEC's enforcement chief, puts it. "In many instances where people are not lining their own pockets you can only explain corporate crime in terms of 'produce or perish.'"[14]

Fortune viewed most unethical business behavior as situational rather than criminally intentional. These were bad situations, not bad people. One executive argued, "I've always thought of myself as an honorable citizen. We didn't do these things for our own behalf...[but] for the betterment of the company."[15]

Whatever the cause of crime, the survey indicates that more than 10 percent of our firms are guilty of *legal* violations. What about all violations, legal and ethical? What figure would we get if we (1) included all crimes, (2) speculated on the percentage that are not caught, *and* (3) added subtle ethical considerations which particularly bother employees and customers but are technically lawful? Would you guess that more than 50 percent of your country's corporations can be accused of poor ethical judgment? That's probably a conservative figure. While it may not be clear whether business ethics have gotten worse, there's certainly room for improvement. To whom should we look for leadership?

The Role of the CEO Is Ambiguous

The *Fortune* survey also noted that the senior executives, particularly the chiefs, are seldom implicated in the crimes. Why? Is this to suggest that top management is not to blame or just careful not to get caught? Does top management simply lack the power to enforce legal and ethical behavior? Or does it imply that top management fails to take any initiative in establishing clear ethical standards?

George Steinbrenner at American Ship Building and Daniel J. Haughton at Lockheed were two CEOs who fell into the spotlight during the multimillion-dollar political bribery scandals which hit many companies in the early 1970s. Steinbrenner was convicted in federal court of election law violations, and he and the company paid fines of $15,000 and $20,000, respectively. Steinbrenner claimed he was pressured into paying what amounted to bribes to political figures. He resigned voluntarily shortly thereafter. Haughton initially defended his actions as essential to save the company. He, too, eventually resigned under pressure from his board and the business community. These men were the exception. Few chief executives lose their jobs because they mishandle ethical issues.

Fred Joseph at Drexel Burnham Lambert (DBL) and Robert Foman at E. F. Hutton were repeatedly lambasted and blamed by both colleagues and the news media for the eventual collapse of their firms. Neither was convicted of unethical behavior nor privately disciplined. Inadequate managerial supervision was the charge. Both retired quietly. This is a more typical result for CEOs who fail legal or ethical tests.

Special tolerance for the chief executive is a tradition at least as old as the great "Commodore" Cornelius Vanderbilt. In the early part of the previous century this brazen and uncouth ship captain terrorized eastern waterways with his cutthroat pricing and bullying tactics. His more socially respectable competitors fought back with legal measures. He sent them a two-sentence letter, finally, assuring them he would not take them to court. Instead, he wrote, "I will ruin you" and signed his name.[16] At the height of his career he was receiving more than $50,000 a month in bribes. He was never convicted of any sort of criminal offense, despite countless days in court. The Commodore never had any personal illusions about his innocence. He accepted total responsibility for his actions. In the eye of the public he was a hero. It was not likely that today's public would so highly regard such a blatant violator of common decency. Maybe the ethic of business has changed for the better. The role of the CEO remains ambiguous, however. Are they to be held totally responsible or not?

Middle Managers Take a Lot of Heat

CEOs are rarely hanged for the crimes on their watch. Who is held responsible, then? Captains of industry typically chart the course and give the orders to hoist the sails. The deckhands—middle managers and senior executives—implement those orders. They are the ones usually caught and sent to jail. While particularly true a century ago, it happened as recently as 1960 in what came to be called the "incredible electrical conspiracy."[17] Eight corporations, including Westinghouse and General Electric, were caught fixing prices on a number of electrical items such as transformers. Upon assuming the GE helm, Ralph Cordiner embarked on a course of precipitous decentralization. With little preparation, executives were suddenly given greater managerial latitude. It became a produce-or-perish situation. Those most fearful of perishing evidently resorted to price collusion. CEO Cordiner denied any knowledge of the unsavory business. (He had sent out memos instructing his executives to obey the laws.) Federal courts convicted several of his vice presidents and managers, however. They were fined and sent to prison. It was a devastating experience for those people and their families. Cordiner, the captain of the ship who exerted the pressure to produce, retired earlier than scheduled. There was no explanation for his early retirement.

The American system punishes actions, not intentions. From a business perspective, corporations usually have noble and worthy goals. From an ethical perspective, their intentions are good, even when a bit greedy. It's the implementation of goals and selection of methods which occasion the bulk of unethical behavior. It would not be surprising, therefore, since methods are the province of middle management, that most cheating on the rules occurs here. Modest research supports this supposition. A survey conducted by *Personnel Journal* revealed that middle managers in their early forties are more likely to be involved in unethical activity. The reason most often supplied is a desire to "make it" before it's too late.[18] While making it may be the personal incentive, the system itself plays a major role. Middle management provides a unique combination of temptations and opportunities. The job of middle managers is to get the work done at virtually all costs. They are less likely to be closely supervised. They have been around a while. They are trusted. They are also relatively less visible in the middle. Their failure, on the other hand, will be very visible. In sum, unethical behavior cannot be simply attributed to "a few bad apples." The system itself is partly responsible. Middle managers are in the most vulnerable position.

Contrast the situation of middle managers with their colleagues at the bottom and top. Entry-level employees, apart from being new and unfamiliar with all the opportunities, are usually under less job pressure and are more closely supervised. Like the CEOs, they're very visible and have less opportunity to cheat without being caught.

Men and Women on the Edge

Cheaters are not just those in the middle, however. They are on the edge, according to James Balog, vice chairman at Drexel Burnham Lambert, Dennis Levine's last employer. "We hire entrepreneurial types, and entrepreneurs always work at the edge." Writers Miller and Selby conclude: "Impelled by their own ambitions, and pressed by the competition, many Wall Streeters are indeed pushing the boundaries of acceptable behavior to their limits."[19] Defenders of the free enterprise system insist that its open, competitive spirit brings out the best in people. It can and does. Intense competitiveness can also bring out the worst in people. Aggressive entrepreneurs, for example, are more likely to take ethical as well as economic risks. And they are not all guys.

Women are moving into positions of corporate leadership. What's the impact of this increased influx of women into corporate offices? Dare we hope that women will bring greater sensitivity and moral insight to business decisions? *Working Woman* magazine conducted a survey of 1400 women in February 1990. They published the responses in the September issue. Those who responded to the survey concluded that fair play is disappearing from the American business scene. Fifty-three percent agreed that successful businesspeople must occasionally break the rules. Seventy-eight percent of those who considered themselves successful also revealed that they were more willing to break the rules. Some were not above using their sex to their advantage on the job: 43 percent admitted to flirting to make a sale, 10 percent to having sex with a client, 29 percent to having sex with the boss.[20] While this poll is far from conclusive (one wonders what percentage of those respondents were victims of sexual harassment), it does suggest that ethics depends on the situation rather than the gender.

Examining the impact of women on corporate ethics is not the only innovative attempt to determine whether business ethics are getting worse. The size of the company also contributes to the nature and likelihood of unethical behavior, according to a study by three Baylor University professors.[21] While the ethics of small firms were stricter on more issues than large firms, some unethical behavior was perceived as "more acceptable" in the small-business group, such as padding expense accounts, insider trading, and copying computer software. Here again the evidence suggests that what's ethical in business is indeed highly situational. Standards vary. Compliance with those standards varies even more. The corporate ethic, in practice, becomes a product of individuals' reactions to each other and any formal standards, written or understood. The question is whether individuals know what the standards are. If so, do they have any intention of following the standards? That takes us into the realm of morals. If we want to know more about the state of business ethics, we'll also have to take a look at personal morals. What do individuals expect of themselves?

Are Moral Standards Declining?

Personal morals and business ethics are different. We have reached that point of cultural sophistication when it proves helpful to sharpen the distinction between the words *morals* and *ethics*. We need to distinguish between what kind of behavior we expect of ourselves and what kind of behavior others expect of us (and we of them). We need words and ways to acknowledge that we live in pluralistic cultures and an emerging global economy with vast differences in manners and mores.

Morals, we will say here, refer to personal beliefs that may be closely tied to religious tenets or similar private convictions. Ethics we will define as those public expressions of negotiated and mutual expectations. This means that a person might have strict personal standards and discover that the company they work for considers them a nuisance. Conversely, the corporate standard may demand more from people than they would do on their own. We will say, and hope that it doesn't sound pejorative, that personal morals may be "higher" or "lower" than the company's ethics. Finally, we would say that a person acts morally when they live up to their self-avowed principles. Similarly, a person acts ethically when they live up to society's principles. Morals are a person's private business. Ethics are everybody's business. Pollsters have tried to probe into the private beliefs of individuals. Let's see if the polls give us any clues.

What the Polls Say.   The Gallup Organization conducted an extensive poll for *The Wall Street Journal* contrasting the opinions of citizens and business executives. The results were summarized in a four-part series of articles entitled "Ethics in America" starting on October 31, 1983, shortly before the Levine-Boesky-Milken insider trading scandals broke completely open. There are several remarkable contrasts in this poll. While both groups believed that moral behavior has declined in the United States, 65 percent of the public share this view with only 23 percent of the executives. Interestingly enough, the business executives interviewed subscribed to higher personal standards than the general citizenry. The two groups handled moral dilemmas differently. The business executives included financial aspects of the situation. The general public maintained that money factors would have little impact on their decisions. One might assume that business executives tend to be more practical, the general public more idealistic. Two ancillary observations emerged. First, the moral aspirations of the "churched" versus the "unchurched" were barely statistically significant, suggesting that religious beliefs, as such, are not an overpowering force in the marketplace. Second, business executives as role models ranked below doctors and lawyers but above representatives to Congress.

Two years later the Roper Organization conducted a "morality survey" for *U.S. News & World Report*. The conclusion is that "many Americans today are stretching the boundaries of traditional morality." Twenty-four percent admit to cheating on their tax returns. Sixty percent or more believe that white-collar crime "is a serious and growing problem that shows a real decline in business ethical behavior."[22] Business executives are generally ranked as "average" for their honesty and ethical standards, compared with "high" for clergy and "low" for car salespeople. The public's confidence in financial services and the legal profession declined considerably.

There Is a Need for Moral and Ethical Certainty. Public opinion is far from conclusive or reliable on the rise or decline of moral standards. Feelings rather than facts are measured. The absence of real substance in the response leads one to wonder whether citizens have abandoned personal moral standards altogether and rely completely on what others expect of them. If so, clarity about the business ethic is doubly important. First, individuals need moral standards to achieve a sense of personal satisfaction. Second, society depends upon moral and ethical standards to maintain order and cohesion. In sum, both individuals and society require some degree of moral and ethical certainty.

The principal aim of management science is to reduce business uncertainty. The principal aim of business ethics is to reduce moral uncertainty—for *all* constituents. Fortunately, more and more executives and corporations are joining the search for better ethics, some hesitantly, others boldly. Unfortunately, even business leaders with fine credentials, benevolent intentions, and ample resources have not been able to unite the community in a common vision. It is undisputably clear that ethical standards for business are on the rise. Compliance with the evolving new standards has simply not matched these rising expectations. Times have changed. The need for good business ethics has become as important as the need for good business management. Instead of making nostalgic comparisons with the past we need to look at the present and the future. On that horizon, change itself warrants careful consideration. Let's explore the dimensions of what's changing.

The Scale and Scope of Change

Change is inevitable. Change is the dominant independent variable in the business ethics equation. We are surrounded by change. Everything's not only changing more rapidly than ever before, the scope of change is different, as Robert Oppenheimer noted.

> The order of society, the order of ideas, the very notions of society and culture have changed and will not return to what they have been in the past. What is new is new not because it has never been there before, but because it has changed in quality. One thing that is new is the prevalence of newness, the changing scale and scope of change itself, so that the world alters as we walk in it....What is new in the world is the massive character of the dissolution and corruption of authority, in belief, in ritual, and in temporal order.[23]

The Marketplace Is Changing

Increasingly, executives and managers are called upon to make complicated ethical judgments affecting their products or services, employees, customers, or the corporate bottom line. In contrast to an earlier age, the best corporate strategy no longer dictates pushing every advantage to its financial or legal limits. It becomes unethical, as with Parker Brothers. A number of additional changes confront management today, each of which creates intriguing ethical implications.

New Products. Thousands of new products of various sizes and shapes enter the market with increasing frequency, developed from technology not always fully understood even by the technicians. The range of new products and services is astounding. With packaged foods approximately 90 percent flunk their market share tests. They are off the market before some customers even hear about them. The variety of products and services competing for the same purchasing dollar is equally astonishing. In a free market system it's pointless to ask whether all these products and services are actually needed. Ethical considerations are more immediate. Are these products worthwhile? Do they deliver what they promise? Are they safe for all potential users? Are there hidden or long-term problems? What is the government's role in supervising or restricting the flow of new products to the consumer?

Affluence. There's plenty of money available to spend on these new products and services, recessions notwithstanding. Installment buying commits the future affluence of consumers. The ethic of thrift and frugality disappeared in the Roaring Twenties. How is this affluence to be managed? Should we continue piling up huge personal and national debt to finance luxuries? How do we justify the income and wealth disparities between the super rich and the super poor? Should we legislate or educate? Is there an "invisible hand" that dispenses our resources ethically?

Marketing Techniques. Techniques to sell all these new products and to reach or even create markets for them have become incredibly sophisticated. Selecting the proper market plan is as vital as the product or service itself. Market differentiation and segmentation are two concepts which reflect the trend away from mass markets toward highly specialized or individualized ones. Result: marketing costs increase; profit margins decrease. These developments tend to increase competition and foster a sense of urgency bordering on hysteria. For example, the fight for shelf space in retail stores is legendary. Martha Farnsworth Riche, national editor of *American Demographics,* calls it the "particle marketplace," caused by stagnant population growth and three nearly equal market segments based on age—youth, midlife, and 50-plus.[24] Intense competition gives rise to temptation. Other considerations, such as consumer welfare, are crowded out by an exaggerated necessity or desire to win. Bribes and kickbacks become a normal way of doing business.

Certain types of marketing and advertising have been accused of promoting personally harmful purchases or misrepresenting the true nature or value of a product or service. Tobacco is an example of the former. Tobacco is an addictive narcotic. Should it even be sold, let alone advertised? Infant formula marketing in developing nations is an example of the latter. Was it marketed to those who least needed it? These issues are commonplace around the world. In mid-1991 the South Korean government banned advertising promotionals on behalf of New Zealand kiwi fruit. Officials argued that the campaign would appeal to those least able to afford this luxury. This process of creating a customer, which Peter Drucker says is the main purpose of business, raises subtle and complex ethical considerations. Is it ethical for pharmaceutical companies to compensate physicians who attend seminars introducing new products? Should lawyers be allowed to prod potential clients into lawsuits with television ads? Do consumers need legislative protection against their ignorance or self-destructive behaviors? If so, how much protection? Is there a cost versus benefit ratio?

Greater Customer Sophistication. Citizens throughout the entire world are better educated, more aware politically, and more deeply committed to shaping the world as they want it. This unwillingness to settle for anything less than the best is always taking new forms. According to a *Wall Street Journal* article, some consumers are now hiring consultants to advise them on big ticket items such as automobiles.[25] The consultants help them get the best product at the best price. For some purchasers this new sophistication tends to focus primarily on price rather than quality issues, such as durability, life expectancy, or all-around safety.

Litigation. New laws have strengthened the legal rights of both sellers and buyers, making the threat of lawsuits extremely real and their occurrence commonplace. By the late 1970s the United States had more lawyers than all the rest of the world combined, approximately one for every 500 citizens. Litigation coerces ethical behavior, essentially. Product liability expert Peter Huber has placed a $380 billion annual price tag on this coercion, $80 billion of it going directly into lawyers' pockets. Economist Stephen Magee calculates the cost as a $500 billion annual reduction in gross national product. Can our society afford it financially? Can we afford it psychically? Does it exacerbate the adversarial characteristics of our society, turning friends into enemies?

Changing Business Relationships. Perhaps the most intriguing shift, from an ethical perspective, is the changing relationship between sellers and buyers. That relationship has lost much of its personal touch. Sociologists describe this as a change from a primary to a secondary relationship. Buyers and sellers do not confront each other face to face. They are typically unknown to each other. In contrast to an earlier era, today's consumer may know very little about the personal lives of those who manufacture, market, or sell their purchases. Trust levels are transformed and symbolic. Brand names are intended to convey the trust once imparted by first-name relationships. The corner drugstore, that venerated symbol of small-town America and free enterprise, is being replaced by national chains such as Wal-Mart and K-Mart. Price is the overriding consideration. Price tags, along with brand names, have replaced friendship, loyalty, and even national pride. CEO Lee Iacocca intuitively challenged this trend with his personal TV appearances on behalf of Chrysler cars. When such attempts to rely on dying traditions are thoroughly exhausted, how is trust to be established in this new age?

Rising Personal Expectations. All of these changes have a profound effect on the core values of individuals and society. Customers want better products. Employees want more respect. The stockholders want more voice. Management wants to be trusted. Environmentalists want more control. Indigents speak of having "welfare rights." George Orwell had it exactly backwards. In 1948, he projected a future of technologically enforced conformity. Individuals in *1984*[26] would function like programmed robots, responding to orders delivered by an all-knowing state. His fictional fabrication captured the imagination of millions. The book became a staple of high school and college literature courses. Eager devotees marked the nation's progress toward this unpromising land. We never arrived. Instead, the 1970s initiated a trend dubbed "do your own thing." Lots of individuals did, giving birth to social and corporate chaos. Burger King commercials captured the spirit: "Have it your way." This same individualism manifested itself in the 1980s with a new spurt of economic entrepreneurship. It was the decade of self-employed consultants. The price tag on individual liberty, leisure, and even license has become very steep. But it has many willing buyers. Orwell was either wrong or we must credit him with cleverly forestalling our enslavement.

Business Ethics Are Changing

The scale and scope of business ethics are shifting beneath our feet as well. It is a societal issue that embraces the entire world for the foreseeable future. Powers and Vogel[27] tell us why:

1. The increased technological, regulatory, and competitive international pressures

2. The growing sophistication of governments at all levels around the world along with their need and ability to regulate business

3. The continued resource scarcity

4. The limitations and even disillusionment with governments, requiring greater responsibility from corporations themselves

5. The increased attention and role of the business corporation in public life

Business ethics are here to stay. The basic issue is easier to state than achieve: what ethic satisfies the demands of relevant and responsible constituents? What rules of the road would you like to see adopted? We stand on the edge of an ethical frontier. We are stumbling through the process of developing new standards as this frontier expands. We have been making up the rules as we go along. We need some guidelines for this process.

The Need for a Business Ethic Is Gaining Recognition

It may not be perfectly clear what's ethical, but more voices are raised in support of finding out. Robert D. Gilbreath, director of advance practices for Theodore Barry & Associates, gives several reasons why ethics will be of increasing significance in the future:

1. The easy decisions, such as cost cutting, layoffs, and reorganizations, have already been made.
2. All business is now public business; nothing is private.
3. Management prudence is the new standard because of new audits, reviews, and second-guessing of corporate action.
4. The list of stakeholders is growing.
5. The hero is vulnerable under the public spotlight.
6. Scapegoats are needed and individuals will be found who can be blamed.
7. Traditional values are coming back, blending intellectual and economic soundness with definitions of the "good."[28]

But why doesn't the presentation of ethics policy receive equal billing with financial matters? Is it resistance to things ethical? Or is it because corporate executives fail to appreciate the intangible factor described by Mark Pastin?

> Ethics is an intangible factor, but it yields tangible results.... Ethics is becoming increasingly important to business, especially large corporations that operate under the intense scrutiny of the media, swarms of regulators and numerous public interest groups. The economic success or failure of these corporations depends on their ability to anticipate the responses of these outside groups to corporate actions and to find some common ground for interactions.[29]

Companies in the defense industry must have listened to Pastin. They sought out their mutual interests following years of continual harassment from government lawyers for contract violations. CEO Robert F. Daniell of Hartford, Connecticut–based United Technologies was the chief instigator of what became the Defense Industry Initiatives. Approximately 25 firms participated in the creation of an 18-point code of ethics. Government officials were consulted in the process. The participating firms then signed it. (Not all participated or signed.) Despite the initiatives, federal regulators continued to prosecute firms guilty of various minor legal infractions and punished them with sizable fines. While the initiatives provide evidence of corporate integrity, good intentions on the part of a couple of dozen firms were not enough. First, the firms were unable to coax all the defense industry companies to unite under their ethical umbrella. Second, they could not deliver ethical compliance from those who took the initial pledge. Third, government regulators were caught in a conflict of obligation between the defense industry companies and the laws which created them. The government was not free to compromise or negotiate in good faith. Legalistic rigidity prevailed.

Progress toward a unifying business ethic has not been smooth or always amiable. Corporate critics have been quick and persistent in calling public attention to the adverse effects of these changes in the marketplace. Some of the finger-pointing has been hysterical. The contemporary equivalent of bearbaiting is cornering corporate leaders at their annual meetings to embarrass or goad them into action. That approach may mitigate moral indignation, but it does not change the fundamental issues. A more positive tack has been taken by several groups. Two are noteworthy.

1. The recently formed Business Enterprise Trust, funded through a blue-ribbon corporate board of directors and headed by Stanford Business School ethics professor Kirk Hanson, is searching for stories of firms that have earned an "A" in ethics.

2. The United Church of Christ, a liberal Protestant denomination that has been aggressively critical of many large corporations in the past, has recently launched a similar program of citing good corporate behavior.

Skeptics are already calling these "good puppy" awards. The criteria used to select the winners are bound to cause some controversy as well. Those pessimistic reactions notwithstanding, it remains to be seen whether this approach will counteract the cynicism of a jaundiced public, let alone inspire fundamental changes in business ethics.

The Search for Common Ground

Why has the common ground been so difficult to find? According to Milton Friedman, business leaders and their critical constituents have a fundamentally different understanding of society. Both abuse the enormous freedoms extended by free enterprise.

> The two chief enemies of the free society are intellectuals and businessmen, but for opposite reasons. Every intellectual believes in freedom for himself, but is opposed to freedom for others. He thinks that, in the business world, because of the chaos of competition and waste, there ought to be a central planning board to establish social priorities. But he's horrified at the thought of a central planning board to establish social priorities for writers and researchers. The businessman is just the opposite. He favors freedom for everybody else, but when it comes to himself, that's a different question. He ought to get special privileges from the government, a tariff, a subsidy or what have you.[30]

Ralph Winter impugns the motives of business critics. He questions their ability to deal fairly with the issues.

> If we have learned anything from the professional corporate critics in the past, it is that their animus against the private sector is so intense that they cannot be trusted to address real problems sensibly.[31]

The motives of business leaders are attacked, too. Allegations of greed and insensitivity on the part of corporate executives, with which some critics defend their animus, are commonplace. The search for a common ground that business and its constituents can share in the shaping of a new ethic for this new age has been extremely elusive, despite increased internal and external pressures. Lack of clear ethical policies and principles affects employee satisfaction and the financial bottom line. The efforts of local, state, and federal governments to legislate ethics have further narrowed management's scope of discretion. Stakeholders or consumer advocates of one stripe or another are turning up the heat under the ethics burner. Business ethics as a business priority is moving to the forefront, but slowly and tentatively. Business executives have not been insensitive to these developments. As we shall have occasion to note, some have been calling for action for decades. More recently, some followed a time tested corporate approach to handling problems strange to the marketplace. They hired outside consultants. Some of these outsiders carried philosophical or religious credentials. Business leaders evidently hoped the philosophers would bring academic stature and benevolent neutrality to the controversy as well as tell them what's ethical. The philosophers did their best: they lectured, wrote books, devised work shops, counseled executives, sponsored business ethics centers throughout the country, and even promoted an international association of business ethicists. Their approaches varied from the highly theoretical to the arrantly practical. They sometimes introduced words and concepts which required a lot of pondering or they simply created codes of ethics that, once written, required little more than passive obedience. Their contributions have been laudable but indecisive for the long term. Such approaches shared a serious limitation. They did not take full account of a dynamic marketplace in a pluralistic society. Executives today need a decision-making instrument they can carry around in their heads for on-the-spot use.

A Model for All Seasons

We live in an age without ethical consensus. The pattern seems to be, act first and defend the action later. Business leaders need a decision-making process that

1. Affirms their individual freedom and responsibility
2. Promotes consideration and respect for all constituents
3. Encourages calculation of the long-term impact of decisions *before* any decisions are reached
4. Is relatively free of religious, cultural, or nationalistic bias

These four elements emerge as crucial considerations for determining what's ethical in this new age. Chapter 2 will introduce an ethical algorithm[32] designed to incorporate these four considerations. It boasts additional strengths. It combines consideration of ends and means from the dual perspective of motives and consequences. It is relatively simple to use: there are only four basic checkpoints, each accompanied by three ancillary questions. It stimulates the kind of reflection that leads to action. If used conscientiously by enough decision makers, it can build ethical commonality in the marketplace. It's an analytical tool designed to be helpful to CEOs and managers in companies like Parker Brothers and Hooker Chemical.

Setting Some Ground Rules

The ethical algorithm requires a commitment to rational thinking. In addition, two assumptions underlie its development.

Business Is a Survival Activity. The survival instinct is unarguably strong in all forms of life. In ancient times human beings were forced to pursue survival at the cost of their lives. In these more civilized times, business is an activity which continues the basic struggle for survival. The name and risks have changed, but the instinct remains intact. People will still defend what they perceive to be their right to survive with unsquelchable zeal. This right to survive constitutes a fundamental principle. Food comes before ethics. The survival issue stirs the most profound feelings. It has turned the gentlest people into vicious animals. How do we reconcile the struggle of innumerable individuals and corporations as each pursues its own survival? Just to put the dilemma in a realistic perspective, how do you negotiate between two vicious dogs fighting over the same bone? Very carefully, obviously. We must presume that everyone will be fighting valiantly to have the eventual settlements come out in their favor. Business ethics sets the rules for survival among presumed equals. It is a serious business. Be prepared to compromise.

Survival Is in the Eye of the Beholder. One person's need is another's luxury and vice versa. Managers and executives who have undergone the trauma of an ethical crisis often have difficulty in describing exactly what happened and why. The analysis or indignation of outsiders rarely pleases them. Their defense finally rests on a statement intended to close debate: "You had to have been there to understand." That's true, but only in part. It's equally true that you had *not* to be there to gain complete perspective on what transpired. The victims of unethical corporate behavior are never pleased with excuses that require them to understand the one who made the decision. Perhaps victims should try to understand, but they don't. They want an explanation. They want managers and executives punished or some assurances that it won't happen again. Sometimes both. Between perpetrator and victim we have two sets of conflicting wants. Can they be reconciled? Only if they follow a process that brings them to negotiation or discussion as equal partners. The ethical algorithm is intended to provide the framework and process to achieve that very end. Be prepared to look at issues from another person's perspective.

In the chapters that follow we will focus on the consequences of corporate actions that have come to be labeled "unethical." We will try to do this as fairly as the available public information permits. We will try to phrase the issues in such a way that even if things didn't happen exactly as described herein there still will be something we can learn.

After looking at the consequences, we will examine the goals, methods, and motives of the major decision makers in order to find the root cause of the problem. In some chapters this framework will be more visible than others. What might have been done differently to avoid the unethical consequences? This smacks of second-guessing, to be sure. But how else can we learn?

We will explore these unethical consequences from the perspective of the decision makers: That is, what were the goals, methods, or motives associated with the undesirable behavior? Were the decision makers content with their actions and outcomes? Then we will try to provide some analysis which helps explain why things happened as they did. Finally, of course, it is up to the reader to form his or her own judgment.

Summary

In this chapter we have suggested that bad things can happen even to good corporations. Further, ethical standards have risen and corporate behavior has not yet measured up to the emerging ethical expectations of a corporation's many constituents. If the moral behavior of individuals has fallen, it may be due to the absence of corporate leadership. The marketplace has changed. Corporate managers and executives must respond to a greater number and greater variety of vocal constituencies today. A century ago their primary considerations in this area were limited largely to stockholders, customers, and governments, in that order. The list has grown to include employees, organized labor, competitive peers, multiple vendors, international competitors, independent professional groups, pension fund managers, community organizations, consumer advocates, religious institutions, more vocal agnostics, and aberrant individuals. That's a long accountability list fraught with complications.

The Protestant work ethic which served the business community so well for so long has lost much of its power to either inspire or constrain. Ethically as well as technologically we have entered a new world. We have not yet come to terms with the ethical side of enterprise. General Omar Bradley was one of the first to observe that "The world has achieved brilliance without conscience. Ours is a world of nuclear giants and ethical infants."[33] We are unprepared to manage ethically in this new world. Where did we get any training or education in business ethics? Not in our public schools! Not in our churches or synagogues! Only recently and haphazardly in our business schools. We should be pleasantly surprised that corporate behavior is as ethical as it is, considering the myopia and cynicism that abounds. Our culture dictates that we be situational in our ethics. The ethical algorithm represents one way that managers and executives can reach sound, long-term decisions that are acceptable to this wide range of constituents.

Footnotes

1. *The Wall Street Journal,* March 2, 1979, p. 1.

2. Ibid.

3. William Mueller, "Who's Afraid of Food?" *American Demographics,* September 1990, p. 42.

4. Peter Drucker, "What Is 'Business Ethics'?" *The Public Interest,* no. 63, Spring 1981, p. 35.

5. Ibid.

6. Peter Brimelow, "The Confusion over Corporate Ethics," *Chief Executive Magazine,* Autumn 1986. Brimelow is a senior editor of *Forbes.*

7. William E. Simon, "A Challenge to Free Enterprise," *The Ethical Basis of Economic Freedom,* Ethics Resource Center, Inc., Washington, D.C., 1900.

8. Frank G. Goble, "Building Ethics From the Classroom Up," *The Wall Street Journal,* Jan. 8, 1988, p. 18.

9. J. Irwin Miller, "Business Has a War to Win," *Harvard Business Review,* March–April 1969, pp. 4, 8.

10. *The New York Times,* Jan. 1, 1990, p. D2.

11. Steven N. Brenner and Earl A. Molander, "Is the Ethics of Business Changing?" *Harvard Business Review,* January–February 1977, p. 57.

12. Ibid., p. 71.

13. W. Michael Hoffman, "Business Ethics Boom Reaches Corporations," *Business Ethics Resource,* vol. 1, no. 1, March 1987, p. 1.

14. Irwin Ross, "How Lawless Are Big Companies?" *Fortune,* Dec. 1, 1980, p. 62.

15. Ibid.

16. Matthew Josephson, *The Robber Barons: The Great American Capitalists,* Harcourt Brace Jovanovich, New York, 1934.

17. Richard Austin Smith, "The Incredible Electrical Conspiracy," *Fortune,* Apr. 18, 1961, p. 132.

18. Reported in *Marketing News,* Nov. 6, 1987, p. 6.

19. Gregory Miller and Beth Selby, "Grappling with the Moral Dilemma," *Institutional Investor,* October 1986, p. 229.

20. "How Ethical Is American Business?" *The Working Woman,* September 1990, p. 113.

21. Justin G. Longenecker, Joseph A. McKinney, and Carlos W. Moore, "Ethics in Small Business," *Journal of Small Business Management,* January 1989, p. 27.

22. "Morality," *U.S. News & World Report,* Dec. 9, 1985, p. 52.

23. Robert Oppenheimer, "Prospects in the Arts and Sciences," *Perspectives USA,* vol. II, Spring 1955, p. 10.

24. Martha Farnsworth Riche, "Countdown to the Twenty-First Century," *Marketing Tools Alert,* a special news supplement to *American Demographics,* September 1990.

25. "Pampering Motorists Proves Profitable," *The Wall Street Journal,* Sept. 13, 1990, p. B1.

26. George Orwell, *1984,* Harcourt, Brace, New York, 1949.

27. Charles W. Powers and David Vogel, *Ethics in the Education of Business Managers,* Institute of Society, Ethics, and the Life Sciences, Hastings-on-Hudson, N.Y., 1980, p. 11.

28. Robert D. Gilbreath, "The Hollow Executive," *New Management,* vol. 4, no. 4, Spring 1987, p. 25.

29. Mark Pastin, "Ethics and Excellence," *New Management,* vol. 4, no. 4, Spring 1987, p. 43.

30. Milton Friedman, "Corporate Governance and Legitimacy," *Public Policy and the Business Firm,* Conference proceedings compiled by Rogene A. Bucholz, Center for the Study of American Business, St. Louis, 1980, p. 92.

31. Ralph K. Winter, "What's *Not* in a Name," *Regulation,* vol. 4, no. 3, May–June, 1980, p. 29.

32. Verne E. Henderson, "The Ethical Side of Enterprise," *Sloan Management Review,* vol. 23, no. 3, 1982, p. 37.

33. Omar Bradley, "No Armistice," speech in Boston, Nov. 10, 1948.

2
The Ethical Algorithm

**A New Approach to
Corporate Decision Making**

"And please protect me from the appearance of wrongdoing."

Drawing by Lorenz; © 1982 The New Yorker Magazine, Inc.

The Ethical Side of Enterprise

Douglas McGregor of the Massachusetts Institute of Technology introduced us to "the *human* side of enterprise" in mid-century. He focused fresh and warranted attention on the vital importance of the manager's attitudes toward their subordinates. A quarter of a century later we are able to identify an *ethical* side of enterprise as well. Ethics focuses our attention on the actions as well as the attitudes of managers toward a growing multitude of constituents. The ethical side of enterprise is intricately bound up with the business side. They are inseparable except for discussion purposes. Think of these two sides as you would a sheet of paper. It is a single item. It also has two sides. Enterprise is like that sheet of paper. It is a single operation that can be viewed from two sides. The business side is typically measured in dollars, revenues, profits, or market share. The ethical side is measured by human feelings of satisfaction, for example, or relative fairness and the long-term consequences for society and the environment. These data are softer, the conclusions often controversial. How can we bring to the ethical side of enterprise some of the clarity and certainty of the profit or loss calculations on the business side? Not easily.

This chapter will focus on the way we make ethical decisions. Our goal is to identify a *process* that will deepen our understanding and increase our confidence in managing the ethical side of enterprise. Let's use a quiz to test our familiarity with this emerging new dimension of business.

What's Your Ethical IQ?

Ethical dilemmas can be very troubling. In the time-honored metaphor known as "being caught on the horns of a dilemma," you face a charging bull. You are certain to be gored. Your choice, as the "moment of truth" approaches, usually comes down to selecting which horn you most wish to avoid. There are two implicit assumptions in dilemmas: you must choose, and you have the power to choose. Not to choose is itself a choice.

Below are 10 true-life dilemmas from business. Each requires a choice. Give your first-reaction answer to each of the following questions by circling either No, Depends, or Yes. Your answers should reflect what you believe you would *actually* do in the situation, *not* what you think you ought to do or believe is the best or most ethical answer. We'll discuss that later. Take only as much time as you think you would have in the situation.

Ethical IQ Test

1. You are a newly hired junior executive in a large manufacturing firm. The business conference you have been attending on behalf of your firm for the last two days is over. You had planned to fly home, but a couple of friends you've made at the conference are driving back by car and have invited you to ride with them. It would be a five-hour drive instead of a two-hour flight, but they would drop you at your doorstep. It would be stimulating to ride back with your new friends and it might benefit the company. You reason that the additional travel time would be out of your pocket, so to speak, not the firm's. You decide to drive back with your new colleagues. You toss $10 into the refueling kitty during the midpoint pit stop.

   Q. **Would you cash in the return flight ticket and keep the money?**   NO   DEPENDS   YES

2. You have a strict code of ethics in your office regarding employee appropriation of office supplies. The most competent and longest-tenured secretary is caught by you, the secretary's boss, taking typewriter ribbons and erasure tapes home in a briefcase. There is a rule against this as well as a clearly established procedure for providing employees with supplies if they do company work at home. The code requires you to fire the secretary on the spot.

   Q. **Would you make an exception for this loyal worker?**   NO   DEPENDS   YES

3. A friend at work asks whether you'd like a take-home copy of an expensive computer software program. You know it is protected by copyright.

   Q. **Would you let your friend make a copy for you?**   NO   DEPENDS   YES

4. You are the senior vice president for public responsibility in a large multinational corporation. One of your long-time friends in the marketing department confides to you that the boss is subtly suggesting that sales representatives give misleading information to prospective clients about a particular product. Your friend is very upset about it and wants your advice.

Q. **Would you encourage your friend
to follow the boss's suggestion?**   NO   DEPENDS   YES

5. You are a public relations professional in a medium-sized midwestern city. Three months ago you set up your own company. Your first big client wants to promote throughout your region a passive exercise machine. The home office in Texas claims the device is "scientifically proven to take off pounds easily and quickly." The manufacturing firm does not have a national reputation and, despite your repeated requests, has been unable to provide you with any scientific proof of its claims.

Q. **Would you continue serving this
firm as a client without the scientific proof?**   NO   DEPENDS   YES

6. You are the director of research and development in your firm. The personnel office has found two candidates for a vacant position in new product testing in your department. The better qualified candidate with more potential for promotion and future contribution to the organization appears to be rather cold and aloof and will likely clash with your personality. The less qualified candidate is your personal choice, even though the company will not be as well served.

Q. **Would you choose the less qualified candidate?**   NO   DEPENDS   YES

7. You are the product manager for one of your firm's largest dollar volume brands. You know that your product will soon be challenged by an improved version from a strong, well-financed competitor. One of your vendors offers to provide you with a confidential copy of the competitor's strategic marketing plan. No price for the copy is mentioned.

Q. **Would you utilize this vital information to help your brand?**   NO   DEPENDS   YES

8. You have recently accepted the top marketing position at a new company. One of your first assignments is to approve an all-expenses-paid trip for the senior purchasing officer of one of your largest client firms. The four-day seminar in the Caribbean, sponsored solely by your company, would include first-class airline tickets for client and spouse, a three-day cruise following the seminar, plus a $500 honorarium. You know that this particular company does not have a written conflict-of-interest policy. You also know

that your new boss is very eager to have this purchasing officer at the seminar.

Q. Would you authorize the expendi-
tures for this client?   NO   DEPENDS   YES

9. You serve as an outside member on the audit committee of the board of directors of a major pharmaceutical company that markets new drugs through practicing physicians. You have secretly learned that your research department has developed an abortion pill that appears to be 100 percent safe and effective. However, it has been repeatedly rumored that your chief executive officer will not let this product be brought to market because of deep religious convictions. Millions of dollars of potential revenue and profits will be lost.

Q. Would you let this secret decision
of your CEO go unchallenged?   NO   DEPENDS   YES

10. You happen to overhear a couple of engineers in your company discussing a radically new product that your colleagues in upper management are anxious to see hit the market on schedule. You accidentally learn that the engineers are also quite concerned about some design flaws that could be harmful to product users, although the probabilities are very remote.

Q. Since you are not directly responsi-
ble for this product, would you
completely ignore their com-
ments?   NO   DEPENDS   YES

TOTAL SCORE: ____   _____   ____

How to Calculate Your Ethical IQ

Total up the number of times you circled each No, Depends, or Yes in the space provided. Take the *highest* number in *only one* of the three categories, multiply it by 100, and then divide by 5. This is your ethical IQ (average is 100; perfect score is 200.)

If you scored *above 160* in any of the three categories, you are a person with a strong and consistent ethical decision-making pattern. Your colleagues will experience you as predictable. If your high score is in the No column, for example, they will likely think of you as a paragon of virtue. Some of your ethical decisions might attract considerable attention because they will seem unfashionable or unpopular. If your high score is in the Yes column, your willingness to make exceptions to the rules on a regular basis might earn you the reputation of being unprincipled. You and some of your decisions may be very popular, however, either because they are adventurous or because you don't "stand on ceremony." If your high score is in the Depends column, you will likely be perceived as indecisive. The popularity of your decisions will rise and fall on a case-by-case basis. In sum, high scores in any of the three columns indicate that you will very visible on ethical issues, one way or another. Furthermore, any time you deviate from your established and predictable ethical pattern, you are likely to attract additional attention, frightening your friends and pleasing your foes.

If you scored *between 100 and 140* in your highest category, you are probably a very thoughtful person as well as a product of our times. You have scattered your responses among the three alternatives. This pattern reflects the high degree of ethical ambiguity in the marketplace today. The most ethical course of action is not always crystal-clear. In fact, we are surfeited with significant choices at every turn. The ethical consequence is a growing number of Depends or Yes responses. It's not as easy to just say No. What's more, it's often very rewarding to say Yes. There's excitement and money.

If you scored around 110 — which for any given group tends to be the mean — you probably sense that principles from the past cannot be applied rigidly and religiously to many contemporary situations. People who are most adjusted, and sometimes the most prosperous, are those whose ethical IQ scores are nearer this mean. They are more willing, evidently, to make the necessary compromises between unyielding principles and harmful impact on people. Maybe there's more to be said for mediocrity than we thought.

If you scored *below 100* in your highest category, you could be either extraordinarily sensitive or insensitive to ethical issues. You may be aware of dimensions to the questions that others overlook or deliberately ignore as irrelevant. At the other extreme, you may not have been aware that there was an ethical issues at all. In either case, there is no strong pattern to your answers so each must be analyzed separately for clues. Ethical consistency — measured here by five or more No, Depends, or Yes responses — is obviously not your top priority, and you're not afraid to act that way, at least on paper. If you consider yourself ethically sensitive, you may have experienced a lot of discomfort in answering the questions. You will certainly be surprised by your pattern of responses. You may be one of those people who see themselves as strong decision makers and conclude that the questions as phrased are too ambiguous. Ethical dilemmas in real life are ambiguous, so ambiguous in fact that we often fail to realize ahead of time that we are about to be gored by one of the horns. Are you trying too hard to give No or

Yes answers? If so, then you should give the Depends response. There are two other types of people with low ethical IQs, the ethically alienated and the ethically confused.

The Ethically Alienated. Some who score below 100 may belong to what Frederick Herzberg labeled as the "confused mixture" (see Table 7-1, p. 212). Herzberg hung this label on the youth of the 1970s. As a group, they were not as easy to categorize as the socially sensitive "flower children" of the 1960s. Ethical behavior is dependent upon either a very strong sense of what's right or sensitivity to how others view your actions, sometimes both. To put it another way, our behavior is either guided by a combination of deeply ingrained principles or perception of anticipated consequences. Again, as a group, it is simply unclear what ethical considerations guide young people entering the work force after the 1960s. There is no broad pattern. Some in this group seem deeply alienated by what they perceive as the ethical ambiguity and antiquated standards in business. They expected better, found worse, and turned cynical. Ethically, they "tuned out" and "turned off." They experience great difficulty giving restricted choice answers to questions they feel they shouldn't have to face. Many in this group feel uncomfortable about even being placed in a situation that requires them to think about such matters as confidential copies of a competitor's strategic marketing plans. They reject the responsibility for the situation. They simply can't give an answer. Their scattered responses reveal some basic, unresolved doubts about the economic system. Questions 4 and 6, dealing with job performance and promotion, are equally vexing. They miss the subtleties: Corporate loyalty and long-term considerations are concepts foreign to this group. As Herzberg noted, their loyalties are sharply curtailed. They are not joiners. They have little sense of time – past, present, or future. In contrast, at least the "now" generation had a sense of the present.

The Ethically Confused. Some test takers, while ethically sensitive, blur the distinction between microethics with macroethics. In Questions 1 and 2 some respondents argue that the company policy is at fault. The company in Question 1, for example, shouldn't be so rigid about keeping track of employee travel expenditures. They're getting more than their money's worth. The strict code of ethics in Question 2, some insist, robs managers of discretionary authority and presumes the manager is an ethical idiot. It's a bad policy so it shouldn't be taken seriously. Maybe so in both cases, but that raises a different issue. That's way the terms *microethics* and *macroethics* are needed in the business ethics lexicon. Microethics focuses on *compliance* with known ethical standards.

Macroethics is primarily concerned with *redefining* the standards in response to changing expectations. The difference between these two
terms is parsimoniously illustrated by a clever turn of phrase in Warren
Bennis's book, *Leaders.*[1] Bennis distinguishes between "doing things
right" and "doing the right things." Microethics is doing things right.
Macroethics is doing the right thing—after you've figured out what it is.
Microethics is compliance. It can range from either blind or minimal
obedience to second-mile efforts to exceed the expectations of constituents. Macroethical considerations, on the other hand, typically challenge or change those current standards, either formally through legislative change or informally through consumer demand and corporate
acquiescence. It's very important to be clear whether you're discussing
the issue of compliance with established standards or a change in the
standards.

Question 9 contains a trap for the unsuspecting decision maker. The
CEO undoubtedly believes he or she is "doing the right thing" by secretly sidetracking development of the abortion pill. The CEO is basing
that decision on highly moral principles—religion, no less. Alas, our
CEO is also "doing things wrong" within the typical corporate ethic. He
or she is abusing the authority given by the corporation and indirectly
by society. While the scale is different, it's similar to requesting a subordinate to do personal, nonbusiness-related favors for you. You are using the corporate power of your position to accomplish a personal
rather than a corporate goal. Some test takers argue that the CEO in
Question 9 is also overstepping the boundary separating church and
state. The fact that action is taken somewhat secretly casts additional
doubt on the ethics of the decision. It violates due process.

The scores alone, we should now understand, do not tell us all we
need to know about our ethical IQ. Good intentions do not necessarily
create good ethics. The business environment is more complicated than
that. Let's see what else we can learn from the test.

What the Categories Mean

Purist. A high number in the No category suggests that you are a *purist.* You follow the rules to the letter. You are the kind of person who
will always act ethically, even if it means your best friend will be fired.
You sense that others count on you to set the standard. Doing your duty
or always doing what you perceive to be the right thing is uppermost in
your ethical calculations. You have high confidence in your strong intrinsic sense of what's good and true. Sensitive calculations are unnecessary. You are one of the first to cry out against unfairness or injustice.
The higher your ethical IQ, the higher your expectations of yourself

and others. You would not authorize the lavish expenses for the Caribbean seminar on behalf of a promising client in Question 8. You would "blow the whistle" on the ethically timid engineers in Question 10. You know what's right and aren't afraid to tell others what you think.

In like manner, if you were the outside board member of the corporate audit committee in Question 9, you would not let the secret decision of your CEO regarding the abortion pill go unchallenged, even if you agreed with it. As a purist you might challenge this action on two counts. First, it violates the established corporate priority on profits. The dominating ethic in business is profit maximization. Second, secret unilateral decisions circumvent board authority. The process is unethical even if you support the antiabortion stance. Some purists push for open discussion and decision.

As a purist, you bring ethical stability and high standards to the groups or organizations of which you are an integral part. Since you are ethically uncompromising, you are more likely to suffer economically in the short run, but you might succeed in the long run. You are happiest in a culture where all others respond ethically as you do.

Expedient.   A high number in the Yes category suggests that you are an *expedient*. You are willing to break the rules if they seem silly and unnecessary or get in your way. You believe you try to do the right thing. But you measure "right" in short-term consequences rather than as some inherent sense of duty. Some will see your decisions as self-centered. Purists will call you "greedy" or "ambitious," which may or may not be true. Like the purist, you have a strong sense of yourself and know instinctively what serves your interests.

For instance, suppose you are the boss in Question 2 who catches the loyal secretary putting office supplies into a briefcase. As an expedient you would make an exception and answer Yes to this question. You probably wouldn't even ask whether the secretary were stealing for personal gain or just ignoring the rules. Mere obedience to a code of ethics is not that important to you. Neither is the cost of the supplies taken. Getting the work done and respecting people's judgments are more likely to receive higher priority with you. Codes of ethics are written for other people. As they say in Boston—a city notorious for scofflaw drivers—the traffic lights and stop signs are for the tourists.

As an expedient product manager in Question 7, you would answer Yes when offered a confidential copy of your competitor's strategic marketing plan. You might have to conjure up a defense for your intuitive response later, such as "they'd do it so us" or "it's ethical if it's not illegal." What's more, you'd feel obligated to "compensate" the vendor with some kind of gratuity. You'd find an appropriate way to handle that matter as well.

As an expedient person, your response here will undoubtedly reflect your age, your ambition, the competitive intensity of your industry, the present market conditions, and the relative strength of your ethical up- bringing versus the pressures of your present job. In all likelihood, there are some years when you'd be more than willing to pay a bribe to get a copy of that plan. In the ethical IQ test, the expedient men and women are forever pressing against the ethical boundaries.

Affluence and the gradual extension of personal freedoms have given birth to ethical pioneers. Despite continuous efforts by governments to leg- islate a new morality, solitary entrepreneurs and aggressive corporations are quick to blaze new trails in the ethical wilderness. Tribal ethical bonds do not hold them fast and secure. They invent and improvise as they go along. They say yes when the folks back home would say no. Increasing competition and deregulation of markets have given rise to unprecedented ethical improvisation, beginning around the mid-1970s. Dennis Levine, Ivan Boesky, and Michael Milken are just three who gained notoriety from their inability to manage the ethical frontiers into which they had wan- dered. They are not alone, however, just better known.

Your ethical contribution as an expedient to groups and organiza- tions of which you are a part is excitement and enthusiasm for change. Since you are ethically adventurous, you tend to be a loner, little influ- enced by the ethics of those around you. If you are economically moti- vated, you will probably be rich, even if lonely and perhaps unhappy. You can thrive in any ethical atmosphere. If your expedient type comes to dominate that culture, however, it will likely self-destruct in a rela- tively short time. You are capable of risky ethical decisions, some of which could be disastrous for all involved. If you are financially success- ful, you might become a benefactor and strong supporter of the purists and their "socially responsible" programs.

Pragmatist.   A high number in the Depends category earns you the epithet of *pragmatist*. Like the purist, you are deeply aware of rules and have a strong sense of doing what is intrinsically right. Like the expedi- ent, you also try to reason through to good ethical decisions. Unlike the purist, you look more carefully at the consequences of your decisions to make sure you don't get your best friend fired. Unlike the expedient, you take the perspectives of other people and the long term into con- sideration. Because you factor so many dimensions into your ethical de- cisions, you are slower to reach judgments and often change your mind. Consequently, you are likely to feel conscience-ridden rather fre- quently. Since others must evaluate your decisions by your actions alone rather than the motives or thought processes behind them, you may ap- pear to them as ethically insecure.

If you were the senior vice president for public responsibility in Question 4, it would take you a long time to answer your friend who is upset about possibly misleading clients. You'd wonder what's really going on. Is your friend exaggerating? You see at least three options. Is the boss really and truly asking the sales reps to lie, or to just not tell all the truth, or to emphasize certain points to the exclusion of others? Furthermore, to what facet of the issues will you respond: your friend's feelings, the boss's intentions (if you know him or her), or the bigger picture, including other sales reps and the boss's boss. Finally, as an employee you have a vested interest in the outcome even though you have no direct authority.

In Question 6, on the other hand, a Depends person would be quick to reach the hiring decision as director of research and development. You would not let your personal preference for a future employee's personality supplant the best interests of the company. At the same time, if that new employee's personality was vital to team spirit, you'd take it into consideration. In sum, you think things through very carefully and use your intuition carefully within some rational framework.

How did you respond in Question 3 when your friend offered to give you an illegal copy of an expensive computer program? Copyrighted software is one of those issues on the ethical frontier. Software is a product of the new technology. So, what did you do? Take the copy? Tell your friend you didn't need it, which might have been a white lie? The responses to Question 3 are invariably divided equally among the three possible responses and hotly debated in discussions afterward. A slight majority of respondents answer Depends to Question 3. Their equivocations are numerous: How much did it cost originally? How well do you know the friend? How old is the software? Who paid for it originally? How important is it to have a copy? Questions bordering the ethical frontier rarely receive consistent answers in random groups of employees. Sometimes it's simply a matter of not having had the opportunity to discuss the question before. Other times you sense strong resistance to such discussions.

Your main contribution to groups and organizations as a Depends person is thoughtfully reasoned, temperate ethical leadership. You can bring the extremes to the center. Because your position is often ambiguous and difficult to explain quickly, you tend to be less vocal. You are reluctant to speak out even though the business community badly needs your moderating voice. You can serve as the catalyst for an emerging and more enduring ethic. The ethical future is in your hands.

Summary of Test Results

This concludes our formal discussion of the ethical IQ test. We should have learned something about how each of us tends to approach ethical issues, how we differ from others, and the complexity of even rather routine ethical issues. The test underscores the dynamics of change and uncertainty in the marketplace. What's ethical can change overnight. The latest bit of scientific research and shifting public opinion are just two of the powerful forces at work. A 10 commandments for business, chiseled in stone and implying permanence, is the wrong medium and message. The marketplace is changing too rapidly. Several conclusions emerge from the IQ test. We discuss them in the next section.

The Spectrum of Ethicality

Sincere people reach sincere differences about today's ethical dilemmas. The ethical IQ test has been administered in one form or another in a variety of corporate settings and among different kinds of industries. Usually the questions are developed from ethical issues unique to that industry, ranging from computer hardware and software, pharmaceuticals, public relations, and management consulting, to banking. Listening to earnest arguments presented by respondents to one particular question or another convinces you that there is a spectrum of ethicality not unlike the rainbow of colors refracted from a single beam of white light by an optical prism. Thoughtful decision makers may lean to the adventurous Yes edge or cling to the cautious No end of the spectrum. The Depends types fall in the middle, of course. However, nearly all are arrayed along a spectrum of varying views which can be called ethical. This evidence of honest differences of ethical opinion leads to a number of conclusions.

There Are No Perfect Answers

As measured by the ethical IQ test, there are no perfect ethical scores today. The most thoroughgoing purist finds at least one question that can't be answered with a simple No. In Question 2, for example, nearly everyone wants to break the corporate code of ethics to avoid sacrificing a loyal worker to a dubious rule. The ethically confident will do so. No expedient test taker has boasted a total string of Yes answers. Those who are willing to accept the illegal computer software insist they are usually motivated by their friend's urging. In sum, we have yet to find responders who are rigidly principled or adventurously unprincipled. We live in an age of ethical ambiguity. Once upon a time the exception proved the rule. Now, the exception *is* the rule. Business decisions in a pluralistic society require thoughtful and time-consuming Depends responses to most ethical questions.

Business Ethics Is Situational

Clearly, every ethical decision has its own peculiar context, depending on the journalistic who, when, how, and why. The ethical IQ test questions described only part of each context. Differences of opinion surface as the situation becomes more specific. Sometimes a combined set of questions from several industries are presented to a mixed group. The results are interesting. Respondents often have a difficult time understanding the ethical subtleties in an unfamiliar industry. It's tough enough, they say, answering the questions that surface on their own turf. What's more, managers and executives sometimes exhibit powerful possessiveness of their ethical turf. They do not appreciate corporate outsiders who try to give expert ethical advice without thoroughly understanding all the nuances. Cynically speaking, the less we know about an ethical issue the easier it is to decide. The more we know, the more difficult it becomes. Ethical decisions in business are an integral part of their situations.

A Foolish Consistency?

Ralph Waldo Emerson warned that "a foolish consistency is the hobgoblin of little minds." His emphasis fell on the word *foolish*. Do you always follow the rule simply because it's the rule? Or do you break the rule because the outcome is more acceptable? Do you fire the loyal secretary because he or she has broken a rule? Or do you make an exception, either because intentions were honorable or because the rule is unnecessarily rigid?

Repeated use of the ethical IQ test with diverse groups sheds some interesting light on this issue of consistence. In the initial scoring by respondents, the Depends category consistently receives the fewest devotees. Eighty percent of the respondents cast the majority of their votes in either the No or Yes columns. In the discussions that followed, many of the No and Yes marks changed to Depends. What's the explanation? Several commented that they felt that their answers *should* be a clean No or Yes. For somewhat the same reason, it turns out, the No voters are slightly more numerous than the Yes. A Depends answer, they feared, might make them appear indecisive. That's a foolish consistency. They began to speculate about the pattern of their responses instead of the issues themselves. In short, the pattern took precedence over the impact of the decision itself. Respondents incorrectly presumed that an ethically principled person is either a No or Yes person.

Consistency is an important consideration. No one would long tolerate ethics or laws that perniciously discriminated among individuals or groups. Ordinary, everyday fairness requires consistency in applying the rules. It's the rule about rules we learn from parents at home, from teachers at school, and from playmates on the playground in the harsh and authoritative world of the third grade. Fair is fair. You challenge this deeply ingrained precedent at your own peril. Ethical inconsistency for whatever reason scares people. It's like moving the furniture in a blind person's house, causing terror and anger when he or she tries to sit in a nonexistent chair or sofa and falls all the way to the floor. Not funny. It's the rule about rules. Be consistent. Nevertheless, the advice of Emerson stands. Don't be foolishly consistent.

It's Tougher at the Top

Ethical decisions become more complicated for respondents higher up the corporate ladder. Lower-level managers tend to answer with lots of Nos and Yeses. Senior-level decision makers answer with more Depends. As you move up the corporate ladder, you can count on the ethical side to expand correspondingly:

1. A greater number of constituents will be affected by your decisions.
2. Your decisions will have increased visibility throughout the company and perhaps beyond.
3. Your decisions are more likely to have a permanent effect on employees, company policy, and the community.
4. Your personal values and ethical perspectives will come into play, especially if you are the CEO.
5. A greater number of options will be available.
6. Doing "the right thing" will depend more on whose perspective you take.
7. One or more constituents are likely to disagree strongly with whatever decision you make.
8. If your firm is transnational or multinational, you will be involved in cross-cultural value clashes.

The increased managerial responsibilities of senior executives impel some corporations to actions that carry covert ethical implications. A senior vice president and branch manager of a major Wall Street brokerage house reported that his job description listed 72 distinct responsibilities. Detailing so many specific duties to a single individual raises another kind of ethical question: Who's protecting whom and from what? Some corporate codes give the insidious message that the company is to be protected rather than the employee guided. This, too, can make life at the top tougher. Nevertheless, managing 72 distinct responsibilities requires at least goal clarity and some priorities. If you want, as did this vice president, to function ethically as well, you will need some sort of quick reference guide or process that encourages and helps you to do so. The rest of the chapter will address that need.

The Ethical Algorithm

Sound ethical decision making in today's business environment requires a lucid and vigorous instrument. The ethical algorithm is such a tool.[2] Its use requires thoughtful examination of the four critical dimensions of corporate action: GOALS, METHODS, MOTIVES, and CONSEQUENCES. Five basic assumptions undergird the ethical algorithm.

The Five Basic Assumptions

1. *Business ethics is a process.* Powers and Vogel, two pioneers in the business ethics field, described ethics as the on-going process of clarifying what constitutes the newest and best definition of society's welfare and mandating the behavior to secure it.[3] In short, what's ethical is always changing, evolving. The word *algorithm* is itself a *process*. Algorithms solve problems. Neophytes soon learn that no significant problem can be solved without a proper algorithm. In the minds of the technologically inclined, having an elaborate and elegant algorithm is more interesting than getting the correct solution! *How* the problem is solved ranks a higher priority than *what* the answer is. Didn't you have an algebra teacher who insisted that you show the entire problem-solving process on your exam paper? Your teacher most likely wanted to be sure you understood the process so that you could apply it to similar problems. The ethical algorithm embodies this concept of *process*.

This emphasis on process is not new. Francis Bacon, often called the father of the scientific method, stressed means rather than ends, the method of inquiry rather than the conclusions reached. Process is the essence of medical ethics, for instance. Surgeons are not merely jesting when they remark that "the operation was a success but the patient died." The ethics of good medical practice is judged by methods followed rather than consequences achieved. Business ethics is moving in the same direction.

Resolution of ethical issues in business is extremely unlikely to receive the kind of certitude we find in science, although comparison of the two might lead to some helpful insights. First, in both ethics and science, solutions that are only a little bit wrong can be very costly, as the *Challenger* space shuttle disaster proved: mechanical failure of a small part led to the explosion. So you always want the best possible answer. Second, both ethics and science aim at solving problems, one way or another. Third, both typically employ some sort of reasoned process with several steps or considerations. Business ethics rarely yields a single, noncontroversial answer. Sometimes there are more suggested solutions than there are constituents! Little wonder that the issue of ethics in business has become a battleground of its own.

The ethical algorithm is designed to bring the precision of mathematics to the *process* of ethical reasoning. Used properly, it can manage the interests of multiple constituents. It can help identify the most ethical options in manufacturing or marketing methods. It can help decision makers explore their personal motives and values.

2. *Human behavior is caused.* This is not intended to provoke some profound philosophical argument. It's a practical assertion that people have reasons for behaving the way they do. Human behavior does not occur randomly. If we are set to judge or evaluate the behavior of others, it is only fair that we try to understand whatever reasons or explanations lie behind it. Why do business leaders act the way they do? What causes unethical behavior?

In the ethical algorithm, the MOTIVES category gets at the deepest and most personal aspects of corporate behavior. MOTIVES encompasses the personal values and leadership styles of the key decision makers. We often have to speculate about the motives of managers and executives. They're not always out in the open and as easy to read as a mission statement or balance sheet. We have to draw inferences. Since motives invade the psychological and private life of managers and executives, it's dangerous to speculate too wildly or confidently about them. It's difficult enough to understand the inner forces that drive ourselves, let alone others. We have even less access to the unrelenting aspirations and ambitions in the hearts and minds of our colleagues. For instance, can anyone be sure why Warren Anderson, when he was CEO of Union Carbide, jumped on a plane and flew to India just a few hours after being briefed about the pesticide leak in Bhopal? Was it true, as some critics insisted, that Exxon CEO Lawrence Rawl was callously indifferent to the Alaskan oil spill? Could anyone be publicly certain about the motives that drove Dennis Levine to violate federal laws, SEC guidelines, and the public trust until he himself gave us the reasons in the *Fortune* story? We must be very careful in exploring the motives of businesspeople. On the other hand, we need to do it. The MOTIVES section of the algorithm often provides the best explanation for the causes of unethical corporate behavior. It is easier to say that behavior is caused than it is to define the cause with certainty and fairness. Nevertheless, the algorithm demands careful probing of managerial motives.

3. *Actions have consequences.* The proverbial pebble dropped in a quiet pond creates wave upon wave of rippling reaction. In today's world that pond is neither quiet nor disturbed by a solitary pebble. It is more turbulent than it's ever been before. The world's marketplace is bombarded by pebbles of all sizes, large and small, good and bad, lasting and fleeting. Reactions can remain beneath the surface for some time before breaking through explosively. For instance, it took decades to document beyond a reasonable doubt the carcinogenic properties of asbestos. The consequences were accumulating unseen. In this case, as in many ethical dilemmas today, we have to wait for developing technology and the painful passage of time to give us an actionable reading of the facts. Only a fool leaps from a tall building and boasts halfway down that "Everything's alright so far." Actions have consequences, even if unseen or delayed.

Some consequences are all too clear but their initiating action is in doubt. In fact, the cause may be more or less irrelevant. During the great Tylenol scare of the mid-1980s, it was reported that Johnson & Johnson executives speculated privately that a disgruntled employee might have injected the fatal dosage of cyanide into its capsules. Employee sabotage is common enough. A smoldering feeling of injustice finally breaks into flames. The underlying cause of the Tylenol episode remains clouded in mystery. Johnson & Johnson executives were forced to manage the consequences, instead. The public seemed to feel they did a good job. They acted *promptly* by assuming full responsibility for consequences that apparently were not their fault. They were *open* with the public about what had happened and what they were going to do. They *compromised* their business goal of making money when it conflicted with their ethical goal of consumer confidence. Eventually, they *modified* the product to reduce the chance of a recurrence. Johnson & Johnson accepted full responsibility for the unanticipated and harmful consequences of their decision to market Tylenol. The ethical algorithm encourages decision makers to anticipate unacceptable CONSEQUENCES when possible and also understand and manage them when the unexpected happens.

4. *What's perceived as ethical depends on the viewpoint of the constituent.* Edgar Schein noted a quarter century ago that multiple clients are a problem in the ethical education of business managers.[4] He listed a half dozen constituents, ranging from stockholders to customers, and then asked: From whose perspective are you going to teach them to be ethical? The beholders today are a large and growing list of constituents. The ethical cognoscenti call them *stakeholders*. We will call them *constituents* here in order to underscore the managerial perspective. Constituents are those to whom business leaders feel responsible. As many experienced executives have painfully learned, the eye of each

constituent perceives what's ethical from a different perspective. Look at a representative list of constituents and imagine how each group might define what's ethical on any given issue.

Customers
Senior management
Board of directors
Vendors
Unions
Professional organizations
Employees
The adjoining community
Special interest groups
State governments
Federal government
Foreign governments
The international community
Stockholders

Executives who take business ethics seriously face an impossible challenge in reconciling those multiple perceptions completely. The ethical algorithm can help.

5. *The need for good ethics rests on our mutual vulnerability.* Edgar Schein also addressed the question of *why* we need to teach managers to be ethical. Why do we need business ethics? His answer is very interesting.

> The *vulnerability of the client*...has necessitated the development of moral and ethical codes surrounding the relationship. The client must be protected from exploitation in a situation in which he is unable to protect himself because he lacks the relevant knowledge to do so.[4]

Vulnerability is the key word. Schein has put it in italics. It could be underscored a couple of times, too. We all know what it is to be vulnerable, to be at the mercy of another. Many consider this a situation to be avoided at all costs. That's impossible. Life means being vulnerable. Moreover, both democracy and free enterprise are systems which permit and foster high vulnerability. Schein's mere mention of it invites the mind to ponder successive dimensions of our human vulnerability: childhood, parents, schoolteachers, school chums, spouses, bosses, buyers, governments, law courts, IRS, etc. Very few people, if any, emerge from these various situations of vulnerability without scars. It's understandable if some reach adulthood possessed by a blinding passion to be invulnerable. We can speculate that the motivation for riches and power might be little more than a desire to be invulnerable! The role of ethics is to mitigate this vulnerability in a manner acceptable to all, from the least to the most vulnerable.

Vulnerability applies to everyone on that constituency list we comprised earlier. We are all vulnerable. No word better conveys the interpersonal need for sound business ethics. No word better explains why some constituents—customers and employees, especially—are consumed with outrage at business misconduct. No word better describes why so many citizens today are possessed by ambivalent feelings toward our technological, impersonal, automated world. No word better conveys why business ethics is more important (and more problematic) than it's ever been before. For instance, individual customers are often intimidated by the sheer size of the giant corporation. Little wonder if big business is distrusted just because it is big. It heightens the individual's sense of vulnerability. Good business ethics, therefore, becomes an effort to bridge the gap created by this vulnerability of size.

Size is not the only consideration, however. Every business client needs and expects a measurably different kind of protection. These differences can be contradictory if not mutually exclusive. The absence of a single set of values and matching ethical behaviors creates value conflicts for managers. So how do you resolve a deep and acrimonious conflict between two constituents? Compromise? Negotiation? Most likely. Such an admission underscores the situational nature of business ethics. The "perfect" answer becomes what the constituents in question agree is an acceptable answer. That's an imperfect, time-consuming process. Again, Exxon CEO Lawrence Rawl's handling of the Alaskan oil spill is a recent case in point. *How* Rawl managed the accident received more public attention than *what* Exxon actually did. Their 1989 annual meeting lasted a record-breaking 4½ hours, drawing an astounding attendance of 2000 stockholders who asked literally hundreds of irate questions. Several stockholders called for Rawl's resignation. Several hundred protesters paraded outside the hotel. We can speculate that the protesters were determined to make Rawl feel as vulnerable as they did. Perhaps this explains why Rawl was unable to restore public confidence in the same manner as had James Burke of Johnson & Johnson during the Tylenol scare. Despite it all, Rawl managed to retain a sense of humor. When Gary Hart was nominated as a write-in candidate for his job, he quipped, "It's terrible to deliver another blow to Gary."[5] Here again, however, Raw missed a sensitive point. He presented Gary Hart rather than himself as vulnerable and the object of ridicule.

How the Ethical Algorithm Works

The ethical algorithm can help us gain a better understanding of the decision processes that create ethical problems. Most important, it can be used as a planning device to help anticipate and avoid ethical dilemmas. Let's take a took at this simple but extraordinary tool.

The algorithm consists of four major interactive elements:

GOALS: What do you want to achieve?

METHODS: How will you pursue your goals?

MOTIVES: What personal needs drive you to achieve?

CONSEQUENCES: What results can you anticipate?

Before we add the ancillary considerations to each of the four elements, let's see how they interact, how changing one affects the others. Shaping a career decision might look like this.

GOAL: Get rich.

METHOD: Rob banks.

MOTIVE: Antisocial drive for financial security.

CONSEQUENCES: Make millions, buy a condo complex in Florida, and retire early.

Now if you had an ethical side to your career, the method of robbing banks would be unacceptable. Similarly, if you calculate the probable consequence of getting caught—i.e., a prison term—you might abandon robbery as a method out of fear, if not ethics. Finally, if you have no ethical side to your goals, select unethical methods to achieve them, and suffer the consequences of getting caught, your motives will likely surface when your case goes to trial. How will you defend your actions? That you're an unrepentant thief? That you robbed to feed your starving family? That you are a kleptomaniac and simply can't help yourself? In short, MOTIVES make a big difference, too. MOTIVES will determine *both* the GOALS and METHODS you select and how you will be judged by others when the CONSEQUENCES of your actions become visible. The four elements of the algorithm represent different perspectives on a single course of action. Changing one will change the others.

MOTIVES will be the hardest to unravel. They are rooted in childhood training, are culturally conditioned, and often are shaped and sustained by powerful religious beliefs. Motives surface in adulthood as a constellation of values. They are still difficult to identify and change. You don't just flip some psychological switch and stop being antisocial, for example. If you could, we wouldn't need prisons. Greed, rooted in deep feelings of financial insecurity, is like a powerful addiction. Only persistent application of the ethical algorithm eventually can bring us face to face with our motives and our human limitations. The algorithm demands an unwavering commitment to an open, reasoned process.

Ancillary Considerations

The algorithm is presented in Figure 2-1. Each major element — GOALS, METHODS, MOTIVES, and CONSEQUENCES — is enriched with three penetrating ancillary considerations which broaden and deepen the analysis. Note, further, that the outline is divided into two columns headed *Business*

	Business Side	Ethical Side
GOAL(S)		
Multiplicity	_____	_____
Compatibility	_____	_____
Constituent Priority	1_____	1_____
	2_____	2_____
	3_____	3_____
	4_____	4_____
METHOD(S)		
Constituent Acceptance	_____	_____
Satisfy or Maximize	_____	_____
Essential/Incidental/ Extraneous	_____	_____
MOTIVES		
Hidden or Known	_____	_____
Selfish or Shared	_____	_____
Value Orientation	_____	_____
CONSEQUENCES		
Time Frame: Short Term	_____	_____
Long Term	_____	_____
Constituent Impact	_____	_____
Exogenous Factors	_____	_____

Figure 2-1. The ethical algorithm.

Side and *Ethical Side*. You recall from the opening of this chapter that an underlying assumption of the algorithm is that enterprise, like a single sheet of paper, has two sides. There is a business side and an ethical side. We separate them for analytical purposes only. Let's proceed with brief descriptions of each of the ancillary considerations under each element of the algorithm.

Goals. *Do you have multiple goals?* Does your firm have both a business and an ethical goal? Typical business goals include making a profit, gaining market share, or simply surviving. Ethical counterparts might include providing a necessary personal or social benefit, such as jobs, health products, legal services. In the former the emphasis is on what you do, in the latter on why or how. Are your two distinctly different goals clearly articulated in a mission statement or code of ethics? More important, what are your goals in practice? Are they operational? Do you really strive for what you say your aims are? It is often easier to quantify the business goals—survival, profits, or market share—since they are measured in dollars or percentages. That hard data stand in contrast to the softer intuitions of ethics. The latter are rooted in values and feelings, which are more subjective and changeable. Moreover, measurements on the business side are collected into a single set of figures. They may be controversial, for one reason or another, but the focus is on facts. Ethical evaluations are spread among a number of often conflicting constituents. Differences might be aired at board meetings or annual meetings but not necessarily resolved.

Are your goals compatible? Are these multiple goals compatible? Can you reasonably expect to achieve both business and ethical goals in the normal course of events? For instance, might you have to sacrifice or reduce profits in order to achieve your ethical goal? What if your ethical goal dictates that you cease manufacturing or stop providing a given product or service? Parker Brothers was placed in that position with its Riviton toy. They couldn't continue to sell the toy and still remain ethical from their own perspective. Their goals proved to be incompatible in practice. They surrendered the business goal.

Which constituents get top priority? Make a list of your constituents, those groups of people to whom you feel accountable about either the business or the ethics of your firm. Stockholders, employees, and management itself might receive the top priority on the business side. Customers, employees, and the federal government might rank highest on the ethical side. Configurations will vary from company to company and industry to industry. In some companies it's possible that the listings and assigned priorities are identical. In practice, rather than theory, a pharmaceutical firm might put the customer tops on the business side and the federal government tops on the ethical side to reflect the role played by the Food and Drug Administration (FDA). Again, in practice, a large, durable goods manufacturer in the *Fortune* 500 might place the stockholder first on the business side and Ralph Nader's consumer advocacy group at the top of the ethical side. These priorities can change with time and circumstances. The business goals tend to be fairly routine and predictable. In contrast, the ethical goals are situational. Who are your most important constituents from an ethical perspective based on the decisions you make throughout the year?

Some corporations tend to view formal ethical considerations as constraints only. Their mission statement does not contain ethical overtones; they probably do not have a written code of ethics. They simply assert that their solitary goal is to show a profit and be perceived as legal and ethical. This is not to suggest that such companies are unethical. On the contrary, they may be exceptionally good and law-abiding. Nor does this imply that some industries are more ethical than others. It does mean that the formal attention given to ethical standards and compliance vary. How aggressively corporations pursue and publicize their ethical positions depends in part on the industry and the situation.

The financial industry provides an excellent example. Prior to the insider trading scandals of the 1980s, brokerage firms gave relatively less explicit attention to ethical codes and individual or isolated violation of them. You were expected to know what it was to be ethical and to act ethically but were given a lot of latitude to act on your own. Brokers (and apparently many savings and loan association executives) were permitted to function as "lone rangers," ethically as well as financially. It came with the territory. However, this approach proved disastrous to E. F. Hutton, Drexel Burnham Lambert, and Kidder Peabody, for example. W. Michael Hoffman at Bentley College has documented a significant shift in the percentage of corporations moving toward formal, written commitments to ethics.[6] A major reason for this shift is simply the cost of unethical activity. Another, he speculates, is the intrinsic satisfaction of doing the right thing. If Hoffman is right on both counts, it could be only a matter of time before corporations will embrace ethics as warmly as they do profits.

Methods. *Do your constituents accept your methods?* Firms have an infinite variety of methods available to reach their goals. Effective use of the algorithm requires only that those methods which may prove to be controversial be examined thoroughly. Review your constituent list with your methods in mind. Who is likely to object? For instance, the handling of chemicals might be objectionable to employees or environmentalists, e.g., Allied-Signal's Kepone operation. Similarly, Nestle's methods for marketing infant formula in developing countries were perceived as unethical by consumer advocates.

Polaroid provides an excellent example of problematic methods. Sales in South Africa were handled by an independent distributor. Polaroid's control over the distributor's sales method was limited. In fact, its only control was to refuse to sell to that particular distributor. Naturally, Polaroid was also unable to control to whom the distributor sold. That became the problem and a point easily exploited by critics. Ninety percent of the distributor's sales were to the South African government for an instant photo identification pass system used to enforce apartheid. The ID pass was equated with the Nazi method of tattooing numbers on wrists of Jews. That image destroyed the possibility of reasoned discussion. Note that neither Polaroid's camera nor sales through a distributor were unethical methods in themselves. In this particular situation, the combination of product use and method of sales created an ethical dilemma for Polaroid. They chose to prohibit sales to any distributor in South Africa. This is a very common dilemma. Executives often face constituents displeased with one or more aspects of their marketing and manufacturing methods. The algorithm helps decision makers anticipate the questionable and possibly unethical aspects of their methods.

Once you have identified the problematic aspects of your methods, look at them from the perspective of that same list of constituents you prioritized under GOALS. Will they find your methods acceptable? What about your stockholders, your major constituents? Will they readily accept your methods because they satisfy their expectation of high dividends? Will all stockholders agree? Will some be happy with less profit and greater sensitivity to employees, customers, or the environment? Run through your listing of constituents on both sides of the ledger. How is each likely to respond to the methods your firm uses? Can you quantify their degree of acceptance? How many stockholders will either buy or sell your stock? How many are likely to protest publicly in some way?

Do your methods satisfy or maximize your goals? This concern measures the aggressiveness with which you pursue your goals. How hard will you push for maximum profits or another percentage point of market share? A lot of unethical behavior occurs when employees are pushed too hard or given extraordinary incentive to achieve. Manufacturing or sales methods which strive to maximize revenues or market share represent self-imposed pressures. Employees under pressure, especially the most creative ones, will invent the necessary ways to get around the rules. Were the money managers at E. F. Hutton pressured into check kiting when a new method of calculating bonuses was introduced? Were senior executives at H. J. Heinz encouraged to jockey the records on income and expenditures in order to maximize the management incentive points that determined their bonuses? Pressure, whether malevolent or benevolent, forces employees to choose. Will they compromise their ethics in order to maximize profits? Or will they compromise profits for the sake of ethics? As a manager, would you put your employees into such situations without discussing the pitfalls or at least calculating the worst possible outcomes? The ethical bottom line is dependent on not only the methods you chose but how much effort you put into them.

Maximizing efforts on the business side of your enterprise can diminish if not squelch the ethical sensitivities of your employees. If you send a message that only results count, that may be the only result you get in return. That return may come in the form of a big surprise. Labor unions, whatever their strengths and weaknesses, constitute an institutionalized testimony to management's determination to pursue its goals at the expense of its workers. While the formation of this adversarial relationship dates to the previous century, modern management has been repeatedly unable to shake its image of employee insensitivity. In similar fashion, Exxon's decision (before the great Alaskan oil spill) to forgo the added expense of double-hulled oil tankers increased its vulnerability to the accusation that it was willing to maximize profits at the expense of the environment. Exxon actually calculated a cost/benefit ratio and plotted it against the probabilities of an accident. Obviously, the double hulls were deemed an excessive and unnecessary expense. Equally obviously, hindsight now yields a different calculation. Should Exxon be taken to task for its miscalculation? Isn't paying for the cleanup sufficient atonement? However you answer those questions, it is still true that Exxon erred on the ethical rather than the business side of enterprise.

Additional examples of corporations giving the principal nod to the profit or market share measure are not difficult to find. Once management sends down the subtle message that profits count to the exclusion of all else, dutiful employees begin to measure their performance against that solitary yardstick. It happens with unfortunate regularity. The ethical ramifications of matching methods with corporate goals are often lost or overlooked in the heat of strategy-setting battles. The ethical algorithm can help you keep tabs on the ethics of your methods. Consider another aspect of the method selection process.

Are your methods essential to achieving your goals, or are they incidental or merely extraneous? Corporations may have more flexibility than they realize in selecting the methods available to achieve their goals. Methods, especially, need to be chosen cautiously and carefully, with the fullest possible consideration of the long-term consequences. If the methods eventually selected can be categorized as essential, it means there is little or no choice available. If the methods can be described as incidental, the algorithm argues that there is some choice and that one method may be more ethical than another. Check it out. If the methods chosen can be labeled extraneous, the algorithm is saying that little or no thought has been given to methods. They have been chosen haphazardly and perhaps dangerously. They might be introduced at the whim of a charismatic CEO or an ambitious junior executive. As such, extraneous methods lack corporate integrity. They bear little or no relationship to what the company's trying to do. In fact, they may become goals in their own right.

Ralph Cordiner was determined to decentralize operations when he assumed the top job at General Electric in the 1950s, according to Richard A. Smith.[7] His rationale was based on his feelings as a junior executive climbing the corporate ladder. He hungered to exercise greater authority and judgment and vowed privately that he would distribute responsibility differently if he ever got to the top. He did, on both counts. It was this decentralization that eventually gave way to the "incredible electrical conspiracy." Junior executives were given new powers with very little instruction on either the business or the ethical side. Divisions were set up as cost centers and told to show a profit at year's end. How was up to them. It was not too clear, in Smith's story, that the corporation had to decentralize in order to achieve its goals. If the decision to decentralize was based on a personal whim of the CEO, we can then say that the methods were at least incidental if not extraneous to the corporation's basic goal. Again, decentralization by itself is not unethical. However, in that situation and the way in which it was introduced, decentralization made the conspiracy easier if not inevitable.

William Farah, long-time chief executive at Farah Manufacturing in El Paso, Texas, was one of the first to modernize his textile plants. His cutting and sewing rooms were models for the industry, although clothing manufacturing is a dirty business. His nonunion workers enjoyed many special benefits, including an above-average pay scale. Farah probably considered his methods as not only ethical but more than employees should expect, considering the nature of the work. Nevertheless, no company in the industry has undergone more bitter and protracted labor disputes than Farah. Why? Briefly put, it comes down to this. William Farah's exemplary production methods were extraneous to his implicit goal of making money for his stockholders, or even surviving. Ultramodern plants actually reduced his profits and cannot be defended as essential to survival. Furthermore, his employees were apparently unconvinced that these modern methods were introduced for their benefit. An outside observer can honestly wonder whether Farah's modern methods sprung from personal pride rather than consideration of others. A case[8] account of this corporate story describes an atmosphere of oppressive control. Farah was unable to see that his employees might be reaching out for the freedom and dignity that they presumed unionizing would bring. Farah's goal appears to be total, personal control over everything and everybody. He was apparently so driven by this inner need to control that he seemed willing at times to destroy the whole company rather than compromise a tiny bit.

Motives. We turn next to the MOTIVES element in the algorithm. It focuses on the inner needs and feelings which fuel the behavior of business decision makers. This element needs some special words of introduction. Ethical behavior is often dependent upon the inner machinations of the human psyche. Socrates asserted that "the life which is unexamined is not worth living." His pupil, Plato, advised, "Know thyself." These venerated adages carry revitalized import for the ethics of business today. Managers and executives who are totally unaware of what motivates them are ethical accidents searching for a place to happen. Motives have become increasingly important in this egalitarian age. They need to be examined from an ethical perspective.

When the algorithm is used to analyze decisions already undertaken, it is imperative that motives be inferred strictly from observable behavior to avoid flights of analytical fancy. What did the decision makers actually do? What specific words or deeds provide clues about the assumptions or values that undergirded their behavior? Why did Dr. Land of Polaroid want to do something about apartheid in South Africa? Was it pure humanitarianism? Why did Lawrence Rawl of Exxon decide not to use double-hulled tankers for the transportation of crude oil through dangerous Alaskan waters? Was it a matter of costs or not caring? These are areas of dangerous speculation, but it is sometimes necessary to push into them in order to understand the root causes of unethical behavior. Sins of omission are easier to forgive than sins of commission. Stealing to feed one's children is perceived as a different sort of crime than cheating to pay for an extravagant lifestyle, as Dennis Levine admitted to doing. Motives are a supremely important factor in evaluating ethical behavior.

Using the algorithm to explore one's motives before a decision is reached is a different kind of calculation. You are staring at an unknown. You are looking ahead at what might be rather than looking back on what is. It's hard to do it. It's hard to teach it. Abraham Zaleznick, a Freudian psychotherapist and professor of management psychology at the Harvard Business School, teaches a course for MBA students that is a powerful stimulant to self-examination. It is apparent that some of the future business tycoons in his classes do not take quickly or kindly to introspection. Probing into one's psyche—privately or publicly—can be frightening, time-consuming, and inconclusive. It can slow the wheels of industry. It is the paralyzing "To be or not to be" soliloquy of the tragic Dane. On the other hand, ignoring the subterranean dimensions of our business decisions can be even more destructive. If you doubt that, ask any of the hundreds of financiers sentenced to prison terms for their misdeeds in the 1980s.

Are your motives hidden or known to others? Do your close business colleagues know why you, as a decision maker, are recommending a particular goal or method? Is the reason self-evident? Is the choice based solely on financial calculations, for example? Is the recommended choice the kind that might lead them to wonder what you're up to? Do they know how you think, what you value, who you are as a person? These questions became very important to CEO Bill Agee after his precipitous promotion of Mary Cunningham to a high-level position at Bendix. There were other qualified executives who'd been around longer. Employees were openly questioning his judgment. He called a company meeting to explain himself to his key employees. Like the silent participant in a free-flowing group discussion, motives that are hidden are always open to interpretation. They invite speculation. James Burke's effective handling of the Tylenol scare at Johnson & Johnson was credited in part to his openness about that ethical crisis. Burke took off the "sterile gauze curtain" that had previously masked the firm's relationship with the public. He let his *motives* become known. Obviously, there are risks in corporate openness. It may account for the cultivated "invisibility" of corporate leaders noted by David Finn.[9] On the other hand, hidden motives invite speculation. These need to be guarded against as well. Members of the news media, for instance, can be especially adept at attributing motives to corporate leaders. Sensitive readers learn to recognize the journalistic pattern: "The chief executive officer has refused to comment to the press on this latest environmental debacle his firm has created, *refusing to believe that the issue is as life-threatening as it is.*" Political leaders, as well as corporate CEOs, are targets of their provocative speculation. "The president will seek legislative action on new benefits for the elderly, *hoping to secure an unforgettable place in history.*" Knowing and communicating your motives to corporate constituents is more than a protective action to forestall cynical conjecture. It is a gesture of trust. It is an investment in the future. It builds a foundation of understanding in the public mind that can help you surmount future unanticipated dilemmas.

Sensitive managers and executives will also want to know how widely known their motives are throughout the organization. Do others know what makes you tick? It was said about Robert Townsend of Avis that he related as easily to the car jockeys as he did to the firm's senior-most executives. It may not be enough, in other words, to share your motives with only a few close colleagues. The whole organization can be strengthened by corporate openness that begins with the senior officers. Society tends to respond favorably to an executive like Lee Iacocca who gives the feeling that he has no secrets.

Are your motives shared by others or are they exclusively yours? Corporations can also be victimized by executives whose motives are so prominent and dominating that they kill the incentive and corrective guidance of colleagues. Employees are treated like slaves, denied any thoughts, feelings, talents, or motives of their own. To be sure, many corporations owe their existence to an entrepreneur driven by an all-consuming passion of one sort or another. Henry Ford falls in that category. There were two ways of doing things: his way and the wrong way. He very nearly killed his company, too. His dictatorial myopia paved the way for takeover of the industry by General Motors. His unethical treatment of employees, including his son Edsel, for instance, is well documented. The lesser-known Stanley Goldblum, CEO of the Equity Funding Corporation of America during its scandalous rise and demise, serves as the epitome of selfish motives. He is presented as an extraordinarily flamboyant and impulsive potentate in a filmed account of that gigantic fraud entitled *The Billion Dollar Bubble*.[10] He relied to some extent on a few colleagues who more or less shared his dreams. When he most needed their business judgment, let alone ethical sensitivities, he was impervious to their suggestions. Goldblum was portrayed as a total prisoner of his own ambitions. The motives he lent to the company could be labeled selfish in the algorithm. Goldblum was sentenced to several years in prison for mail fraud to reflect about his motives.

An enduring and ethical business is dependent upon leaders whose motives can be shared by everyone on the team. This is becoming even more true as the egalitarian spirit in our economic system grows stronger. The "team" is no longer just the guys and gals at work. It's the whole country. Firms led by executives whose motives cannot be widely shared may survive, but not for long. This means that unchecked greed must be tempered. The Drexel Burnham Lambert story provides a dramatic example. CEO Fred Joseph is an awfully nice guy. DBL's services to the financial community were exemplary. The team spirit and corporate loyalty among all levels of employees have been reportedly high. Their star player, Michael Milken, gained early fame for his astonishingly generous support of worthy causes. The charges that resulted in his 10-year prison sentence appear to be legal technicalities. Dozens of other charges were dropped. At the deepest level, what is there about this story that most disturbs the nation? There's a saying on Wall Street that it's not the bulls or the bears that give the stock market a bad name, it's the pigs. It's untempered greed. The Drexel Burnham Lambert case centers finally on the huge sums of money involved. Michael Milken's $600 million salary and bonus package in one bountiful year, for example, was the controversial lightning rod for many observers. It was just too much. It was scary. Even Milken's kindest critics could not justify this large a share of the treasure. Few outsiders could vindicate its size, none its dubious source. They could not identify with Milken's motives. His motives could not be shared.

What is your value orientation? Values has become the current buzzword in discussions of business ethics. That's understandable. What you value as a decision maker provides the foundation for what you think is ethical. If you place a high value on personal integrity, for example, you will consider business bluffing unethical. If you believe all laws should be followed to the letter, you will not go through a red light in the middle of the night. Values have become such a central issue, however, because of cataclysmic changes in our world. Urbanization, technology, and population growth aside, visions of a better world are emerging everywhere, from within the family to political giants like Russia and China. Individual and national expectations have multiplied geometrically, forcing changes in what's considered ethical. Marital and political turmoils occupy the ends of the spectrum. In between there are many other issues in the public domain which press for change. The deterioration of the environment, the growing disparity between rich and poor, the rapid depletion of natural resources used for soon-to-be-obsolete material goods, perceived salary inequities between various groups — men and women, whites and blacks, athletes and teachers, nurses and doctors, CEOs and assembly workers — all feed the flames of controversy. Only the naive believe that any sort of change is easy. There is an extended history of decisions that have created the present system. It is important for executives to have dreams of "the best of all possible worlds." If they don't, who will? Isn't this what leaders do? At the same time, big dreams become reality in bits and pieces, brick by brick, decision by decision. Discussions of values take on significance only when they are tied to specific situations.

Values in real life are like mercury, slipping away the moment you try to put your finger on them. How would you answer a newspaper reporter who asked you to name some of your values as a business leader? Words such as honesty, fair value, contribution to society, family life, respect for the individual, corporate loyalty, or even patriotism fall rather easily from the lips. Some of the same people who purportedly subscribe to one or more of those fine values are serving prison sentences. Why? Because the values that we really and truly hold as decision makers surface in the midst of crisis. If you are unaware of your values or hold them tenuously, ethical dilemmas will rip them from your grasp. Your ethics as a tennis player, for example, are most tested on a close line call at set point. The same is true for your opponent, of course. Recall some of those pressure points in your business life and take a reading. Are you happy with the outcomes? What do those decisions under pressure reveal about your values? Are they merely dressing to be removed when the going gets tough? Or do they support and shape your decisions?

Finally, how will your peers, your stockholders, or your customers respond to your values? After all, what's going to be perceived as ethical will be determined largely by your constituents. They may share your goals and objectives, say, but not your values. Your constituents may be either less or more demanding in your shared search for profitability. Sharing goals is not the same as sharing values.

Consequences.   Setting business goals and selecting appropriate methods influenced by your motives will eventually create one or more consequences. Anticipating those consequences is the last and most critical step in the algorithm. From the business side you may be calculating the probability of survival, certainly the likelihood of profit, including how much and how soon if it's a new venture. Similar calculations, even though less exacting, need to be noted on the ethical side.

Is the time frame of anticipated consequences short- or long-term? Business regularly uses short-term and long-term calculations on financial matters. Learning curves in manufacturing processes, the entry of new competitors into the market, the future cost of capital, the potential impact of new technology, and changes in the labor pool are just a few of the business questions with differing short- and long-term answers. Take time to ask the equivalent questions on the ethical aspects of your business. Look again at some of those business calculations and probe for an ethical dimension. For instance, does the period of the learning curve place extraordinary pressure or stress on a few employees whose health may be impaired? Or how will you handle the threat of competitors?

A decade ago it was common practice for computer software manufacturers to announce a new product long before it could reasonably be delivered. Why? To hold buyers out of the market in the short term. Was this a case of bad judgment or poor ethics? It was poor ethics when measured over the long term: when delivery deadlines were not met or the product proved to be less than advertised, the credibility of the industry suffered, customer confidence fluctuated, and a climate of disrespect contributed to software piracy and violation of copyrights. People who would not steal a candy bar from a supermarket were stealing computer software.

The labor pool issue is fraught with short- versus long-term ethical ramifications. The fact that we have a minimum wage law suggests that an awful lot of corporations are calculating only the direct labor costs over the short term. To be sure, the pressures are there. Your competitors are hiring the cheapest labor possible. It seems you have no choice. But there are long-term consequences. Federal and state minimum wage legislation is one. Unemployment compensation is another. The movement of labor-intensive industry to foreign countries is the most damaging. What you're doing may seem ethical in the short term. But what about the future? The savings and loan crisis is one product of a short-term mentality. Failure to calculate the long-term effects of poor business decisions eventually forced S&L executives to compromise their ethics as well.

Assuming you're ethical now, how long can you afford to stay that way? This question reverses the priorities in the cartoon that heads this chapter. In the cartoon, survival comes *before* ethics by several years. Cynicism notwithstanding, neither ethics nor profits are an either-or calculation anymore. Effectively calculating the ethics of your operation over the long term could become a matter of corporate life or death. Ask the Manville Corporation. Or Equity Funding Corporation of America. Or E. F. Hutton, or Drexel Burnham Lambert. There are many others.

What impact will your anticipated consequences have on your constituents? Try to put yourself in the shoes of each of the constituents you named under your GOALS. Go down the list, one by one, and imagine how your constituents will respond to the consequences you have anticipated. Will they be happy? All of them? Probably not, given the conflicting ethical expectations that characterize a corporation's constituency list today. Is there anything you can do at this point to mollify the unhappy ones that might reconcile them to your decisions? Should you alter your plans in some way? Can you explain anything in greater detail? Failure to anticipate constituent reaction proved to be very expensive to the nuclear energy industry. Some argue that the industry's failure to comprehend and manage the fears and objections of the general public will have very serious long-term costs to the entire nation. Know your constituents. Anticipate their reactions.

Are there any likely exogenous factors? Exogenous factors are those people, powers, or events that are either uncontrollable or unpredictable. Weather is an obvious one. Murphy's law—what can go wrong will—is the humorous analogy to this ancillary consideration. If something can go wrong, what is it likely to be? For example, the formation of the OPEC cartel in the 1970s was experienced as an exogenous shock to many nations. It was both an event and a coalition of powers beyond the negotiational reach of the victimized nations. Cartels were outlawed in the United States by antitrust legislation. Most western countries took similar action after World War II. Oil industry leaders assumed those legal precedents would not be violated. They were. Now this is not to suggest that OPEC was unethical as well, although undoubtedly some people and nations still think so. It was simply an event far beyond the imagination of all but a clairvoyant few.

This last step in the algorithm amounts to imagining the unimaginable. Could the Manville Corporation have imagined the carcinogenic properties of asbestos? Could the nuclear energy industry have fathomed the depths of public fear of atomic reaction? Who was talking about global warming 50 years ago? Alvin Toffler's *Future Shock* and John Naisbitt's *Megatrends* have given fortunetelling new respectability. Soothsaying might well become the newest addition to the curriculums of avant-garde colleges, universities, and business schools. That's not as farfetched as it sounds. Walter Coddington, a consultant with Persuasion Environmental Marketing, notes an attitude shift in environmental management from mere compliance to one of "let's anticipate the future."[11] Note that this shift in approach also turns the ethical focus from microethics to macroethics, from compliance with established standards to changing the standards themselves. Figure 2-2 presents the algorithm with some questions you might consider when you use it to analyze your own ethical dilemmas.

How to Increase Your Ethical IQ

Let's practice using the algorithm on some of the questions in the IQ test. Put yourself in the position of the PR professional in Question 5. You have just started up your own business. Your basic goal is to survive and make lots of money. Perfectly ethical. Let's say you haven't thought much about an ethical side to your enterprise, at least formally. You presume you'll function ethically. At this early, vulnerable stage in your corporate life you need clients more than anything else. An unheard-of Texas company wants you to promote their exercise machine, a new product of unsubstantiated benefit. At last you have a potentially large client who can take you giant steps toward your goal. But there's an ethical risk. Claims for the product may be unjustified. You know this presents a dilemma. You ask for documentation. It is not forthcoming. Are you still eager to use this questionable method to turn a profit? How desperate are you? Desperate and eager enough to try to anticipate the consequences? What's the best and worst that can happen? The product might be very successful, in which case your fledgling firm benefits

	Business Side	Ethical Side
GOAL(S)		
Multiplicity	Make money only?	Be ethical?
Degree of Compatibility	Both goals doable?	Do they fit?
Constituent Priority	Stockholders?	Customers?
	Management?	Employees?
METHOD(S)		
Constituent Acceptance	Will they like?	Will they like?
Satisfy or Maximize	Sacrifice profits?	How ethical?
Essential/Incidental/ Extraneous	Alternatives?	Intentional?
MOTIVES		
Hidden or Known	Do others know?	Publicized?
Selfish or Shared	Just top management?	All constituents?
Value Orientation	Hardnosed?	Softhearted?
CONSEQUENCES		
Time Frame: Long/Short	Next quarter?	Next decade?
Constituent Impact	How affect them?	All happy?
Exogenous Factors	Unforeseen?	Unanticipated?

Figure 2-2. Using the ethical algorithm.

enormously. Or, it might be fraudulent, in which case your reputation could be badly tarnished. How do you decide?

Pioneering, entrepreneurial firms are more vulnerable than mature companies with established reputations and a large working capital. Their goal of simply surviving is very real and problematic. Their size and youth reduce the number of constituents about whom they must be concerned. They are more likely to be a target for clients who will take advantage of this vulnerability. Small venture firms are still building their client base. There's more pressure to select methods that provide for short-term rather than long-term needs. A constituent at hand seems of greater worth than the proverbial two in the future. The motives and associated values of entrepreneurs play a vital role in determining the eventual consequences. Figure 2-3 presents the algorithm in outline form on the basis of the information available at the outset of the dilemma found in Question 5 of the ethical IQ test.

Our public relations professional in Question 5 faced two kinds of risk: financial and ethical. These were the horns of her dilemma. She

	Business Side	Ethical Side
GOAL(S)		
Multiplicity	Make money	Nothing formal
Compatibility	O.K. so far	Conflict ahead
Constituent Priority	1. Firm survival	1. Future clients
	2. Self	2. Reputation
METHODS(S)		
Constituent Acceptance	Texas firm + Self	Buyers unhappy
Satisfy or Maximize	Maximize money	Take a chance?
Essential/Incidental/	Need this client	Push for facts
Extraneous	very badly	from client
MOTIVES		
Hidden or Known (To Self)	Pure survival?	Conscience?
Selfish or Shared	How will you look?	Who else shares?
Value Orientation	Buyer beware?	Consumer trust?
CONSEQUENCES		
Time Frame: Long/Short	Survive/Short	Doubtful/Long
Constituent Impact	You're happy	Customers happy?
Exogenous Factors	New law prohibits	Who might tell if
	sale through mail	it turns out badly?

Figure 2-3. The ethical algorithm used to analyze Question 5 of the ethical IQ test.

had to calculate the risks and make her choice. The dilemma surfaced in the methods available to her. When she couldn't secure the factual data, the risk became even greater. Her motives consisted of a strong conscience regarding the customer. In real life, our young entrepreneur turned down the account. She concluded that the ethical risk was too high when her attempts to secure substantiating information failed. She was gored by the financial horn, but not mortally wounded. She lived to tell her tale.

Borland International, a successful computer software company, rather boastfully acknowledged it employed unethical methods to manipulate its first big break. In order to secure favorable credit terms, managers bamboozled the salesman by misrepresenting the size of their staff as well as their true advertising aspirations. Founder Philippe Kahn implied that they adopted these methods out of "necessity."[12] It was the only way they could edge out powerful competitors. They believed the situation forced them to be unethical. Maybe so. What do you think? In any case, the Borland story is an excellent example of the centrality of methods in the real world of business. Their methods became the focal point for an inordinate goal and powerful personal motives. Our PR entrepreneur in Question 5 was less aggressive, shall we say, on both sides of the equation. With Borland International, the financial and ethical risks have paid off...so far. Will their now-it-can-be-told-truth-telling haunt them? Is this a blatant example of bad business ethics? Is this why critics joke that business ethics is the ultimate oxymoron? Free enterprise in the United States gives businesspeople a lot of ethical discretion. Borland International is a company that bears watching. They aren't afraid to take big ethical risks.

Let's flex our ethical algorithm muscles with another example. How about Question 1? The junior executive was a newly graduated MBA in the top of his class from a well-known business school. He cashed in the return flight ticket and kept the money. The consequence: He was fired within a month. He'd worked for the company less than six months. Needless to say, he did not use the ethical algorithm. He did not anticipate the consequences. He was blind to his own motives.

Question 1 occasions a rich variety of responses from discussants. What advice would you have given the junior executive at the point of his dismissal? This experience nearly ruined his career. He was personally devastated by the firing. He had great difficulty explaining the sudden discharge to other potential employers. He believed that he had done nothing really wrong and was extremely frustrated that the company refused to see it his way. His peers *outside* the company tended to agree with him, exacerbating his indignation.

Critics more neutral than his friends suggested that the junior executive failed to follow the company's uncompromising ethical policy. He didn't have to agree with it, but as an employee he should have followed it. He should have checked the matter with his boss before taking action, in any case. Some of these same critics describe the younger generation as self-centered and ethically insensitive. They are perceived as hostile to big business and lacking in company loyalty. Another group of discussants cite this episode as a perfect example of the need to include courses in ethics at business school. Business schools teach a measured and reasoned approach toward manufacturing and marketing with such instruments as linear programming and sampling techniques. The same kind of researched and reasoned approach is necessary on the ethical side. Intuition and good intentions are not enough in today's marketplace. A variation on this theme asserts that the junior executive in question based his decision on gut feeling rather than careful analysis. A final reflection turned on those situations either where company policy is lacking or where employees are less closely supervised, as with outside salespersons or brokers. It's not certain that these various responses would have satisfied the perplexity of the junior executive. Perhaps only the passage of time, the dissipation of his present frustration, and additional maturing experiences will bring this young man a broader perspective.

What emerges most clearly from this example is the ongoing need to anticipate how one's decisions will be viewed by others over the long term. The ethical algorithm is one way to accomplish this task both simply and quickly. The goals of the young MBA in Question 1 were fuzzy and short-term. The prospects of additional corporate or professional benefit from continued contact with those new-found friends appear rather dubious. Absence of goal clarity creates a power vacuum and functions like a magnet for unethical actions. The method selected to achieve this questionable goal—a five-hour drive in their car—is very casual and suspicious. An arresting feature of his method is monetary gain for himself. It makes you wonder what his goal really was: get better acquainted with potential friends and/or clients or make a few bucks? Instead of a reasoned decision, the junior executive reached a flimsy rationalization for doing the wrong thing. Lack of goal clarity with ill-considered methods, as in this story, accounts for an astonishing amount of unethical activity. Such an activity resembles an ethical accident rather than a calculated misdemeanor. The perpetrators look foolish rather than evil. In sum, goal clarity matched carefully with appropriate methods is the first step toward avoiding ethical dilemmas with potentially disastrous consequences.

It is difficult to address the motives of our junior executive from Question 1 with so little information. We can speculate that he was self-centered to a fault. He values only what benefits him, apparently. His inability to accept the company's judgment suggests a misplaced confidence in himself and lack of trust in others. He appears incapable of viewing his actions from any perspective other than his own. Ethically, he is all sail and no rudder. He is probably fearless, likes to be on the edge of things. He likes to take risks. He pushes into the ethical frontiers in part because he is unaware of ethical boundaries. He is likely to be either a big winner or a big loser—like Bernard Baruch or Ivan Boesky. How he responds to his recent predicament will largely determine which path he follows.

Looking Backward

The algorithm can be used to analyze decisions already made, as we have just been doing with a few of the IQ test questions. When so used it's helpful to look at the unethical CONSEQUENCES first. What's happened?

Is there an ethical dilemma or an unethical action? From whose perspective? In Question 2, for instance, the manager is caught in a dilemma. Should he or she follow the code of ethics to the letter and fire the faithful secretary? Or should the manager do what he or she thinks is right and make an exception? In Question 4 an employee is caught between conflicting obligations to the boss and conscience. Both *obligations* are ethical but the consequences might not be. In Question 3, at least one consequence of accepting the illegal software program could be viewed as ethical—you don't want to offend your friend. Question 9 is especially complicated. There are deep and honest differences of opinion about the ethicality of abortion, the role and responsibility of board members, the authority mandated to the CEO, decisions reached in secrecy. The consequence which launches these considerations, however, is lost revenues and profits. As the marketing executive in Question 8, your definition of a conflict of interest may be stricter than that of the firm or industry. Company policies, stated or unstated, vary widely. Well-intentioned individuals may disagree on their answer to this question. Again, it is an anticipated consequence which creates the dilemma for executives in this position. They fear they might create an unethical obligation in their clients. When analyzing events in the past, start with the consequences.

Remember that motives especially demand attention in an analysis of the decisions of others. Motives are difficult to pinpoint with any certainty. They call for a probing of the psyche and deeply rooted values of key decision makers. Executives and managers rarely articulate personal predilections publicly. Motives must be inferred from observable behavior. Be careful when generalizing as to why people behave as they do. *What* people do becomes a matter of public record. *Why* they do it may remain a perpetual perplexity.

Looking Forward

The algorithm is most helpful when used to analyze pending decisions. Start with GOALS. On the business side these are usually fairly standard: survive, show a profit, gain a specific market share, make an economic contribution to society by way of jobs, products, or services. What are you going to fill in on the ethical side? Nothing? A code or mission statement with an ethical flavor, like giving the customer top priority? Or, are you going to simply acknowledge certain legal or ethical constraints? It's your choice. You'll have to face the eventual consequences.

METHODS typically provide more options on both sides of enterprise. Will you pick a method that all your constituents can accept, customers and employees alike? Is your ethical goal stated strongly and clearly enough to help you and others resist bribes as a method? Are your values under MOTIVES such that you will follow the corporate ethical goal? Are you willing to sacrifice profits for the sake of ethics? Are there alternative methods which are less risky from an ethical perspective? Methods often prove to be the key element creating unethical CONSEQUENCES: bribes, kickbacks, dangers to employee health, environmental hazards, unfairness (a course chosen to please a personal whim at the expense of other constituents). Select your methods carefully.

The Legal Side of Enterprise

The focus in this chapter has been on the ethical side of enterprise. There is also a legal side of enterprise. But what is it? Is it simply incorporation, a legal status companies acquire by filing incorporation papers? Former Chief Justice John Marshall of the United States Supreme Court apparently thought so. He remarked that the corporation is "an artificial being, invisible, intangible and existing only in contemplation of law."[13] Does this mean that an unincorporated company is somehow illegal or "unlegal"? Does the legal side of enterprise begin and end with incorporation? Not quite. This artificial, invisible and intangible being mobilizes the work lives of millions of people and amasses billions of dollars in assets. The legal aspects of a corporation are only the tip of the iceberg, yet they have assumed a dominant role that is neither fully understood nor seriously questioned.

First, incorporation usually proves to be an expensive proposition, aside from the filing expense. As incorporated companies grow larger, their legal departments seem to grow disproportionately. In general, they consume far more corporate resources than the ethical side. Second, as embittered cynics have noted, large corporations use the protective umbrella of the law to exploit the human and natural resources of the world. The legal side of enterprise has not been confined to expensive protection. Its relationship to the ethical side has been blurred.

A central question is how the legal side relates to the ethical side of enterprise. Why is it, for instance, that ethical issues are often delegated to corporate legal departments? Do executives believe that ethics and law are virtually synonymous? If so, that is a false and precarious presumption. True, both focus on defining and monitoring acceptable corporate behavior. But the emphasis is very different. The legal side essentially protects and promotes the interests of the corporation. The ethical side *should* protect and promote the interests of society in general and the corporation's constituents in particular. Delegating ethical considerations to legal departments creates a conflict of obligation.

Whose interests should they serve? Employees, particularly, sense this dilemma intuitively. They know that ethics and the law are not necessarily the same.

Protection is certainly one aspect of the legal side of enterprise. Christopher Stone underscores this point in an historical review and analysis of the modern business corporation, interestingly titled *Where the Law Ends*.[14] The early impetus driving merchants to incorporate was to limit their financial liabilities. Stone's embryonic example was the eighteenth-century British East India Company, formed by entrepreneurs to spread the risk of sailing ships facing the double jeopardy of piracy and stormy seas. (Note that even then the risks were spread unevenly: captain and crew risked their lives; merchants risked their capital.) While Stone does not draw a clear or deep line of distinction between the legal and ethical sides of enterprise, he argues that the power of the law to promote ethical ends is limited. There is a point "where the law ends" and ethics must take over. Law and ethics serve different clients, utilizing different methods.

Law itself has many facets. Practically speaking we can distinguish between legislation—which creates laws—and litigation—which shapes their implementation. Controversy invariably accompanies both processes, pressing our attention ever closer to the letter of the law rather than its spirit, the justification for law's initial creation. This pernicious tendency of legal matters to follow the flight pattern of the kiwi bird can turn vicious. Again, the asbestos tragedy suffered by Manville Corporation employees provides an illuminating illustration: calamity was compounded when lawyers' fees began to exceed payments to victims. The cause of justice is lost in the myopic minutia of diverting detail, professional ambition, and inducement to self-centeredness in victims. The fundamental virtue of law is its capacity to limit damage as well as liability when applied properly. In contrast to ethics, the law has considerably less ability to inspire and promote generosity of spirit and consideration of others. Parties to legal controversy become adversaries rather than friends. Good ethics strengthens the bonds of personal and social relationships. Law takes advantage of the vulnerability of the opponent. Ethics responds sensitively and helpfully to the vulnerability of one's clients and constituents rather than probes them for exploitation.

Finally, the cost of legal action and its failure to deliver when and where it counts underscore the need for better business ethics. Let's consider these points briefly.

Federal legislators became proactive more than a century ago when they set up the first powerful regulatory agencies. This pattern continued through the 1930s. After World War II a new pattern emerged. Beginning in the 1960s, both federal and state legislatures spawned literally hundreds of new restrictions for businesses, ranging from equal employment for minorities, employee safety, health benefits, pensions, and whistle-blowing to environmental pollution. Murray L. Weidenbaum calls it "social regulation." He estimates that 85 percent of the federal agency budgets are directed at this newer form of regulation.[15] The emphasis has shifted from how businesses treat each other to how they treat their employees and the environment. The shift itself represents a monumental rise in ethical standards. These new standards have neither been firmly embraced nor fully developed. Allocation and fair distribution of the costs of higher ethical standards occasion considerable controversy.

Legislation is ethics with the managerial discretion removed. The only choice is to obey or not to obey. It is a costly process. In addition to the federal and state budgets supported by taxpayers, it was estimated in the mid-1970s that the paperwork compliance costs alone cost companies more than $100 billion a year.[16] There are other kinds of costs. Sears & Roebuck spent millions of dollars successfully defending itself against an illegal employment lawsuit by the federal government. Atlantic Richfield filled nearly an entire floor of their sunny, downtown Los Angeles skyscraper with lawyers whose job it was to anticipate the moves of state and federal governments. ARCO is proud to be known as "the oil company that wants to be loved" according to *West* magazine. It consistently ranks among the top 10 in the corporate charity charts, too. It spends a lot of money to stay legal and ethical.

The legal profession has been perhaps the greatest benefactor of this new social legislation. A few facts will give use some perspective.

- At the end of the 1980s there were 13,000 registered lobbyists in Washington alone, a great many of them lawyers. Divide that number by 100 senators plus 435 representatives. Each member of Congress ends up with an average of 24.3 generously compensated advisers. If we assume the average lobbyist's salary to be $90,000, the figure for senators and representatives, we arrive at a total of approximately $1.2 billion per year. That figure is only salary, not expenses.

- In complex and/or hotly contested cases the number of lawyers involved, and hence legal fees, can be staggering. The adjudication of all the lawsuits against the Manville Corporation over asbestos injuries has allocated the lion's share of payments to the lawyers rather than the victims. The lawyers flocking to Bhopal, India, and Valdez, Alaska, in the wake of those tragedies was well publicized.

- The United States now has more lawyers numerically and per capita than all the rest of the world combined. Japan, an ardent competitor of the United States in many industries, has only one-fiftieth as many lawyers. Sony founder Akio Morita attributes Japan's economic successes to the absence of lawyers in their business operations.

The differences between Japanese and American management styles is a subject of countless discussions. One not-so-funny caricature presents the differences this way. For a given problem that requires 400 new people, the Japanese hire 100 engineers, 296 workers, 3 managers, and 1 lawyer. Americans hire 1 engineer, 3 workers, 100 managers, and 296 lawyers. The lawyers as lawyers are not to blame for this situation. But as citizens they carry the same responsibility as the rest of us for the long-term consequences of these developments. Corporate managers must ask whether there are alternatives to expensive, time-consuming, and unsatisfactory legislatures and law courts. Isn't it about time they took full responsibility for the ethics of business?

Summary

Business is a survival activity. It's what we do to put food on the table, a roof over our heads, a feeling of well-being in body, mind, and soul. In primitive times our ancestors ventured forth with necessary regularity to hunt and kill in order to feed themselves and their families. Civilization has changed only the methods used, not the underlying need or the sense of moral urgency the hunters feel in pursuing their needs. By primitive standards, the hunting tools and methods taught by our business schools today, for example, are sophisticated beyond measure. Sophisticated methods notwithstanding, the need to "bring home the bacon" is still the same.

Something else remains the same. Even tribal societies had rules governing their survival activity. For example, you might steal from other tribes, but certainly not your own. Myriad rules have evolved along with the changing methods of survival. The biggest change? The tribe today is the whole world. Everybody. Business today faces essentially the same kind of question primitive tribal leaders asked following one of their celebrated mammoth hunting expeditions: "How many warriors got killed?" So your company made a profit and survived? How many of our citizens were hurt or harmed?

Footnotes

1. Warren Bennis and Burt Nanus, *Leaders: The Strategies For Taking Charge*, Harper & Row, New York, 1985, p. 21.

2. Verne E. Henderson, "The Ethical Side of Enterprise," *Sloan Management Review*, vol. 23, no. 3, Spring 1982, p. 37.

3. Charles W. Powers and David Vogel, *Ethics in the Education of Business Managers*, Institute of Society, Ethics and the Life Sciences, Hastings on Hudson, N.Y., 1980, p. 1. "In essence ethics is concerned with clarifying what constitutes human welfare and the kind of conduct necessary to promote it."

4. Edgar H. Schein, "The Problem of Moral Education for the Business Manager," in *The Art of Managing Human Resources*, Oxford University Press, New York, 1987, p. 101. Originally appeared in *Sloan Management Review*, vol. 8, no. 1, Fall 1966, p. 103.

5. *The Wall Street Journal*, May 19, 1989, p. A3.

6. W. Michael Hoffman, "Developing the Ethical Corporation," in W. Michael Hoffman and Jennifer Mills Moore (eds.), *Business Ethics: Readings and Cases in Corporate Morality*, 2d ed., McGraw-Hill, New York, 1984, p. 628.

7. Richard Austin Smith, "The Incredible Electrical Conspiracy," *Fortune*, April 1961, p. 132.

8. Frederick D. Sturdivant, "Farah Manufacturing Corporation," in *The Corporate Social Challenge: Cases and Commentaries*, Irwin, Homewood, Ill., 3d ed., 1985, p. 4.

9. David Finn, "Public Invisibility of Corporate Leaders," *Harvard Business Review*, vol. 58, no. 6, November–December 1980, p. 102.

10. *Billion Dollar Bubble*, BBC Horizon, Films Incorporated, Chicago, Ill.

11. "'Green' Executives Find Their Mission Isn't a Natural Part of Corporate Culture," *The Wall Street Journal*, March 5, 1991, p. B1.

12. "Management By Necessity," an interview of Philippe Kahn by the editorial staff of *Inc.*, magazine, March 1989, p. 32.

13. Chief Justice John Marshall, *Dartmouth College* versus *Woodward*, Supreme Court case, 1819.

14. Christopher Stone, *Where the Law Ends: The Social Control of Corporate Behavior*, Harper & Row, New York, 1975.

15. Murray L. Weidenbaum, "The Changing Impacts of Government Regulation of Business," in *Public Policy and the Business Firm*, proceedings of a conference compiled by Rogene A. Buchholz, Center for the Study of American Business, Washington University, St. Louis, 1980, pp. 21–44.

16. Chase Manhattan Bank estimates the corporate costs to be 20 times the total budgets of all the federal agencies, which at that time was approximately $5 billion.

3

Who Decides
What's Ethical?

*"Miss Dugan, will you send someone in here who can
distinguish right from wrong?"*

Drawing by Dana Fradon; © 1975 The New Yorker Magazine, Inc.

In Chapter 2 we learned that what's ethical in business depends on whose perspective you take. In this chapter we will look more closely at those various perspectives, beginning with that of the decision makers themselves. What's the mentality that leads to unethical behavior? We will see that doing the right thing is more than a matter of having good intentions. It's knowing the perspective of others and learning to anticipate changes in the marketplace. The change factors alone make staying ethical a complex process. A conceptual framework is provided to help you understand the process of change from an ethical perspective. Coupled with the ethical algorithm, it should help you anticipate and thus avoid ethical dilemmas.

Ethics Is the Art of Doing the Right Thing

But What's Right?

How do you know when you've made a sound ethical decision? Is it the kind of thing you feel, an intuition? How do you know when you've made an *un*ethical decision? Do feelings of apprehension and even cold fear creep over you? If so, of whom or of what are you afraid? Of being found out? Exposed? It's hard to answer such questions, isn't it? And sometimes, unfortunately, when the answer comes, it's too late to change the outcome. Our intuitions have proved to be wrong. Where privately we might have been only uncertain and hesitant, once our actions become public we suddenly know exactly what's right and wrong. Why couldn't we have known before?

Not being completely sure about what's right or wrong is more commonplace than you may think. In moments of uncertainty it's easy to follow the line of least resistance, whatever that might be. When we sense we are walking a tightrope, our intuitions tell us to stick with what seems familiar. If we act ethically, the business consequence is usually lost opportunities or diminished competitive advantage. Or if we act unethically, we may feel pushed into what we only dimly sense are the gray areas by powerful fears that all will be lost if we don't act in this way. In either case, when the consequences of our ethically significant decisions are eventually on public display, they always present a new and different perspective. Ethics has been described as the art of doing the right thing. It starts with what we feel and ends with how others respond. Let's look at some specific cases and issues and see if that's really true.

Unethical Birds Come Home to Roost: The Equity Funding Corporation of America

The Equity Funding Corporation of America (EFCA) will long be remembered for the most enormous and egregious insurance policy fraud of the twentieth century.[1] It is a classic case study in misguided personal ambition and blind employee loyalty, plus the dangers lurking in risky financial instruments. EFCA was a small conglomerate with financial interests in real estate, oil, minerals, and insurance. The insurance business was the source of its demise.

EFCA developed the ingenious concept of packaging life insurance with equity funds. It carried strong appeal among younger families with limited funds who wanted to build an investment portfolio and simultaneously secure insurance protection. Equity Funding provided the perfect instrument. Your annual contributions leveraged you into a special mutual fund which paid dividends and accrued capital gains—as long as the stock market kept rising. Your mutual fund stock also served as the collateral against which you borrowed to purchase your life insurance policy. On paper, you were richly in debt. Dividends from the mutual fund would pay down the insurance policy loan. Your mutual funds would increase in value *if* the stock market kept rising. That turned out to be a very big "if." Nevertheless, sales were brisk.

Sales charts released to the public projected a strong upward slope well into the future. The Equity Funding Corporation of America went public and quickly became a Wall Street favorite. It was too soon to tell whether these sales forecasts were the product of sound marketplace research or the unfounded aspirations of aggressive and power-hungry executives. Rather soon the company faced some hard decisions.

1. *They laid an egg bigger than they could hatch.* First, a stagnant stock market dimmed the glamour of mutual funds. Equity fund sales sank steeply. Next, accountants for the whole company presented top management with the possibility of a totally unanticipated year-end deficit of nearly $10 million. It was only a possibility, they stressed. It was hard to get a clear picture of their true financial position. For example, on the insurance side they were in the process of switching all the accounts to computer operation. They ran into serious problems retrieving accurate information during this changeover. If these problems became public, the executives calculated, both their mutual fund stock and

policy sales would plummet further. Worse, other EFCA divisions had become increasingly dependent on equity fund policy sales as their primary source of operating cash. The whole company teetered on the brink of collapse.

2. *The horns of the dilemma emerge.* The annual stockholders' meeting was approaching. Was the possible deficit real or not? How were stockholders going to handle that? Executives faced a dilemma. Should they be gored by the horn of pessimism or optimism regarding the deficit? They chose the latter and fell back upon that ancient accounting technique known as "fernow," as in good enough "for now." After all, they argued among themselves, "once we've got our new computer program operating properly we may be able to show record profits! Who knows?" Based on this uncertainty, the chief accountant was encouraged to adopt a record profit figure and "work backward" to justify it.

3. *They reached a point of no return.* The $10 million deficit turned out to be real. State auditors arrived unannounced. Suddenly the company needed policies to back up the doctored revenues. Top management hastily contrived another ill-conceived and vaguely implemented solution. They spun out bogus policies on the magical computer. The scheme was elaborate enough to warrant a code name, the "99 business."

Senior executives rationalized this creation of "paper policies" as a temporary "advance" from sales, like a loan. It would tide them over until the market recovered. When sales picked up, as they surely must, the paper policies would be retired or converted to real ones. These hopes never materialized. Those fake policies were later sold to reinsurance companies to bolster a cash flow depleted by increasingly cavalier senior executives. They successfully skirted every opportunity to confront the reality of negative cash flow and an increasingly suspicious marketplace.

4. *If we could only see ourselves as others see us.* *Time/Life Books* created a docudrama of the Equity Funding Corporation scandal.[2] The startling impact of public exposure emerges very clearly in this film. The perpetrators of the 99 business facetiously calculate in private that "in another 10 years we will have insured everybody in America." They laughed. It's all very funny until the state insurance investigators walk in. Then, and only then, does it dawn on them what kind of fraud they've perpetrated. The senior accountant hangs his head and mutters, "I'm so ashamed." This is the emotional high point of the film for viewers. Groups who have been watching in detached silence invariably guffaw with the delivery of that line. It is a response of incredulity rather than hilarity. The partners in crime have finally come to see what the rest of us have seen all along. They had been blind to the long-term

consequences of their actions. They'd lost perspective on what they were doing. They had mothballed their consciences. *Their crime did not appear wrong to them!* Finally, catching that first glimpse of how others viewed their actions made the difference. This pattern of ethical insensitivity or blind faith in good intentions is amazingly common. We often recognize our unethical birds only after they've come home to roost. Robert Burns pleaded for it poetically: if only we had the gift to see our deeds through the eyes of others.

5. *The cost of blind loyalty is high.* Four senior EFCA executives were sentenced to fines and imprisonment. The charges were mail fraud, not conspiracy. There was no evidence that their illegal and unethical activity had been planned. No one had actually given any specific instructions. Cooperative employees had simply done their best to help top management achieve their goals. Loyal employees responded thoughtlessly to unvocalized expectations. This, too, is a prevalent pattern in large-scale unethical activity. Guilt is elusive. Everyone presumes that somebody else will bear the final responsibility.

6. *New business tools can be very seductive.* The computer played a key role in this scandal. It served as the facile facilitator of deception. It stamped an imprimatur on fraud. It worked like magic. A single EFCA technician could crank out a thousand bogus policies a day with the clandestine cooperation of only a few employees. The computer genius christened his machine a "people maker" in the *Time/ Life* version (*Billion Dollar Bubble*) of the EFCA case. Instruments, however, are ethically neutral. They may make large-scale crime possible but neither necessary nor inevitable. The power to deceive resides within human beings, not their tools. Let's look deeper into the nature of that deception.

Analysis by Algorithm. The computer may have been the instrument of fraud, but the actual fingers on the keyboard belonged to the top executives. This crime was no minor mishap. Neither was it a precisely planned and executed fraud. Their presumed corporate goal was to make lots of money. That's hardly unusual or unethical. Their method was an innovative packaging of equities and insurance. Not wrong in itself. The illegal and unethical consequences were rooted in motives and values of the most senior executives. Their motives are portrayed in the film as blind ambition. Their refusal to acknowledge the stark realities of the marketplace suggests a myopic management. Dreams of fame and riches perhaps crowded out all other values. Creatively ambitious but ethically shortsighted businesspeople drove this firm to disaster. They backed into crime.

Unexamined Assumptions Are the Parents of Fraud.   The EFCA scandal rests upon a broad foundation of unexamined assumptions. There was no clearly articulated ethical side to this enterprise, in either its goals, methods, or motives. There were numerous occasions when company executives could and should have paused to ask ethical "what-if" questions. They could have anticipated the possibly harmful consequences of their goals, methods, and motives. Failure to explore these checkpoints thoroughly left them hostage to some unexamined assumptions.

1. *Their GOALS lacked an ethical component.*   They assumed the ethical side would take care of itself. It didn't. Top management should have created a mission statement that specified the nature of their commitment to customers, stockholders, and employees. Instead, it was top-heavy on the business side: revenues, profits, market share, acquisitions. Without a stated commitment to function ethically in pursuit of fame and riches they proved unable to handle the threat of market adversity. The painful realities of a recession presented them with a dilemma for which they were ethically unprepared.

2. *Their METHODS rested on three dangerous assumptions.*   On the business side they assumed that the mutual fund market would keep rising. It didn't. The potentially lucrative bundling of insurance with equities is coupled with high risk. The market has to keep rising steadily in order to capture and hold the interest of both policy buyer and policy seller. *What if* the market doesn't keep rising? Clearly, sales are likely to fall off. That's the financial risk the company takes, but is that all? No. Undoubtedly, falling sales will bring incredible pressure to bear upon sales personnel and marketing executives. Suppose the salespeople have private agendas that induce them to minimize the risk? Suppose a member of the sales force is threatened with personal bankruptcy? Others might be driven by a strong need to achieve. How are these types likely to react when the going gets tough? What kind of leadership and guidance will they need at that point? Will they get it? If top management asks the what-if question before inaugurating the plan, they will be better prepared for the worst, if and when it occurs. They will have anticipated the response of their subordinates, mitigated the pressures upon them to cut corners, to cheat a little here and there, or to fall into major fraud. Inordinate financial gain is always accompanied by financial risk. Thoughtful decision makers can anticipate this.

Second, the equity funding method is flawed on the ethical side, too. For the prudent investor it is an extremely risky financial transaction for policyholders. A falling stock market reduces both capital and dividends, diminishing the buyers' investment and possibly requiring additional, unanticipated payments on the insurance premium. Don't sales personnel have an ethical obligation to warn buyers of the potential hazards of their purchase? Isn't it unethical to conceal such information about your product or service? It's like selling a potent drug without warning the user about harmful side effects. Clients should be warned. Even the salespersons need to be aware that their income can fall off rapidly if the stock market slumps.

Third, top management failed to ponder the full scope of the possible consequences of the risky methods. The middle managers to whom the growing dilemma was delegated functioned in an ethical vacuum. Not surprisingly, with no ethical guidance from the top, middle managers drifted into an unethical solution. These middle managers who actually created the scheme assumed they could keep their secret secret. They never asked *"What if* our 99 business becomes public?" That question was eventually forced upon them by the state auditors. The time for what-if questions had now passed and the time for "what-now" questions had arrived. The fatal CONSEQUENCES would now be dictated by the law courts.

3. *Their* MOTIVES *were suspect.*   What motivated the senior-most executives at EFCA to assume blithely that a $10 million deficit might be attributable to an accounting error? Why couldn't they calmly ask whether the deficit was real? After all, every business suffers some adversity. Why did they hastily delegate the deficit dilemma to junior executives without thoroughly probing its probable cause? The EFCA junior executives, for their part, happily joined in the cover-up. Were they feeling guilty about creating the alleged deficit because the computer changeover was delayed? If so, they were ethically vulnerable. Their primary objectives would be to atone for any implementation shortcomings along with a normal desire to please their bosses. Resolving the deficit itself would be a secondary consideration, at best. Each set of executives, in other words, had their private motives for not wanting to face the real truth. Both top and middle management truncated their ethical sensitivities through preoccupation with their personal agendas, conveniently ignoring policyholders, stockholders, and the professional ethics of accounting.

The code language is a powerful indication that something's wrong. With EFCA it was the 99 business. In the incredible electrical conspiracy of the late fifties, the code language used in telephone calls included phrases like "decorating the Christmas tree" (creating collusive bids) and "sending in your Christmas card" (phony bid). Code language pushes the panic buttons on trust and confidence in those from whom the truth is hidden. It proves that you have something to hide. The vulnerable customer, especially, wants to know what.

Code language should not be confused with corporate secrecy based on proprietary information. IBM, for example, is often described by the media as a secretive company. They do manage their press releases with utmost restraint. While journalists may be unhappy with this aspect of Big Blue, it is a secrecy that other constituents and competitors can understand and accept. In contrast, it fosters a certain kind of trust and respect.

Algorithmically, this leads us to the conclusion that the MOTIVES of EFCA's top managers were unmitigated greed cloaked in delusions of grandeur. These motives were hidden and selfish inasmuch as they could not be discussed or altered in light of changing market conditions. Likewise, top management's cardinal value was the mere appearance of financial success, being "the biggest" as measured in stock market dollars. Such motives are out of place in the insurance business. The need for public trust and the presence of state auditors leave little place for colossal egos. We can further speculate that these ethically flawed motives determined their sales and management methods. Failure was inevitable.

The Art of Ethics Is Anticipation

Doing the right thing depends on how well you anticipate the consequences of your business decisions. It calls for a clear and complete vision of your financial canvas. That will always be an inexact calculation. In this sense ethics is more like art than mathematics. Ethics is imprecise because it changes with time and place. Your early vision, nevertheless, can serve as a still life, painted upon a canvas large enough to include all your constituents. Your sensitive rendition of a probable future is an attempt to freeze an ever-changing scene. That's a tough scene to sketch, let alone finalize in oils. Who will appreciate what you have drawn? As the creator, you are certainly entitled to a measure of personal satisfaction from your product. Your constituents have both rights and interests in what you are drawing, however. In the business world they are also entitled to an opinion. Good business ethics requires a high degree of satisfaction from all.

Begin as an artist by selecting a good, large canvas. (See the ethical algorithm, Figure 2-1, page 56.) Pencil in your answers to the four major and 12 minor checkpoints of the ethical algorithm. Be sure to use the two columns which distinguish between the business versus the ethical side of the enterprise. Fill in the GOALS, METHODS, and MOTIVES as you see them. List at least four constituents of significance in your GOAL structure, i.e., stockholders, employees, management, customers. Assign priority rankings. Who's your number 1 constituent, your number 2, your number 3? Next, play out in your mind the most likely short-term and long-term CONSEQUENCES of your GOALS, METHODS, and MOTIVES.

List them on paper. Are you still satisfied? Note especially if there are measurable differences between short and long terms. Will you stay out of jail while achieving your business objectives? Now, calculate the likely impact of your decisions on the constituents named in your GOAL structure. Add to your constituent list those who might be affected in any way: vendors, consumer advocates, environmentalists, competitors, the press, foreign countries, federal and state agencies, and so on. How would they view your GOALS, METHODS, and MOTIVES if they were privy to them all? How will they respond over time to the probable CONSEQUENCES of your actions? Once you've gone through this process thoroughly, you'll have done about as much as you can to anticipate "what's right."

The EFCA case teaches us that doing the right thing is a lot more than responding to your intuitions or gut feelings. These can get us into trouble. Doing the right thing requires anticipating the best and worst outcomes and looking at events from the perspective of others.

Creating a Corporate Ethic

The concern about corporate ethics has risen considerably in recent years. Some senior executives have responded with sharply focused in-house programs to create an "ethos" that guides and sustains employees in their decision-making responsibilities. J. Irwin Miller followed this path when he was CEO of Cummins Engine. He observed that it takes about 10 years to develop a corporate ethic that captures the allegiance of every employee. Unfortunately, he wryly confessed, one employee in one day in a single decision can bring it tumbling down. A corporate ethic, whether formal code or informal understanding, can be a fragile creation. Let's see how and why.

How Not to Build Your Corporate Ethic

A large financial conglomerate hired an outside consultant to enrich its work ethic. Management wanted to inspire employee compliance rather than demand conformity through a written code of ethics. The consultant utilized the following group exercise for new employees. The trainees are divided into groups of approximately four each and given the following list of 12 persons:

A retired military officer

A high school science teacher

A professional basketball star

A college-educated handicapped person

A bank loan officer

A hippie do-it-yourselfer carpenter, plumber, electrician

A computer programmer

An unwed pregnant woman

An ordained clergyman

A nuclear physicist

An environmental specialist

A cold climate survival expert

The trainees are asked to imagine that they are facing a nuclear ho-locaust. The single available survival shelter will hold only six persons. Each trainee is to review the list and select the six persons he or she thinks should be saved. These individual choices are then discussed and negotiated with the other members of your group to create a team an-swer. The entire exercise is intended to take about 45 minutes.

The firm's intentions in authorizing this exercise were admirably threefold: build teamwork and company loyalty; sharpen analytical skills; and, most important, convince employees of the benefits of group discussion and support when faced with tough decisions, including eth-ical dilemmas. The right structure is there. Each person does his or her own homework, then shares it with the group, and a group solution is negotiated. Analytical skills will come into play as participants argue the relative merits of youth versus experience, intrinsic individual worth versus potential value to the group's survival. The final decisions of each group undoubtedly called for uneasy compromises. Participants gained insight into the values and reasoning processes of their col-leagues. They probably did feel better about making such tough choices in a group. Responsibility for who lives and who dies was shared. The question is, What did these trainees actually learn?

Sounds like a reasonably innocent and stimulating game, doesn't it? Let's try to imagine what might happen. Will participants treat the is-sues strictly as a thought-provoking exercise or will some highly charged emotions come into play? Suppose there are persons in the group mil-itantly driven to base their selections on moral character, for example, rather than on survival usefulness, the broader ethical consideration? It's going to be more difficult to negotiate such conflicts if some base their decision on who's worth saving while others base theirs on who can best help the group to survive. More than likely, groups will argue their choices without realizing that they do not share the same goals, let alone values.

How to Avoid a Pandora's Box of Controversy

Training exercises that focus on employee values are a two-edged sword. They are capable of cutting against the intended grain as well as with it. Changing attitudes and altering behavior are both difficult and complicated. It is a profound activity that can reach deeply into the human psyche. It is usually easier for individuals to act their way into a new way of thinking than to think their way into a new way of acting. Setting high ethical expectations can lead to deep disillusionment if ideals fade or fail. Once the initial training period is over there is a natural inclination for the newly converted to revert to "their old sinful ways." Therefore, it's especially desirable to anticipate as fully as possible the potential long-term consequences of employee training, management incentives programs, or executive development. Thoughts and actions are highly situational, dependent on who you are, who you are with, and the pressures and temptations that surround you. The most imponderable issues are the long-term effects of any exercise. What are likely to be the long-term effects of this financial conglomerate's trainee exercise? What reflections are participants likely to entertain in the following weeks and months? Will they get an unintentional message from the bank officer about who's valuable, for instance? Is it possible that the training will have the exact opposite effect, that employees might be inspired to act unethically? Will the training create ethical dilemmas that weren't there before? Specifically, will some people be inclined to trust group decision making less rather than more? Yes, all of these are possible.

Be Careful about Labels.   There is an insidious superficiality in the labeling of individuals on the list. The unwed pregnant woman might be an experienced doctor as well, for example. Labels are always descriptive, not definitive. To suggest otherwise invites acrimonious argument and shifts the focus to personal rather than team values. Moreover, the labels in this exercise weren't strictly survival-oriented. Some are likely to subvert thinking about survival to value judgments about the people rather than the task at hand.

Be Careful about Inviting Invidious Comparisons.   Imagine you had been part of this exercise. The training period is over; you've been assigned to your very own set of clients. You're pretty busy each day just dealing with customers and keeping track of your accounts. Your job requires you to function in isolation from your colleagues most of the time. The same is true for them. You are all alone together. Then you have one of those days: the customers have been irritating; the account doesn't tally; you're going to be here all night straightening it out. What's more, you've had quite a few of these days recently, the more you think about it. Suddenly, feeling underpaid and underappreciated you recall how inspired you were during the training days. You remember the holocaust game; you start talking to yourself. Hey, there's no teamwork around here. How come I'm always the last one to leave? Nobody cares. It's everyone for themselves. That game wasn't about teamwork, anyway. What they were trying to tell me is I'm dispensable if I don't get the job done. Well, the hell with them. We'll see who survives and who doesn't. If the job itself doesn't promise a lot of team activity, it's a mistake to imply that it does.

Be Careful about Individual Differences.   People are different. They respond to training in different ways. High achievers, for example, often turn out to be types who can fake cooperation while secretly pursuing their private agendas. It makes little difference whether those high expectations are intrinsic to the individual or stimulated by training exercises. When thwarted, such persons become prime perpetrators of unethical behavior, whether selling cosmetics in a department store, making loans in a bank, or marketing stocks on Wall Street. High achievers take ethical risks. Sometimes those risks are excessive and they end up in jail. If we misread their cooperation as genuine, we're often surprised by their behavior. How often have you heard the reaction: "I just can't imagine how such a nice person could do something like that."

Low achievers, in contrast, tend to rely excessively on group support. They avoid risks if they can, and might even duck all responsibility for their actions. The team becomes a crutch which can hobble their growth and stunt corporate achievement.

Be Careful about Demanding Excessive Loyalty.   Would this exercise make you wonder how much of your soul you're selling to the company store? Does it ask you to compromise more of your personal values than the job actually requires? Are recruits likely to whisper to themselves "this company's trying to brainwash me"? Today's younger generation is less willing to accept corporate interference with their beliefs and values. Some resist the company's need to govern superficial social behavior, such as dress, hair style, and deportment on the job. They are even less anxious to make value judgments about the worth of their colleagues, in or out of the workplace. Use training exercises that focus on the work.

Be Careful about Simulations That Are Too Theoretical. Does this exercise raise some throbbing ethical issues that push the discussion far beyond the ordinary business environment? What sort of ethical sophistication is required to distinguish among candidates for nuclear holocaust survival versus membership on a relatively straightforward job? Would it start you worrying that a measurable percentage of persons in our society are perceived as having relatively little social utility? Would you begin to fret that you will be "dispensed with" when any crunch comes? Furthermore, might it occur to you that somewhere in the country someone is already at work "making a list and checking it twice." Value training should match the needs of the job—no more, no less. It should focus on real issues that require real-life decisions. Raising survival questions in the workplace can arouse deep feelings of guilt and fear. Be careful. Company-sponsored discussions are never "innocent" to a potentially beleaguered employee.

Be Careful about One-Shot Training "Packages." American General Corporation (AGC), a large insurance company headquartered in Houston, Texas, has developed a unique training system for its 8000-plus employees. All employees receive continuous, practical training that matches corporate needs. Each of 10 modules builds on previous learnings, fostering individual growth, respect for others, and high productivity. Training is a weekly event for nearly all employees at AGC. Outside consultants are used very sparingly.

Human nature responds well to regularly scheduled events. It is no accident that the major world religions call the faithful to weekly reinforcement of their beliefs. Employees need regular reminders of your corporate goals and ideals. The IBM T-H-I-N-K signs served this purpose. Schedule reinforcing exercises at the same time as you plan the initial events. Teams need not only to be built but constantly rebuilt. Regular revitalization is essential.

If you are unable or unwilling to make training a regular part of corporate life, it is still wise to avoid one-shot exercises. As J. Irwin Miller implied, the corporate ethic is owned and created by the employees in response to the way work is designed. It is exceedingly difficult to change that ethic directly. It is easier and more effective to change the design of work. The employees will then create their own ethic.

Be Careful of Creating Unspoken Expectations. Make sure that your expectations of your employees do not induce them to make unethical choices. The Equity Funding scandal and, to a lesser degree, the conglomerate training exercise share a fascinating characteristic. Employees were invited to respond to unspoken expectations. The subordinates responded conscientiously. *They acted in response to what they thought was being asked of them. At the same time their bosses could claim they never asked anybody to break the rules.* So who's most to blame? Take your pick between bosses and subordinates. Who are the victims? Thousands of people: customers, stockholders, employees, management, even the free enterprise system itself. Everybody loses when ethical boundaries are unclear and expectations unarticulated. This phenomenon is more common than we suppose.

Who Really Decides What's Ethical?

The Equity Funding Corporation case reveals what happens when senior management fails to decide what's ethical: the employees create their own ethic in response to unspoken expectations. The financial conglomerate case reveals what happens when senior management selects a poor training exercise to decide what's ethical: employees are confronted with multiple and conflicting expectations. So who decides what's ethical? Everyone. All constituents participate in determining what's ethical in an open, democratic, and pluralistic society. This creates a situation which is confusing, conflicting, and constantly changing. We live in a time when truth is no longer spelled with a capital T nor ethics with a capital E. What's ethical is what people are led to believe is ethical. President Franklin D. Roosevelt gave political credibility to this notion when, paraphrasing Winston Churchill, he remarked that it was not the facts that count, but what people think are the facts. There are philosophical and linguistic roots to this development.

Ethics Evolves from Situations

Humans interpret reality in whatever way best ensures or justifies their survival. The little boy who gets caught with his hand in the cookie jar might avoid a spanking by a contrite "I'm sorry mommy, but I was so hungry." Humans create elaborate belief systems based on their interpretation of reality. Meanings grow out of experience, in other words. Josiah Royce, professor of philosophy at Harvard at the turn of this century, averred that the true meaning of a word was what others did in *reaction* to it, not what it says in the dictionary. True meanings are situational. The following story illustrates this principle.

Back in the days when brigantines sailed the high seas the ship's captain was required to keep a record of disorderliness or unseemly conduct by the crew and report it to the ship's owners upon returning to home port. It happened that on one ship the chief mate was drunk with contemptuous regularity. The captain duly entered in the ship's log: "The chief mate was drunk today." The chief mate, sharing equal access to the ship's log, was aware of these entries and became increasingly worried as they neared home port. One day an ingenious solution occurred to him. He entered into the log: "The captain was sober today." What the chief mate wrote was absolutely true. What he hoped, however, was that the scrutinizing owner would read a different meaning into the sentence and conclude that the captain was drunk more often than he. Human beings seek to create meanings most beneficial to their situation.

Incidents like the drunken ship's mate occur regularly on the job. Managers and leaders unintentionally misread or are intentionally mislead. As Royce observed, what people hear *becomes* what you've said, even though you may *not* have actually said it. There is an ethical counterpart to this principle operative in today's marketplace. Namely, what a growing majority begin to believe is ethical, *becomes ethical* for all practical purposes. As our society has become more fragmented and pluralistic, predicting how subordinates will respond to managerial directives has become more problematic. That, however, is only the beginning of the challenge. Employees are only one of many constituents.

Managing the ethical side of enterprise evolves from a host of constituent expectations at every managerial level. Business ethics is evolving into an ever-changing social contract that both formally and informally spells out the rules by which the business game is to be played. Sometimes these expectations remain latent or poorly articulated until they are blatantly violated or erupt explosively, such as in insider trading on Wall Street and massive oil spills stimulating new environmental concerns. Other times the expectations change in light of new technology or consumer taste, such as with new miracle drugs and health foods. Failure to anticipate and manage these new ethical frontiers can result in debilitating lawsuits; at the least they create distracting internal dissension and costly problem solving. The business environment, like that of sailing ships of old, is a dynamic one, subject to sudden and violent changes. Moreover, it is still a world of pirates, predators, and competitors. The captains of industry face an awesome challenge. Consider some major changes in how society today decides what's ethical.

Change Is Inevitable: Anticipate It.   A growing portion of the manager's job is anticipating and managing the changing expectations of their many constituents. More and more of these expectations create ethical dilemmas of one sort or another. Constituents differ in their interpretation of what's ethical, plunging managers into conflicts of obligation. They want to satisfy both constituents fully, but it's impossible. Or one constituent offers a powerful inducement — such as a bribe — to swing a decision in their favor, plunging managers into conflicts of interest. The interests of one constituent are secretly sacrificed to benefit another constituent. Also, the prevailing notion of what's ethical may change in light of new technology, research, or new definitions of the common good. The contemporary marketplace has been likened to Chinese baseball, which permits the defending team to move the bases after the hitters start their run. The Manville Corporation can tell us what it's like to have the rules changed while the game is in progress. Managers today face the additional challenge of *staying ethical* over the long term in times of rapid change.

The Ethic of Business Is Unique.   Business has an ethic of its own. It is not the same ethic you practice at home, at church, or in other social gatherings. In addition, there are ethical differences between small towns and big cities, between small companies and large ones, between banks and car dealers, between product manufacturers and service providers. Not only does the ethic vary, parts may be unwritten, not universally honored, and sometimes violated unintentionally by the uninitiated. The business ethic is definitely different. It is also more dynamic.

The Ethic of Business Is Situational.   In Chapter 2 we noted the ethical problems presented by Edgar Schein's[3] multiple constituencies: from whose perspective will you decide what's ethical? We also noted the Powers and Vogel[4] dynamic definition of ethics: deciding what constitutes the most comprehensive and equitable level of social well-being is a constant process. What's ethical depends on the people and their evolving visions.

Business leaders themselves provide the evidence that business ethics is situational. They are far from united in their definitions of what's ethical. In the seventies the *Harvard Business Review* carried an article entitled "Is Business Bluffing Ethical?"[5] The author pointed out that many managers considered bluffing a norm, even though it might not be ethical in some sense. The article ignited a storm of controversy, generating a record number of letters to the editor. *HBR* responded in a subsequent issue with another full-length article about reader responses. The controversy continued for months, some respondents insisting that bluffing is unethical and should be banned, others arguing that ethical or not, it's basically a harmless norm. A very practical implication emerges from this brouhaha. Businesspeople should be very clear about the rules by which their various constituents and competitors play the business game, or else they'll be destroyed. What's ethical depends on who's the constituent or competitor.

There Is a Spectrum of Ethicality. One explanation for this controversy about what's ethical is that the opinions of business leaders fall across a rather broad spectrum.[6] These shadings within the spectrum represent honest differences of conviction about what's ethical. Corporate decision makers simply disagree. It is no longer possible to insist that there is only one ethically correct answer. Ethical choices will vary with corporate strategy and the values of the key decision makers. For instance, IBM pays its sales force a commission. Digital Equipment Company does not. Digital CEO Kenneth Olson believes commissions (the IBM approach) are unethical because the welfare of the client is more likely to be sacrificed to the monetary greed of a salesperson.

Some companies choose to work within a more demanding set of standards than others. It may give competitors a potential advantage. Abbott Laboratories wrote its own, more demanding 15-point code of ethics for sales of its infant formula to developing nations.[7] The alternative was a World Health Organization standard. Abbott sacrificed market share and revenues in an effort to do more than was mandated by the World Health Organization.

Some companies subscribe to a demanding ethic but still experience severe censure. The Vietnam war put many executives and companies in this bind in the 1960s. Their public positions undoubtedly affected their financial bottom line, in some cases. Dow Chemical was the prime supplier of the napalm B the U.S. government used in that war. Dow refused to bow to public pressure to stop production and sales of this deadly weapon. They managed it as a conflict of obligation between their country and dissenting stockholders.

Also arrayed within the spectrum of ethicality are companies and managers whose compliance can be labeled minimal or marginal. Their corporate behavior is strictly legal. They subscribe to the equation, "If it's legal it's ethical." Allied-Signal, Sears Roebuck, and American Telephone and Telegraph were three firms that initially fought the legal charges brought against them. Allied was convicted of improper handling of toxic waste and polluting the James River with its processing of the substance Kepone. In time, they not only corrected the violation of the new Environmental Protection Agency (EPA) standards. The episode launched a whole series of new policies and ethical practices regarding handling of toxic waste. Sears Roebuck and AT&T were brought to court by the Equal Employment Opportunity Commission for race and sex discrimination, respectively. Both firms were convinced that they were in compliance with the law. They fought their cases at considerable expense and won and lost, respectively. All three firms were at the legal minimum end of the spectrum initially. Each was newly positioned following their bout with government agencies and concerned constituents, in this case, employees and communities. It is important to recognize that the firms thought their behavior fell within the ethical spectrum. The boundaries and characteristics of the spectrum became more sharply defined as a result of these cases. They did not change the fact that there are a great variety of corporate responses to changing ethical expectations. The definition of what constitutes minimal compliance is changing.

Pressures Mount to Legislate Ethics. Customers in today's changing marketplace are becoming increasingly aware of corporate behavior that aspires only to living up to the letter of the law. One result is increased pressure upon legislators to change the laws. More and more corporate executives wake up on a given morning to discover that they have been ethically repositioned. Ralph Nader surprised General Motors in this fashion with his book *Unsafe at Any Speed,* an exposé of the Corvair sports car. This celebrated case eventually led to congressional investigations, legal actions, and the inauguration of consumer advocacy. General Motors had neither anticipated nor prepared itself to manage such adversity. More recently, Chrysler CEO Lee Iacocca discovered that some of his executives were driving company cars and then turning back the odometers and selling them. The news media gave this story front page coverage. It was not clear whether the news media was Iacocca's initial source of information, but he responded publicly and instantaneously. He is an outspoken defender of American values and direct and honest dealing with customers. He let it be known that he was as surprised as anyone to learn that his company could be guilty of such actions. While he maintained that the practice was part of an effort to increase product quality, he denounced it as "stupid" and censured the executives. Customers did not have to resort to legal action, thanks in large part to Iacocca's ethical sensitivities and immediate action. This is not always the case.

It's easy to make a long list of corporations whose reputations were shattered by a single event or product that turned the public against them. The list of beleaguered companies and products and services victimized by shifts in the ethical wind continues to grow. See Table 3-1.

This is not to suggest that the public's judgment is entirely correct. The production and marketing of these products seem to have been undertaken with good intentions: provide a safe, useful product at a reasonable price and fair profit. Public opinion, however, was a reality with which the company had to wrestle. Each was eventually forced to estab-

Table 3-1. Companies Beleaguered by Shifts in the Ethical Wind

Company	Product or service area in question
Manville Corporation	Asbestos manufacturing
Firestone	Radial 500 tire
Ford Motor Company	Pinto gas tank
Revlon	Rely tampon
A. H. Robbins	Intrauterine device
Parker Brothers	Riviton toy
Metropolitan Edison	Nuclear energy accident
McDonnell-Douglas	Cargo doors on DC-10
Hooker Chemical	Handling of toxic waste at Love Canal
Procter & Gamble	Rely tampon
Union Carbide	Pesticide processing
Philip Morris	Downtown cigarette
E. F. Hutton	Check kiting
Drexel Burnham Lambert	Mergers and acquisitions
Kidder Peabody	Insider trading
Exxon	Oil tanker leading to Alaskan oil spill

lish a more ethical position, much as if they were marketing a new product. The threat of legal action was either present or potential. Not surprisingly, the firms handled their challenges differently.

Manville, for instance, chose Chapter 11 bankruptcy as a means of resolving the asbestos lawsuits. The intention, according to a press release to *The Denver Post*, was to funnel more money to the victims and less to the lawyers. (The then-CEO was formerly general counsel for the firm.) Union Carbide publicly demonstrated its concern for victims of the pesticide gas leak in Bhopal, India, when CEO Warren Anderson embarked upon what the media viewed as a spontaneous sympathy flight to the disaster site. A generous financial settlement from Union Carbide for a mistake which they believed not to be theirs satisfied some constituents. Many, most notably families of the many thousands of victims, were unappeased. E. F. Hutton misread public reaction and treated their check kiting as a public relations issue. They hired Bill Cosby, at a cost of more than $1 million, to recapture their reputation. They understood the importance of public perception, alright. However, I think they failed to see that their problems were internal. They needed to spend some money on themselves, sensitizing employees to ethical issues. Exxon tried to buy its way out of ethical trouble with generous settlements awarded to victims of the Alaskan oil spill. The courts and some of the public remained unsatisfied.

Each of these firms had to identify and articulate an ethical position which satisfied the ethical expectations of a number of their constituents, including themselves, of course. They had choices. There was no single, perfect answer. In no case was every constituent fully content with the eventual corporate position. Moreover, it's easy to imagine that different decision makers at a different point in time may have established a different position and still remained within the spectrum of ethicality. The fact that there are no perfect answers which completely satisfy all constituents places even more pressure on the process of reaching ethical positions. *How* you reach your spot within the ethical spectrum becomes as important as *where* the exact position falls. For example, how long does it take to reach your solution? How open is the process? How inclusive of the interests of your multiple constituents? How considerate of individuals or environments? Is there public dialogue? How long is the time frame of your perspective? How self-serving does your final solution appear? The key is a matter of sorting through the options until you find answers that satisfy the dominant constituents.

Dubious Responses to Changing Expectations

Some business leaders responded imaginatively to the growing insistence for new ethical standards in the process of creating society's products and services. These senior executives dug deeply into their personal values and beliefs in order. They brought the best of intentions to this turbulent marketplace. Unfortunately, some of the responses have turned out badly. They encountered unanticipated consequences. Fate determined the outcomes. Robert Dorsey assumed the helm of Gulf Oil in the early 1970s. He was one of the first to call publicly for broader measures of evaluating a corporation's contribution to society. He stated in an address to the American Manufacturers Association in 1972 that the time had arrived when corporations should "measure their contribution to stockholder wealth by something other than just profits....they need to be socially responsible."[8] Five years later Dorsey resigned in disgrace from Gulf. Unethical hanky-panky by subordinates eventually forced his resignation before his visionary leadership had much impact. There was always some question about the real reason for his demise as a corporate executive. Was it the ethical scandal or ethical innovation at the expense of corporate dividends which occasioned stockholder disenchantment?

Robert Townsend focused on the work ethic of his employees at Avis. He turned second place into a winning combination. He motivated employees with an appeal to their desire to achieve and sense of fairness. He gave them a clear and worthy target to shoot at and rewarded them generously for hitting it. The base salaries at Avis were stair-stepped at modest increments right up to the top. Most varied by less than 10 percent. Townsend keyed bonuses to performance measured by a formula. "Changes in formula should be resisted," he wrote. This was a matter of ethics to Robert Townsend. Employees needed to know what to expect from the company and vice versa. "Fairness and full disclosure are the two keys to making the system work."[9] Townsend left Avis shortly thereafter and the company became a victim of successive takeovers, and his noble efforts were lost.

It's How You Finish That Counts

Things are changing faster than they have ever changed before, noted physicist Robert J. Oppenheimer in the late 1950s. Changes in what's ethical share in this dynamism. The shift in how their product or service is perceived can be very disconcerting to business executives. The product or service itself has not changed. Only the perception has changed. Business leaders plan, commit millions of dollars to manufacturing and marketing, build plants and employ thousands, borrow from hundreds of thousands of stockholders, and then discover that their product is legal but unethical or vice versa. It's been estimated, for instance, that strict enforcement of OSHA (Occupational Health and Safety Administration) and EPA regulations could close down every major manufacturing business in the United States. That's frightening. Canadian business faces a similar challenge. Executives became even more alarmed when environmental issues began to receive worldwide media attention in the late 1980s. It was only one of the forces in the marketplace calling for expensive and extensive alteration of business practices. In short, business entrepreneurs must ask how ethical their product or service will be perceived not only initially, but for how long. When might public perceptions of what's ethical change, perhaps putting them out of business? New technology, advancing research, or misuse of the product by consumers partly accounts for these market disasters. The cost in time and money to every constituent—company, stockholder, employee, and society—behooves the decision maker to make a studied effort to anticipate consequences. One place to begin is with a conceptual framework which catches the contradictions and dynamism in the decision-making process.

The Conceptual Framework

The conceptual framework (see Figure 3-3 on page 105) is one way of tracking the decision-making process from the perspective of multiple constituents. This framework evolves from the perceptions and assumptions enumerated in the previous pages. It attempts to organize the ethical complexities in the marketplace. What characterizes the decision-making process that corporate executives follow in order to produce or provide a service? Next, how does the public respond, initially and over the longer term, to that product or service? How can we distinguish between what's legal and what's ethical? Are they always identical? Are there any clues as to how public reaction can be anticipated and managed? The conceptual framework addresses these questions. Let's look at the decision-making process first.

Anatomy of a Decision

Business decisions typically begin with a single idea or a constellation of ideas within the privacy, maybe even secrecy, of the corporate boardroom or its equivalent. (With Jobs and Wozniak of Apple Computer it was a garage.) Eventually these ideas take shape as marketable products, and the public responds. They buy. Purchase constitutes the first level of public acceptance for most products and services. In the conceptual framework this first stage is called the *manifestation period*. The product or service is visible enough for one or more constituents outside the corporation to develop a reaction. Is it favorable? That initial response constitutes an unofficial ethical judgment. It may not last, but it's a beginning.

Prescription drugs are an exception that still prove the rule. They enter the manifestation arena when a product is first presented to the Food and Drug Administration (FDA) for approval. A second level of manifestation occurs when the drug becomes available to doctors and patients. Pharmaceutical firms face double jeopardy as they enter the manifestation arena. The FDA could deny their certification. Competitors might get hold of valuable proprietary information about the product and use the typically lengthy FDA evaluation period to develop viable alternatives. Entrepreneurs face similar risks when they bring new products to market which rely heavily on proprietary knowledge. Governmental intervention in the manifestation arena can create additional ethical and legal problems for firms. How much technical information should companies provide their customers? What kind of warnings protect corporate interests without alarming the buyers? Will product differentiation be offensive to not-targeted customers?

A second level of public acceptance occurs as the product or service matures and use increases. The product or service becomes fully accepted, ethically and legally. This time-proven formal response is called the *codification stage*. Acceptance is not the only response, however. Perhaps the product is misused with lethal result. Perhaps advancing technology reveals previously unknown and harmful side effects. The result might be a boycott, a lawsuit, or formal legislation, sometimes all three. At this second stage, public acceptance becomes codified, one way or another. See Figure 3-1. Each level represents a widening circle of opinion.

It's Legal But It's Unethical

What our framework needs now is some way of categorizing the codification responses. Is the product or service perceived as both legal and ethical? Does it stay that way? Not always. There's hardly a product on the market today whose manufacture, use, or disposal hasn't been legally contested somewhere along the line. Perhaps it's only a single in-

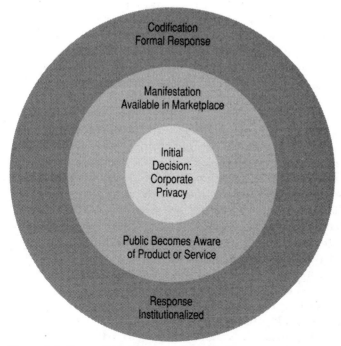

Figure 3-1. Stages of acceptance in decision making.

gredient that's been tested, such as the pesticide used in growing the wheat for a loaf of bread. Or, consider the case of the now ubiquitous polyvinylchloride (PVC). It poses no great danger when used in sewer pipe, but the manufacturing process is extremely hazardous and the substance does not decompose readily. Once a product is launched, it remains indefinitely at the mercy of countless and continuous ethical and legal evaluations, sometimes bouncing around much like those huge ball bearings in pinball machines. It takes a lot of managerial finesse and luck to avoid a "tilt." Scoring big with such products is equally problematic.

The challenge for the ethical manager is thus both gaining the initial acceptance and then keeping it amidst the vicissitudes of the marketplace. High degrees of ambiguity accompany this process. Public reaction may be divided. Some individuals or groups may brand your product as unethical even as they must acknowledge that it is presently legal. That happened with pesticides. There was a measurable interval between early discoveries of negative side effects and legislation regulating pesticide production and use. Those laws do not exist in many countries. That fact might explain why Union Carbide located a large plant in India.

Looking at these issues from both a legal and an ethical perspective creates some interesting configurations. One employer could have exercised his legal right to discharge an employee for cause. However, the employee was permanently disabled. With discharge, hospital insurance would have ceased as well. This employer elected to continue paying the insurance, not because it was legally required but because it was ethically desirable.

Determining what's ethical in business can be a highly volatile calculation. After that initial business decision, both the technological facts and the public's ethical perceptions of your product can change. Worse yet, facts and perceptions may be conflicting. That's been the battle the nuclear power industry has had to face. To the industry those opposed to nuclear power often sound as irrational as those who once believed the world was flat and you could sail off the edge. Figure 3-2 conceptualizes this dynamic process. It uses the recognizable coordinate plane to plot the changing and relative pluses and minuses of business decisions. The x and y axes constitute the legal and ethical demarcations, respectively. The four quadrants created by the intersecting axes are numbered and labeled as shown in the diagram.

An underlying assumption in the framework is that the decision maker will seek to provide products and services for public consumption which fall into Quadrant I, Legal and Ethical. Furthermore, you'll want them to stay there in the customer's eyes. Alas, that doesn't always

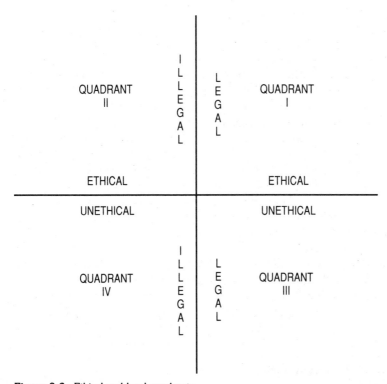

Figure 3-2. Ethical and legal quadrants.

happen. These products and services you have brought to market at measurable expense not only move from quadrant to quadrant over the short term. Over the long term the legal and ethical axis may move up and down or left and right in response to either new technology, public perceptions, or both. Overnight, virtually, your business venture can become illegal and unethical. Ask Dow Chemical how quickly the public mobilized opposition to its manufacture of napalm B. The government said its manufacture was legal. Protesters against the Vietnam war said it was unethical: Quadrant III. Ask Philip Morris about the speedy public reaction to its planned marketing of a cigarette called Downtown because it was targeted exclusively for the black community. Again, Quadrant III.

It's Illegal But It's Ethical

Ask the tobacco companies about legislation that pushed advertising on television into Quadrant II from their perspective, but into Quadrant

IV for Congress, the FCC, and nameless others. Similarly, recent congressional rulings on the use of pesticides nudges them into Quadrant II for farmers, the chemical companies, and much of the rest of the world. It's illegal but ethical. The old cliché that "it's not how you start but how you finish" takes on an ethical perspective.

Environmental issues are presently filling up the Quadrant III space. Anticipated clean air legislation in 1990 was projected to cost an additional $21.5 billion annually. U.S. industry already spends more than $33 billion a year on air pollution control. The market dislocations represented by this newest figure will be far-reaching, possibly outlawing products like hairspray, aerosol room fresheners, furniture polish, and perfume. What's ethical in business has never been more difficult to calculate. If we superimpose one diagram upon the other, we get the panoramic view of the rugged ethical frontier business managers face in bringing their products and services to the marketplace (see Figure 3-3). Corporate decisions are reached. They enter first the manifestation stage and eventually the codification stage. Corporate constituents will position those products or services in a particular quadrant. Naturally, corporate decision makers hope it will be Quadrant I—forever! One more dimension requires consideration.

Cross-Cultural Considerations

Transnational and Multinational Corporations Are Unique. They function in markets where the quadrants don't match up. What's legal and ethical in one country might be quite different in another. Such corporations will experience a real clash of values. Nestle's ran into this ethical quagmire while marketing in Kenya, among other places, an infant feeding formula developed for the United States and Europe. Distributing free samples of the product encouraged nursing mothers to switch to formula; when the formula ran out babies suffered malnourishment because their mothers could no longer nurse and couldn't afford to buy the product.

Cross-cultural issues have gained increased attention in the last decade. InterMatrix has built a large and successful consulting practice helping large corporations anticipate and manage cultural value conflicts. The ethical frontier they confront consists of two frameworks as pictured in Figure 3-3. The trans- or multinational corporation is sandwiched between the differing cultures. Because the quadrants do not match up, the corporation easily gets caught in turf battles and legal machinations. French and Italian wine exporters discovered anew how tough the United States FDA can be. The FDA found traces of the fungicide procymidone in samples of Asti Spumante in early 1990. Use of

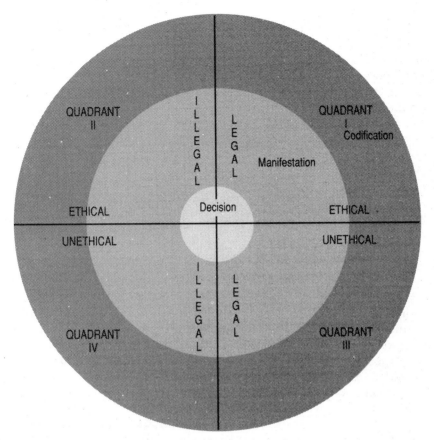

Figure 3-3. The conceptual framework.

procymidone is illegal in the United States but not in Europe. The FDA immediately widened their investigation to other wines. Wine merchants in all three countries have a lot at stake, as do wine customers. Such international conflict will most likely increase in coming years. How will it be resolved? Will the standards of trading partner countries be accepted? If not, how will these cross-cultural clashes be negotiated? These are time-consuming tasks, a strain on one's patience and pocketbook. Nevertheless, managing the ethical side of international business continues to challenge executives. Not only do they function in two often contrasting and conflicting ethical systems, constituents in both bring ancillary considerations to bear on their decisions. One of the most vexing examples of an international corporate challenge is discussed in the next section.

The Ethics of Apartheid in South Africa. The problems confronting transnational and multinational corporations is amply illustrated by foreign firms in South Africa. IBM, for instance, was one of more than 300 U.S. corporations doing business in South Africa. In 1948 a newly elected government legislated racial partitioning of blacks and whites in a system that came to be called apartheid or "separate." IBM opened their first office there in 1952. They have employed as many as approximately 286 native blacks, some of whom occupied managerial positions. The jobs required high-level technical skills. They were guided by the same IBM ethics in South Africa as they were at home. Like nearly all the American corporations functioning in South Africa, IBM was a signatory of the Sullivan principles. These principles, developed by Philadelphia Baptist minister Louis Sullivan, provided ethical justification and strict guidelines for U.S. firms doing business with this otherwise ethically condemned country. The independent and international consultant firm of Arthur D. Little, headquartered in Cambridge, Massachusetts, ranked corporations annually on their progress toward full compliance. IBM always ranked near the top. Microethically, it always complied with the known standard in South Africa.

In the early 1970s many Americans began to protest the presence of American firms in South Africa. They argued that the firms' mere presence perpetuated apartheid. This growing antiapartheid chorus filed stockholder resolutions for corporate annual meetings, arranged boycotts of offending company products and services, and even inspired investment portfolios which excluded companies with South African affiliations. It was of little or no significance to those ethical radicals that many of the firms, including IBM, complied with the Sullivan Principles. They were not concerned with microethics, or compliance. Their focus was macroethics, that is, changing the rules of the game.

The difference is considerably more than semantic. Many firms, especially IBM if you give credence to its public statements, viewed apartheid as unethical. They believed they were as committed to changing the system as their more radical colleagues. They shared the same goal, in other words. Their methods and motives were different, however. The firms wanted to stay in South Africa, motivated by both good intentions and a desire to make money. The radicals wanted the firms to leave South Africa, motivated by moral abhorrence of apartheid and a desire to end it. Common recognition of a shared goal but different methods might have moderated discussions of an issue which often approached that of a sandlot shouting match.

The apartheid system in South Africa began to unravel in the late 1980s. Sullivan himself put the government on notice in 1987 that he would withdraw his protective umbrella unless immediate action were taken. A year later he was forced to do precisely that. IBM also withdrew from the direct investment there. It specifically stated that it was withdrawing for economic reasons only, implicitly implying that its ethical perspective had not changed. It's possible that the two major parties to this controversy will claim that their respective policy of either staying or leaving South Africa contributed most to the eventual demise of apartheid. As noted, the goal was shared. While their methods and motives were different, it might appear that the consequence of defeating apartheid is also shared. That's partly true. The final consequence, however, is not simply the destruction of apartheid. It is the rebuilding of the country along different ethical lines. So, we must now ask, which position contributed most to that longer-term task? The ethical considerations continue. A new dimension emerges as an outer one is peeled off.

Summary

Business is a survival game with its own set of rules. Those rules are changing around the world. Managers must learn to think deeply rather than simply react, anticipate for the long term rather than simply hope for the best, include all constituents rather than the dominant financial ones.

What's ethical depends upon the situation. Situations can be as rich in variation as a child's kaleidoscope. A slight turn brings a new scene to view. Perceptions of what's ethical can change overnight and become illegal in a matter of weeks or months. Finally, we've reached that pinnacle of worldwide egalitarianism whereby a supposedly less influential and significant nation or individual can have a powerful impact on shaping the business ethic. Who decides what's ethical? Everybody. Business ethics is the art of anticipating and negotiating solutions acceptable to all constituents.

Footnotes

1. Frederick D. Sturdivant, "Equity Funding Corporation of America," in *The Corporate Social Challenge: Cases and Commentaries,* 3d ed., Irwin, Homewood, Ill., 1985, p. 101.

2. *Billion Dollar Bubble,* BBC Horizon, Films Incorporated, Chicago, Ill.

3. Edgar H. Schein, "The Problems of Moral Education for the Business Manager," *Sloan Management Review,*" vol. 8, no. 1, 1966, p. 3.

4. Charles W. Powers and David Vogel, *Ethics in the Education of Business Managers,* The Hastings Center, Institute of Society, Ethics and the Life Sciences, Hastings on Hudson, N.Y., 1980.

5. Albert Z. Carr, "Is Business Bluffing Ethical?" *Harvard Business Review,* January–February 1968.
6. Verne E. Henderson, "The Spectrum of Ethicality," *Journal of Business Ethics,* vol. III, no. 1, 1984, p. 163.
7. Frederick D. Sturdivant, "Abbott Laboratories: Similac (A)," in *The Corporate Social Challenge: Cases and Commentaries,* Irwin, Homewood, Ill., 3d ed., 1985, p. 21.
8. Robert Dorsey, "New Standards for Corporate Accountability," address to American Management Association, October 1972.
9. Robert Townsend, *Up the Organization,* Knopf, New York, 1970.

4
Dilemmas Facing
the CEO

*"I told him it wouldn't kill him to try to be nice
once in a while, but I was wrong."*

Drawing by Weber; © 1988 The New Yorker Magazine, Inc.

Lives of the Rich and Powerful

The chief executive officers of major corporations appear to have enormous power. Those in the *Fortune* 500 command hundreds of thousands of employees and manage budgets in the multibillions. Many are chauffeured in limousines. Some travel in private jets. A few are on personal terms with presidents and prime ministers. They are the kings and queens of free enterprise.

Do business leaders today really have power? What kind of power? Is it too much? Is the power grossly or regularly abused? Are the critics of corporate wealth just jealous? Can we believe those CEOs who belittle the resources at their disposal and cite their dependence on colleagues? Are silence and secrecy their best insurance against criticism? It's doubtful that a marshaling of facts will settle questions of executive power to the satisfaction of every reader. In this chapter we will give the formal analytical tools a rest and simply look at the lives of several famous chief executives. What dilemmas did they face? What personal and corporate goals guided them? What can we learn from reviewing their history that will enlighten present and future executives? How did they handle the incredible wealth and power which fell into their hands? What kind of human beings were they?

The Conscience of the CEO

The year is 1905. In the eyes of others, you are the young founder and chief executive of a rapidly expanding oil company in the United States. In your own eyes, you're simply a businessman trying to make a living. The Justice Department has just launched an investigation of your firm for possible violation of the Sherman Antitrust Act. This new piece of legislation is actually 15 years old but has never been given a real test. You certainly favor its major tenet: "Every contract...in restraint of trade...is declared to be illegal." To your amazement you are accused of "conspiring" to do just that. Federal attorneys apparently believe you have used questionable tactics to gain control of several railroads. It looks to you as if these young government lawyers are just using you as a test case for the new law and building reputations for themselves at the same time.

How Would You Choose?   The court trial is held in remote Key West, Florida. You are in the witness box. The prosecuting attorney asks,

"Was there a Southern Improvement Company? Were you not in it?" The attorney does not have the name of the company quite right. He should have said "South Improvement Company." You *are* the founder of that legal entity. The attorney has clearly made a big mistake. How would you respond? The emerging horns of the dilemma suddenly reveal sharp, pointed tips. You ponder the alternatives, quickly. You would be technically correct if you said "no." The lawyer is wrong. He doesn't have the name right. He doesn't really know what he's talking about. He's legally wrong, too. Free enterprise means the government shouldn't interfere with commerce. On the contrary, this new law should help business, not haul innocent businesspeople into a law court. He's ethically wrong as well. What you've been doing is in everyone's best interest. Your motives are the best. Everyone knows what a regular churchgoer you are. You even teach a Sunday school class occasionally. Now, some of those other characters you compete against should be the ones on trial. They're picking on you because you're honest. You silently conclude this court case is not likely to benefit anybody except lawyers. You clearly have solid grounds for a no answer. That would end the lawyers' fishing expedition. But what about the other horn of the dilemma?

You could offer a correction of the company name, and answer "yes" to the intent of the lawyer's question. This would likely lead to additional questions about your business practices and strategies. You definitely do not want to share this information with your competitors. Moreover, a yes answer appears to be both risky and fruitless. A court conviction would damage your personal reputation if not your business interests. Besides, only the legal and ethical purists would answer yes. The horns of the dilemma are clearer and nearer. It's either no or yes. The letter of the law allows you to say no. The spirit of the law demands a yes.

It's a Double Dilemma.   What would you have done in the above situation? Would you have said no or yes? How would you defend your answer? Would it occur to you that you are sandwiched between two dilemmas? One dilemma is a *conflict of obligation* between your business interests and society as represented in the new antitrust law. That's a common occurrence in free enterprise. It's usually considered a fair fight. You have a right to defend your best interests. Society has a right to pursue what it perceives as its best interests. Viewed from this perspective your dilemma is nothing more than a conflict of obligation. That means that both horns of the dilemma are ethical. Compromise is possible. You can answer no in defense of your own worthy interests and force the other party to defend theirs. However, there is another dilemma. It is a *conflict of interest*. You've been brought up to tell the truth. And the truth of the matter is that you *are* involved in a company with a very similar name. The lawyer might not have the name quite right but the rest of his story checks out. This dilemma pits the truth against a technical falsehood. Letting falsehood triumph is unethical. In a court of law it is illegal. How would you decide?

Is It a Lie Not to Tell All the Truth?   Chief executives regularly face such dilemmas. Free enterprise bestows upon them both the freedom and responsibility to choose between self-interest versus the public interest, between truth and falsehood, between the subtleties of what's ethical versus what's legal. The consequences of their decisions shape the destiny of a nation. Their conscience is always on the line. It's been that way for a long time.

Businesspersons have confronted similar dilemmas for centuries. Donald Hill recalled the dilemma facing a merchant during a food shortage and famine in ancient Rhodes.[1] The merchant landed on the beleaguered island with a shipload of corn for which, under the circumstances, he could have demanded and received an exorbitant price. He alone was aware that other traders were also sailing from Alexandria to Rhodes in ships laden with grain. The dilemma, as phrased by Hill: "Ought he to tell the Rhodians the truth? Or should he say nothing and sell his stock at the best price he can get?" With today's market efficiency, the dilemmas facing modern senior executives may be more subtle and complicated. Nevertheless, their resolution must eventually emerge from the same source: the conscience of decision makers. Their values, motives, and sensitivity to other human beings shape both the short- and long-term consequences of their deeds. Extraordinary powers and responsibilities fall into the hands of men and women who control the economic survival or well-being of others. The full dimension of their conscience emerges in direct ratio to their success. Wealth and power have a way of revealing the underlying character of a person. Let's look more closely at the lives of a few internationally famous enterprising entrepreneurs. What kind of people were they? How did they justify their decisions and wealth?

"God Gave Me My Money."   John D. Rockefeller was the man in the witness box in Key West, Florida. His turn-of-the-century assertion that God made him rich is often perceived today as religious arrogance. Others read it as the epitome of capitalistic egotism. In fact, his pious assertion represents his understanding of the Protestant principle of predestination. That doctrine, a potent ingredient in the work ethic, averred that our human destiny is predetermined by divine forces before our birth. Worldly success is merely evidence that our manifest destiny is being fulfilled. From that perspective, it is God's decision that

Rockefeller is rich. If God hadn't decided to make him rich, he'd be poor. Through no fault of his own, he's been selected by divine power to be wealthy. It is his duty to fulfill that destiny. That's powerful moral motivation. It can provide justification for lots of questionable deeds. It's the flip side of "the devil made me do it." For predestined Protestants, Rockefeller's insistence that God gave him his money is nothing less than an expression of profound ethical responsibility and humility. It's not unusual for people with deep religious convictions to sound arrogant, even in their humility and with or without riches. Rockefeller's inordinate success and stories of how he achieved it undoubtedly colored his pious assertion in the eyes of others. Some people envy success. Others imitate it. We will try to understand it. What inner hopes and dreams drove these striving entrepreneurs to their larger-than-life successes? Motives are the key.

Rockefeller's business colleagues never described him as either ethical or humble. Without the slightest hesitation he answered a quick and simple no to the question about the Southern Improvement Company. He took advantage of the technical loophole created by an attorney's ineptness. (He also escaped conviction.) His takeover of Colorado Fuel and Iron was nothing less than mob brutality. His pressure tactics in assembling the companies which eventually became Standard Oil were criminal by today's standards. His ethics in those early days of his career rarely extended beyond the letter of the law, and some of his business tactics often violated the law, certainly the spirit of fairness and generosity. Those decades before and after 1900 acquired a rough-and-tumble business ethic of their own. Rockefeller was a major contributor to that ethos. Was that whole ethos also God's intention? Indisputably, it is now a matter of history. Where did John D. develop his conscience?

Rockefeller's first business ventures occurred in and around Cleveland, Ohio. He was one of five children in a poor family. His father was an itinerant salesman of various products, including medicinal merchandise of dubious efficacy. On occasion the father was an official fugitive. One revealing episode from his youth suggests a possible source of the son's reputed toughness. Rockefeller's father once confessed to an interviewer that "I cheat my boys every chance I get, I want to make 'em sharp. I trade with the boys and skin 'em and I just beat 'em every time I can. I want to make 'em sharp."[2] He succeeded. Rockefeller was indeed sharp. Andrew Carnegie called him "Reckafeller." It is not clear that Rockefeller actually initiated any of his many battles with competitors and regulators. It *is* clear that he knew how to fight and win. Every confrontation seemed to increase his power and wealth.

Rockefeller fell victim to a personal dilemma eventually. He came to realize that his intentions and self-image did not match the public's perception. This is not altogether unnatural. We judge ourselves by our intentions while others must judge us by our behavior, and we them, too. Highly motivated and talented individuals are especially susceptible to this particular dilemma. They can lament with poet Robert Burns: "If we could only see ourselves as others see us."

John D. Rockefeller tried. He met a Lutheran clergyman from Minnesota in the late 1880s. The young Reverend Frederick T. Gates rescued John D. from both the embarrassment of his riches and the court trials which exposed his ruthless methods. Gates encouraged and aided Rockefeller in his giveaway programs, bankrolling schools and churches, initially. Together, they inaugurated the large-scale, nineteenth-century exercises in corporate charity. One of Rockefeller's first gifts, amounting to $600,000, launched the University of Chicago in 1890.

Rockefeller was not suddenly converted to benevolence after he became rich. His diary records a steady stream of gifts of nickels and dimes to his church while he was still poor. He taught Sunday School at a Baptist church in Cleveland. This private Rockefeller, however, was not the man the public knew. Reverend Gates helped the private John D. go public.

John D. Rockefeller's story invites speculation as to how many contemporary corporate executives share his dilemma. How many are misperceived by the public? You wonder whether Willie Farah, CEO of Farah Manufacturing Company in El Paso, Texas, appreciates the newspaper descriptions of his autocratic personality. Did Frank Lorenzo resign as CEO of Texas Airlines because he finally caught a glimpse of the nearly universal hostility directed toward him? Was Peter Cohen of American Express totally blind to the impression he made on his peers? It's relatively easy to make a list of corporate executives whose notorious public images possibly obliterate a contradictory private picture: Robert Foman of E. F. Hutton; Frederick Joseph, Dennis Levine, and Michael Milken of Drexel Burnham Lambert; Ivan Boesky; Martin Siegel of Kidder, Peabody & Company; Warren Anderson of Union Carbide; Daniel Houghton of Lockheed; George Steinbrenner of American Ship Building Corporation; and John ("Neutron Jack") Welch of General Electric. Chief executives are doomed to public visibility for one reason or another: decisions, dilemmas, their presumed power or wealth. They have a choice, as did Rockefeller. How do they wish to be perceived? What do they wish to do about it?

The Sound of Silence. Inordinately successful corporate executives are virtually compelled to be visible with their private convictions and public charities. As Socrates noted centuries ago, "If a rich man is proud of his wealth, he should not be praised until it is known how he employs it." In this new age, praise is only one of the reasons for using wealth publicly. Silence is a powerful sound. Remember the playground proverb, "Sticks and stones may break my bones but words can never hurt me"? Ironically, it's not words but silence from the rich that hurts, that breaks the heart of those who benefit less generously from the system. What is the sound of silence? In the short run the answer lies in how silence affects the people. What does the public believe and how will they react if you say nothing? Rockefeller donated all the initial funding for the University of Chicago. He secured matching gifts from meatpackers Swift and Armour. His gifts to religious charities were numerous, but best known is probably Riverside Church in New York City. The huge fortune Rockefeller amassed has fueled worthy projects for more than a century.

In the long run the sound of silence affects the system itself. Rockefeller not only rescued his name and reputation by going public. He pronounced a wordless benediction on free enterprise. He let his money do the talking. He gave it away. Silence from the rich and the powerful violates the spirit of free enterprise. The system was not primarily designed to endow certain people with inordinately generous benefits. That is a by-product. It was intended to *free* everyone to pursue opportunities and utilize skills without interference from suffocating authorities. You can debate the ethics of a system that permits and even encourages the accumulation of millions of dollars into the hands of a relatively few individuals, of course. Presently the votes to change the system are not there. A recent *Fortune* article reported that less than 24 percent of those polled believe there should be a law limiting the amount of money an individual can earn in a year.[3] However, the health and well-being of our system rests on the ethical sensibilities of those into whose hands the lion's share falls. Their public attitudes and actions are critical. When those whom the system inordinately benefits respond publicly with gratitude and generosity, a powerful ethic is nourished. Whatever it's called — enlightened self-interest, sharing, economic justice — it injects new enthusiasm into the system. The system is the people, all the people.

Measured generosity from the fortunate few can inspire hard work and generosity from others. That is not the best motive for benevolence, however. There is no guarantee that the generosity will be appreciated. Some of those Bible-pounding Baptists believed Rockefeller's money to be irrevocably tainted. They cast their sectarian ballot to reject his gifts. That's another dilemma accompanying great personal wealth. On the one hand, not giving is sure to arouse the enmity of those who expect generosity. On the other, giving will not guarantee a grateful recipient. The best motive for benevolence rests on an inner conviction that great wealth is not a thing to be grasped but a gift to be shared. Rockefeller certainly shared his wealth, even if his motives were unclear. Another famous capitalist, discussed in the following section, shared both.

The Saint of Capitalism

The lives of business tycoons always invite sensitive questions. Should we presume that they were merely products of their eras? Or were they such forceful creatures of destiny that they literally created their times? Did their actions spring from impulse? Or were they guided by a carefully wrought master plan? What were their motives, their values? Did they deserve to be called "captains of industry" because they provided essential and excellent leadership? Or were they "robber barons" who victimized the weak and poor and stole from the public coffers? How can we account for some of their decisions and evaluate their sensitivity to ethical considerations?

Andrew Carnegie was an independent, wily Scots Presbyterian who showed little interest in the risky and exciting world of corporate gamesmanship. He never became dependent upon investment bankers for growth capital. It's true he borrowed the requisite $217.50 for his first investment in Woodruff's Palace Car. It paid off in short order. He also took a flier, using insider information, on some acreage in Pennsylvania after oil was discovered in Titusville in 1859. But he built his steel empire using retained earnings for expansion. That was to become the good old-fashioned way. Carnegie quietly tended to his steel plants, anticipating or responding quickly to market changes while others endeavored to manipulate them. Carnegie Steel grew larger and larger.

When J. P. Morgan finally decided to absorb Carnegie Steel to form U.S. Steel, he opened the conversation by offering Andrew an opportunity to retire early and then asked him to name his price. Carnegie responded by memo, giving a figure he considered fair. Morgan accepted it without argument. There were no further negotiations. No team of lawyers was needed. The Morgan syndicate pocketed a profit of nearly $60 million. While Carnegie got what he asked for, he later remarked he probably could have gotten another $100 million if he had asked for it. Carnegie didn't ask. Morgan didn't offer. Each was guided by a set of deeply held personal values. Their personal motives and public objectives guided them through a potentially destructive ethical dilemma which pitted manners against money. Neither regretted the transaction.

Andrew Carnegie did retire after selling out to J. P. He then devoted himself full-time to charitable work in the education field. In 1901 he started the Carnegie Institute of Technology, followed by a stream of gifts to institutions and educational enterprises in both his native Scotland and the United States, including Booker T. Washington's Tuskegee Institute. By 1918 he had established more than 2500 libraries in small towns and cities throughout the United States. In the course of all this beneficence he was guided by his own theory of wealth.

> This, then, is held to be the duty of the man of wealth: to set an example of modest, unostentatious living, shunning display or extravagance; to provide moderately for the wants of those dependent upon him; and, after doing so, to consider all surplus revenues which come to him simply as trust funds, which he is called upon to administer...the man of wealth thus becoming the mere trustee and agent for his poorer brethren.[4]

Carnegie Faced a Dilemma. Andrew Carnegie's big dilemma was managing his immense wealth. Should he give it all away or keep some of it? The greatest sin, he once remarked, was to die rich. The wealthy man should carefully arrange to dispose of his riches before death. By this standard Carnegie died a sinner in his own eyes. He was unable to give it all away. Nevertheless, in the eyes of the public, then and since, Andrew Carnegie has the best credentials to be called the saint of capitalism. It was Mark Twain who first addressed him as Saint Andrew in a tongue-in-cheek letter written to Carnegie requesting a $1.50 contribution for a hymnbook.[5]

Carnegie demanded a great deal from his managers and steel workers — too much, some said. But he expected no less of himself. The single, large blotch on his record, in his own estimation, centered around the handling of strikebreakers at his Homestead plant. There, a favored, trusted subordinate exercised cruel coercion rather than Carnegie compassion while Andrew was enjoying an extended visit to Scotland. Despite his wealth and worldly acclaim, he was sobered by the rebellion of workers. He returned home to manage it. In his day such a trip was a powerful gesture of compassionate responsibility. Carnegie was generally forgiven, even though the episode was not forgotten. In a public apology he acknowledged full responsibility for the debacle since he was "the lord of the manor."

Carnegie's beneficence gradually spread beyond Pittsburgh. People in the small towns all across America treasured their Carnegie Public Library as *the* priceless community luxury, unashamedly reflecting a subservient appreciation. Andrew Carnegie *was* a saint in their eyes. He established a powerful ethic of corporate responsibility and charity. Try to imagine the impact of his name and generosity upon unnumbered millions of young people.

Men and women of even moderate wealth continue to face the Carnegie dilemma: How do you respond to an economic system that has so favored you with its abundance? Free enterprise places extraordinary wealth in the hands of a few people. It spawns conflicts of obligation between self and family and society. How much should you keep for yourself? How much should you give away? Fortunately, unlike conflicts of interests, conflicts of obligation are negotiable. Both horns of the dilemma are legal and ethical. You can compromise, as did Andrew Carnegie. He was open and generous with all that he had received from America. He brought an integrity to every decision and deed such that, unlike Rockefeller, it was difficult to accuse him of merely dispensing a small portion of ill-gotten gains as either remorse or a public relations stunt. Rockefeller was not treated so kindly by the public. This difference might root in the temperaments of the men. Rockefeller was a more private, uncommunicative man. He is not on record for any apologies for his behavior. He lacked Carnegie's public display of warmth and human compassion. Andrew Carnegie lays unquestioned and unchallenged claim to the title "the saint of capitalism."

The Fine Line between Greed and Gratitude. Carnegie had difficulty living up to his own benevolent ideals. So did the general public. Carnegie's Bible advised him that it's more blessed to give than to receive. There's also a sense in which it is easier to give than to receive. The giver feels blessed, powerful. Giving has great potential to enhance the human spirit. In contrast, if you receive out of desperation, you may feel unblessed and powerless. Gratitude does not rise so easily to the heart or lips. Receiving has great potential to demean the human spirit. A century of personal philanthropy has pushed gratitude to the other end of the ethical spectrum for both givers and receivers. After all, the dispensers of charity are beneficiaries of the system. They are receivers, too. Did the givers start feeling less gratitude? Something changed. The Wall Street crash of 1929 demolished many of the big fortunes. That harsh reality added the motive of fear to that of greed and turned many into hoarders. Personal and corporate philanthropy declined. The public attitude shifted. People were less willing to receive from the hand of the rich, less subservient toward wealth. Strident voices began to demand that wealth be shared in the name of social "rights," economic justice, or corporate responsibility. Unfortunately, these terms were never well defined within the context of our economic system. The "free" in enterprise was diminished. The nation discovered that gratitude is not an instinctive human characteristic. It must be carefully and continuously cultivated by a society fortified with lofty and enduring values. For both those who give and those who receive, this line between greed and gratitude has become exceedingly fine.

Proper gratitude on the part of both those who give and those who receive was very much a part of the business ethic personified by Andrew Carnegie. He measured his wealth by what he gave away rather than what he kept. Is it fair to say that the spirit of free enterprise has turned mean in the midst of more plenty than the world has ever known? The challenge to the modern moneyed crowd is recovery of the Carnegie heritage of unconditional generosity.

The Trust Builder

United States Steel was the first billion-dollar company in America. John Pierpont Morgan was its founder. The year was 1901. When finally assembled through purchase of several smaller firms, U.S. Steel controlled 60 percent of the productive capacity in the nation. It was virtually a monopoly. Mergers and acquisitions were becoming increasingly frequent among the railroads, meatpackers, and assorted manufacturers. As happened again in the 1980s, investment bankers dominated this remarkable period of financial history. J. P. Morgan was the unchallenged figure among investment bankers. Like Carnegie, he embodied the business ethic that prevailed in his time.

The creator of U.S. Steel had lots of irons in the fire: he was intimately involved in shaping General Electric, AT&T, International Harvester, and the Erie, Pennsylvania, and New York Central railroads. One of his contemporaries called him "the boss of bosses,...the ultimate American sovereign."[6] Another remarked that his power "rivaled kings and presidents as an object of interest, respect, and hate."[7] He rescued the United States monetary system in 1895 and then five years later, in an apparent and unusual display of ego, fell into an uncontrolled bidding war with Edward Harriman for Northern Pacific railroad. Eventually this episode occasioned one of the first Supreme Court decisions based on the Sherman Antitrust Act. Toward the end of his financial career as U.S. Senate investigation disclosed that Morgan indirectly controlled more than 100 corporations worth in excess of $20 billion. What was the ethic of a man with so much power?

Morgan Trusted in Trust.   J. P. Morgan stated in public testimony that commercial credit was really based on a person's character. "Money cannot buy it....Because a man I do not trust could not get money from me on all the bonds in Christendom."[8] Most of Morgan's transactions were sealed with a handshake. The deal for Carnegie's steel company required even less. It was handled through an intermediary. Morgan sent a deputy by the name of Charles Schwab to negotiate that buyout. J. P. Morgan had a different style. At least one observer implied he was just lucky: "Not once was he subjected to strictures of 'tainted wealth' nor at any time had he to fight an inimical public opinion such as Jay Gould had to in his day, and as Rockefeller encountered throughout his active career."[9] Morgan set the ethical standard for investment bankers for his time.

J. P. Morgan's religious affiliation was a matter of public record during his day. He was a pillar of his local Episcopal church in New York City. His love of hymn singing, booming baritone voice, generous contributions, and activities at the diocesan level are the stuff of legends. Morgan did not have the coercive, abrasive style of Rockefeller. He displayed considerable tolerance for ambiguity in his personal relationships. With the exception of the bidding war for the Northern Pacific railroad with Edward Harriman (a man he reputedly disliked), we never get a strong picture of a man who abused his power. Rather, the keystone to Morgan's ethics was trust. His mediating efforts on behalf of the Pennsylvania railroad interests provide a typical example of trust building. He coaxed the conflicting parties aboard his yacht and let the relaxing perspective of a sea voyage cool their tempers and warm their feelings of trust. Trust building was a contagion for J. P. The aura of trustworthiness eventually enveloped his every business action. Morgan was the epitome of an honest businessperson. This is not the same, however, as saying that he was ethically sophisticated.

Ethical considerations as such occupied a very small place on Morgan's agenda. His approach to ethics is revealed in his attitude toward lawyers. Elbert Gary, J. P. Morgan's lawyer, once advised him, "I don't think you can legally do that." Morgan replied: "Well, I don't know as I want a lawyer to tell me what I cannot do. I hire him to tell me how to do what I want to do."[10] Truisms thrived: if it was legal it was ethical; if you had the power you had the authority. Any deeper ethical considerations resided entirely within the conscience of the individual executive. Ethical behavior was merely an assertion of people's moral inclinations, if they had any.

There are no stories of Morgan carrying his religion into the marketplace by raising his voice on behalf of the ethics of business. Why, at the height of his power, did Morgan confine his attention to the business side of enterprise? Might he have done more to create nationwide support for higher ethical standards? Is money the only contribution rich individuals can make to society? Why is there no record of J. P. Morgan taking to the pulpit once in a while as did J. Irwin Miller.[11] Morgan's dilemma was not in what he did but what he didn't do. He had an unparalleled opportunity to deliver a few sermons to his colleagues. As the sole college graduate among the business titans of his age, he could have delivered speeches or authored articles that might have made stellar contributions to the ethical standards for an entire century of enterprise. Morgan had a unique opportunity to create an ethical legacy based on the importance of trust in business. He left only his money.

The modern term for what Morgan might have done is *institutionalizing ethics*. It is a cumbersome phrase, possibly misunderstood by both those who favor it and those who find it irksome. Oversimplified, institutionalized ethics is like leaving an inheritance on the ethical side of enterprise. It can be used or abused. It can be squandered or nurtured and passed on once more to a succeeding generation. Like money, there is no guarantee it will be spent wisely or will last forever. Each generation must accept it with appreciation and gratitude. Individuals can use it to enrich their work lives, although it is not a complete substitute for their own efforts. Morgan's generation was also Rockefeller's and Carnegie's. These three powerful figures on the Eastern seaboard were unable to bestow a rich ethical heritage upon their children. What was happening in the west?

The Pacific Quartet

The Civil War awakened both easterners and westerners to the business opportunities beyond the wide Missouri. The painful memories and constant reminders of the ravages of war were not so prevalent there. The west invited exploitation by resourceful entrepreneurs who were undaunted by the endless space or impassable terrain. The west presented risks and dangers on a totally different scale than the east or midwest. Rugged individualism gave way to collegiality. Government functioned as a friend rather than a foe.

The mythology of the western frontier includes stories of businesspersons masked as politicians who used advantageous position to loot the public coffers. That, at least, is the perspective of Gustavus Myers.[12] In typical American fashion, the public never agreed on who they were, what they had done, or whether they should be brought to trial and punished. Friend and foe were often indistinguishable. These alleged exploiters of national resources were never caught or unmasked. Mythology aside, what were some of the facts and faces on this frontier?

Collis P. Huntington controlled the finances and served as leader. Charles Crocker supervised construction activities. Mark Hopkins handled office details. Leland Stanford, educated as a lawyer, assumed responsibility for legal and political matters. They were an awesome foursome, alternately dubbed the Pacific Quartet or the Pacific Associates. Their objective, other than to get rich, was to monopolize the development of the railroad system in California. They succeeded on both counts. Their first major achievement was the formation and funding of the Central Pacific railroad.

The Civil War fanned the flames of enthusiasm for a coast-to-coast railroad. Enterprising entrepreneurs were buying land, surveying potential routes, and signing up the towns through which the "iron horse" would pass even as the war was raging on the east coast. In 1869 the Central Pacific railroad was joined with the Union Pacific railroad at Promontory, Utah, completing the transcontinental connection. It had taken five years for the Pacific Quartet to establish their foothold in California's railroad system.

The bulk of what little capital launched their venture was contributed largely by Huntington from his hardware and miner's supply store in Sacramento, their initial center of operations. The Central Pacific railroad entered the world penniless, like its founders. The source of its assets grew through a careful allocation of city, county, state, and federal funds, secured by delicate manipulation of influential politicians and the naive newcomers to the state. Stanford played a key role in this process. He served as governor of the state of California during the Civil War. The contacts and influence he enjoyed as the highest elected political official in the state served the interests of the Pacific Quartet exceptionally well. Those were raw and worrisome years on the west coast. Secret deals and misrepresentation of facts were commonplace. Trust levels were nonexistent. Stanford was the lead negotiator in most of the deals. His business ethics matched those of his colleagues and competitors, according to Gustavus Myers, which is to say they looked better in context than in retrospect.

The quartet was already rich, but they wanted more. They moved their headquarters to San Francisco, a growing port city that had happily played host to Barbary pirates in an earlier era. Vigilantes had recently restored peace to the city after the murderous pre-Civil War decades. In the course of the next decade the quartet used their success and influence to extend the railroad to Los Angeles via the Southern Pacific railroad. Seven major transcontinental railroads eventually converged on the City of Lights. One way or another the pioneering efforts of the quartet were involved in all seven. All four were now rich beyond measure. They had tamed a portion of the west. What kind of ethics characterized their business dealings? Let's look at a single member of the quartet.

The Leland Stanford Story. In 1885 the California state legislature sent Leland Stanford to Congress as its senator. All senators were so appointed in those days. The U.S. Senate earned a nicknamed as "the Millionaire's Club" because so many successful businessmen were selected to represent their states. (The system was changed in 1910.) Stanford had little problem in securing that appointment. He was wealthy. He had connections. His voting record was predictable.

Leland Stanford was an imposing senator. He was a huge man with an outgoing personality. His annual salary was a paltry $5000, yet his estimated expenses during each legislative session totaled approximately $75,000. He tossed $20 gold pieces to the newsboys.[13]

In the same year he was appointed senator he founded Leland Stanford University with a $30 million grant and 9000 acres from his ranch. The school was named for his only child, Leland, Jr., who had died the previous year at age 15. Despite this largess, at his own death Stanford left an $18 million estate to his wife, Jane. That was an extraordinary sum of money in 1893. Exactly how Stanford accumulated such a fortune will never be precisely known.

The Stanford story is as clear a case as we can find of a businessperson successfully using political office to transform public resources into an immense private fortune. He was a clear beneficiary of governmental largess. Leland Stanford's skill at effecting the transfer of communal property to private pocketbooks raises a fundamental ethical question. Did he benefit at the public's expense or did both benefit equally? Unlike Rockefeller or Carnegie, Stanford did not set up a family or financial dynasty. Everything he accumulated eventually found its way back into the public coffers. He gave more to the university in memory of his son than he kept for himself. His widow continued their generosity toward the university until her death. Was Stanford's behavior ethical?

Stanford Was Caught in a Conflict of Obligation.   Stanford had an obligation to his Pacific Associates as they built and profited from the extension of railroads across the western frontier. At the same time, he had an obligation to those who elected him to protect and advance the public interest.

Conflict of obligation was not a phrase in the vocabulary of these western entrepreneurs. They had a wilderness to tame and were given considerable ethical latitude to get the job done. It was a different era, underscoring again that what's ethical depends on the situation. The story of the Pacific Quartet, because they were so clearly obligated to serve the public interest, discloses an ethical principle that's *not* situational. Namely, business always has an obligation to its constituents in every era and every place. Rockefeller, Carnegie, and Morgan, each in his own way, delivered on this obligation to serve the public interest. Their enterprises were less dependent on direct governmental funding or legislation, at least initially. It falls upon the chief executive to invest sufficient time and energy to determine the full scope of that obligation. Failure to respond to constituent obligation increases the likelihood of public indignation. Then, governments legislate what's ethical.

The Search for Business Ethics

These early captains of industry did not inherit an ethic for their business dealings. They relied upon whatever sense of right or wrong they'd learned at home. Some followed these principles at work. Some did not or had little to bring. The United States was an ethical melting pot. Gradually, the marketplace created its own ethic. It was a crude, uneven piece of work, honored only by those who chose to honor it. Powerful and successful executives like Rockefeller, Carnegie, Morgan, and Stanford could make their own rules, creating a cynical parody on the Golden Rule: whoever has the gold makes the rules. Laissez-faire ethics did not please everyone.

Charles Francis Adams, scion of two U.S. presidents, succeeded to the presidency of the Union Pacific railroad in 1882. He was second-generation management. Adams was appalled by the ethical chaos he inherited in his new job. He testified before a Senate committee that "Everywhere there is an utter disregard of fundamental ideals of truth, fair play and fair dealing."[14] The big corporations that emerged from this era were not sustained by an idealistic ethical foundation. Business leaders were bent on economic monopoly amidst moral diversity and ethical chaos. J. P. Morgan's reliance on trust was an exception to the rules. In hindsight, it was inevitable that public indignation would find its voice through politicians and legislated ethics.

Ironically, the early decades of government action against these consolidated financial interests carried the epithet *trust busting*. This theme carried President Theodore Roosevelt into the White House at the start of the century. The issue defeated his bid for reelection when business interests split the Republican party and rallied behind William H. Taft. The relationship between business and government had turned adversarial. It did not take ambitious politicians long to discover that they could get elected on either an anti- or a probusiness platform. Obviously, this further eroded the trust base and delayed the development of a sound corporate ethic. The general public suffered while government and business leaders engaged in political horse trading as a substitute for bona fide ethical standards.

Personal trust among businesspeople dissolved. Lawyers became a necessary corporate adjunct. The Protestant work ethic and its associated values were less visible around company headquarters: inherited wealth replaced earning it the old-fashioned way; "buy now pay later" nudged Puritan frugality aside; saving for that rainy day was gone with the wind; professional managers replaced the founders and owners. The ethical counterparts of Carnegie's stewardship of wealth and Morgan's dependence on personal character and trust did not flow as easily or as copiously from the lips or actions of their successors. Even though the old ethic began to erode, there is no evidence of a concerted effort to redefine a deeply rooted, contemporary business ethic for either the United States or the world. Little wonder that corporations a half-century later functioned in an ethical vacuum. C. Wright Mills saw it this way.

The moral uneasiness of our time results from the fact that the older values and codes of uprightness no longer grip men and women of the corporate era, nor have they been replaced by new values and codes which would lend moral meaning and sanction to the corporate routines they must now follow.[15]

Business ethics in America has always been a highly individualized happening, dependent in the extreme on the beliefs and performance of one or more key persons, usually the CEO. In countries such as Japan and Sweden, in contrast, the business ethic is rooted in ancient, venerated traditions. While such traditions do not preclude unethical activity entirely, standards tend to be more widely accepted and uniformly followed in these cultures. The United States, in contrast, is an open, pluralistic society. Ethically, the style in America is still "rugged individualism." Ethically, we rely upon the boss to set the tone. The tones we hear today are cacophonous rather than harmonious. It's very difficult to gain consensus on any issue in business, especially ethics: widespread attention, yes; widespread agreement, no. It has been stated boldly.

At no time has there been a content of thinking, a set of beliefs, or a body of opinion to which all businessmen subscribed.[16]

There Were Two Dirty Decades

It's a little eerie to recall that the 1880s, like the 1980s, was a decade of unparalleled dirty dealings. Both can lay convincing claim to the epithet "the dirty decade." At that earlier time business leaders failed to act on the need for higher standards. They seemed unable to help themselves. A scandalized and outraged public demanded action. The federal government came to their rescue. The first major piece of legislation regulating business created the Interstate Commerce Commission in 1887. The Sherman Antitrust laws followed in 1890. A century-long tradition was set. The nation's businesses have demonstrated a consistent inability to define ethical conduct precisely and inspire compliance uniformly. Senior executives today face the same ethical dilemma as their colleagues of a century ago: self-regulation or government regulation.

There are at least two major differences between these decades. First, the government is now far more practiced and entrenched in its role of protector of the public interests. This is not to suggest that our legislative bodies write good regulative laws. Rather, they become adept at securing passage of regulatory bills. For instance, when the Occupational Safety and Health Administration (OSHA) was formed in 1970, several dozen smaller agencies with a total of over 4000 rules were thrown together and immediately expected to police 2½ million corporations. Such bureaucratic undertakings may explain the origin and popularity of that evocative phrase "a can of worms." Executive, judicial, and legislative powers were bestowed upon the Environmental Protection Agency (EPA) in defiance of our traditional separation of those powers. Government regulation introduces an often debilitating degree of uncertainty.

Second, international competition introduces a new set of vital considerations and a role reversal for government. The various branches of the federal government have become the protector of business interests. They are friend rather than foe. The founding of the Business Roundtable in 1972, that exclusive gathering of the top 200 CEOs in America, heralded a new relationship between business and government. It was to be cooperative rather than adversarial, partnership rather than partisanship. Taken together, the question spanning the century between these decades echoes with monotonous regularity. On which horn of the bull do you wish to be gored: self-regulation or government regulation?

Regulation alone is not destroying the system. The Wall Street scandals and the savings and loan fiascoes, for example, connote new heights of the self-destructive greed and trust-busting in the name of free enterprise. Billions of dollars have been lost by investors, billions more have been paid in fines, thousands have gone to jail. We are setting new records for corruption every day. It seemed as if the spirit of deregulation opened the prison doors to those heretofore legally restrained. Many were unprepared or unable to handle freedom responsibly and maturely. They resembled first-year college students finally freed from restrictive home lives.

A century ago it was possible for a powerful figure like J. P. Morgan to whip his friends into shape. He resolved the railroad crisis in Pennsylvania by virtually imprisoning the combatants aboard his yacht *Corcisa* until they negotiated their differences. No single business leader has achieved such leadership authority in recent decades. Senior executives must work together as never before. Providing good personal examples, as many of them do, is simply not enough. The business battlefield of the last century is strewn with idealists who have tried to put firm indelible shape to a corporate ethic. These individual efforts have failed. Senior executives of the world, unite. You have nothing to lose but your regulatory chains.

Dilemmas Facing Current CEOs

Have present-day executives been able to profit from the experience and example of their forebears? Have they learned to see themselves as others see them? Have they been able to anticipate ethical dilemmas, avoid unethical consequences in their corporate decision making? Current CEOs face measurably different dilemmas. Rockefeller, Carnegie, Morgan, and Stanford, for instance, faced the challenge of amassing the dispersing large *personal* fortunes. They were founders-owners who accumulated incredible resources. Their power was virtually unlimited and uncontested. Today, CEOs face the challenge of managing and deploying huge *corporate* resources. Their power is limited. In a sense, they are trustees. They are accountable to a greater number of demanding constituents. Employees have greater expectations. Stockholders are more vocal. Local, state, and federal governments play a more active role. Competition is vastly more intense. It's a new age. Ethical issues are more subtle.

The Uninformed CEO: G. William Miller

G. William Miller, former CEO of Textron and Secretary of the Treasury for President Jimmy Carter, inadvertently provided a revealing glimpse into contemporary corporate management. During his confirmation hearing before the Senate Banking Committee Miller was asked whether Textron had ever bribed any clients. Initially he answered in the negative. Later, on the basis of information presumedly provided him by an executive in Textron as well as other testimony which surfaced during the hearing, Miller was forced to recant. Textron had indeed paid out some handsome bribes while Miller was the CEO. It was never entirely clear, however, whether Miller was guilty of calculated misrepresentation or honest ignorance.[17] Who should be held responsible for unethical consequences? The CEO? Or the employee who actually implements the action? What emerges from the Textron story with astonishing clarity is how difficult it is to trace the threads of responsibility for unethical activity.

Necessary attention to the ethical aspects of enterprise will require a reordering of priorities in some firms. Senior management functions under severe time constraints. Increasingly, CEOs are pressed to give more of their time and attention to issues in the external environment—the macroethical level. Rogene Buchholz gives some convincing examples of the changing priorities of the CEO's daily calendar. At least one CEO reported spending 40 percent of his workweek on regulatory issues.[18] These executive are focusing on the macroethical issues that determine the rules which affect the conduct of business. Some are struggling to maintain managerial discretion, trying to limit governmental interference. Others may be seeking legislative action that will benefit their competitive position. In either case, a high priority is given to macroethical considerations. External constituents — whether governments or consumer advocates — warrant a high priority. They have a legitimate claim on the CEO's time and energy. Few critics can question whether these efforts are necessary. It is not a question of whether, but how and how much.

Suppose Miller and Textron had managed their *internal* constituents better. Suppose greater priority had been given to *micro*ethical issues. Suppose the climate inside Textron had been ethically sound. Miller's embarrassment — or malfeasance — would never have occurred. If firms fail to set and enforce high ethical standards, investigations and possibly legislation become virtual certainties. Assigning a higher priority to good business ethics can forestall legislation, embarrassing inquiries, and an inordinate allocation of time and energy to outside constituents. CEOs have a choice. If they wish to be perceived as ethical, how do they wish to spend their time, preventing fires or putting them out? If they choose prevention, they'll need to send louder and clearer messages to their employees about the ethics of business.

The Naive CEO: Robert Foman

Robert Foman was suddenly thrust into the media spotlight when the check kiting scandal at E. F. Hutton was uncovered. He had served as chief executive for about a decade and a half. He had enjoyed a reputation as a "nice guy" executive, a father figure to those who knew him well. They described him as loyal and lovable. Foman had majored in English and anthropology at the University of California, not exactly a typical background for a Wall Street executive. He was hired at Hutton after being turned down by Merrill Lynch and Dean Witter. Foman triumphed over John Shad, later SEC chief, for the top job at Hutton. He joined an elite crowd. George Ball, later CEO of Prudential-Bache, and Fred Joseph of Drexel Burnham Lambert fame, had also moved through the halls of Hutton. Foman was practicing management by walking around before Tom Peters created the concept. He had little confidence in corporate structure and even less interest in learning to use it. How come bad things happen to such good people? Is it pure chance? Foman was stunned by the accusations of mail and wire fraud. His remarks betrayed an astonishing innocence.

> I never thought ethics was something that could be formally taught. I thought ethics was something you learned growing up at home, in school, and in church.[19]

Alack and alas, it also never occurred to Robert Foman that unethical behavior was something that could be learned at a relatively advanced age. Moreover, it is still not clear to many corporate executives that organizational design and culture can do the "teaching." CEOs find it difficult to appreciate this perspective. Good people will learn to do bad things when there is sufficient incentive. Vigorous and perceptive ethics programs are becoming essential to firms of every shape and size. Look at what happened at E. F. Hutton from the perspective of the CEO.

Robert Foman inherited rather than created the organizational structure at Hutton. The major brokerage firms are customarily classified as "street level" bureaucracies. There is no "high rise" or steep pyramid to their organization chart. The CEO has ample opportunity for close supervision and team building. Hutton, unlike some other brokerage firms, was a loose federation of independent branch offices which, from an organizational design perspective, was all sail and no rudder. Foman became captain of the ship as cataclysmic change struck the brokerage business. Competition was growing in intensity. Business fell off. Brokers in the branch offices were hurting. It was at this point that top management decided to base commissions and bonuses on cash management as well as brokerage transactions. It is not clear whether Foman knew of this plan. Presumably, the new method would motivate managers and strengthen corporate loyalty. It certainly motivated them to manage cash flow. They earned millions of dollars by delaying accounts payable, utilizing transcontinental time differences, and stretching their reputation and banker's patience to the limit. This method turned out to be short-term and shortsighted. Someone blew the whistle.

Foman invited former Attorney General Griffin Bell to conduct an investigation. Bell traced the problem to insufficient supervision on the part of a dozen or more senior managers. Financial accountability between departments and branches was lax. He concluded they were guilty of what they didn't do rather than what they did—sins of omission rather than commission. Interestingly, Bell did not fault Foman, the incentive plan, or Hutton's organizational style. Bell did not dig deep enough into the root causes of Hutton's problem.

Foman simply failed to manage the ethical side of his business. He presumed, as he admitted, that ethics would take care of itself. It didn't. Foman had the authority, power and responsibility to set ethical standards and discipline any unruly subordinates. He did not see the need, then. After it was too late he instigated an ethics program of sorts. He insisted that the ethics program "isn't to impress anyone on the outside,"[20] a comment which suggests a lack of understanding and commitment. He *does* need to impress outsiders. He *does not* need to make excuses for a training program that will help his employees. Foman took early retirement. A new president was brought in, but it was too late. Hutton was eventually absorbed by Shearson. Its demise is directly attributable to its unethical activities. It's very important to understand that neither Foman nor his various managers deserve the epithet "bad apples." It was the situation. Under pressure they selected a method which ignored the legitimate ethical expectations of other constituents. Everyone suffered the consequences. The challenges facing the CEO today *are* both different and devious. Managing ethical issues properly is a major part of that challenge.

These vignettes from the corporate lives of chief executives bear a single common thread. Namely, they failed to devote sufficient time and attention to the ethical side of enterprise. You can't know enough about *what's really happening* at the operations level. You *can't presume* that ethical matters will take care of themselves. You *can't simply trust your intuitions or good intentions* to create desirable or ethical consequences. Ethics has to be managed thoughtfully, consistently, and futuristically. The ethics of business—whether viewed locally, nationally, or globally—is emerging as the supreme challenge to modern managers. By what rules and procedures of fairness and due consideration are our corporate lives going to be governed? Will they be legislated by law or elicited by good corporate leadership and example?

The Dilemma Facing Future CEOs

The business tycoons of a century ago not only amassed big fortunes. They forged the details of the big picture for America: growing energy monopolies in oil, coal, and gas; billowing smokestacks of a mighty steel manufacturing empire; the youngest nation in the world emerging as its financial capital; railroads stretching across the entire nation. America's development as an industrial country was simply astonishing. A new kind of nation was being carved out of a wilderness. The business leaders of that era were both praised for their achievements and damned for their ethical insensitivities. Often, if *what* they did was deemed acceptable, the *way* it was accomplished occasioned criticism. Their wealth invited envy. Their deeds inspired emulation. Few people have had such an unusual opportunity to shape the destiny of a raw nation. Few people have had such a powerful effect on the future of their society. They moved mountains, literally. They changed the face of the nation. They created a model that became the envy of the world. As the twenty-first century dawns, business leaders face a different sort of challenge. This is a challenge not for the hands—industry—nor for the head—technology—but for the spirit—people throughout the entire world working together in trust and harmony. It is a huge challenge. It is also a dilemma. CEOs must choose. Will they accept this challenge of the spirit or not? Either way there are risks.

In the very earliest days of free enterprise, the boldest entrepreneurs risked their personal fortunes. They had little choice. Large, wealthy corporations and indulgent governments didn't exist. A major impetus leading to the creation of the modern corporation, in fact, was risk diversification through limited liability.[21] English merchants, for instance, pooled their funds in order to share the enormous gamble of ships sailing stormy seas swarming with pirates. This evolving system often paid high dividends to individuals who were willing to ante up a secure career or even their lives as stakes for the gambling tables on the high seas or the wilderness of Africa and the Americas. You were not rewarded for your talent or skill. Lots of individuals possessed those qualities, and they stayed home. You were rewarded for taking risk.

As the free enterprise system matured, executives and managers found it increasingly easy to be highly rewarded without taking comparable personal risk. Trying to reduce risk or the odds against failure is as old as the mammoth hunters. That's not unethical in itself. How you reduce your risk is another question entirely. Risk avoidance in today's asphalt jungle takes many unfortunate forms. At one extreme are the cheaters who stack the deck in their favor by doing ethical end runs, as did Boesky and Milken. At the other extreme we have executives securely ensconced in the harness of a "golden parachute," disguised as protection against corporate predators. In between are the nameless thousands who quietly scale the slippery corporate pyramid. They manage their careers as cautiously and carefully as possible. A few may take risks as whistle blowers. Risk is never really averted, of course. Cheaters get caught. Golden parachutes can fail. Worst of all, the system collapses from the weight of these risk-adverse fortune hunters. The risk and challenge facing CEOs today are nothing less than saving the system itself.

Have corporate lions lost their courage? In a simpler era today's corporate managers and executives would be our tribal chieftains and captains. The tribe looks to them for selfless leadership and abounding courage. Cheating, golden parachutes, and excessive preoccupation with one's career deprive society of desperately needed guidance. Warren Bennis strikes this note in *The Unconscious Conspiracy: Why Leaders Can't Lead.*[22] Bennis reveals how seductively easy it is for leaders to become victims of trivia, the status quo. They concentrate on "doing things right" instead of "doing the right things." Thus, they become leaders in name only, simply clipping the hard-earned coupons of their founding entrepreneurs. The basic survival risks have been confronted and conquered by their enterprising progenitors. They now bask in the sunshine of their forebears' achievements instead of pushing into new frontiers.

The golden parachute has become a symbol of the challenge facing corporate America, in the minds of some constituents. It represents a perversion of the free enterprise ethic. Executives are rewarded for *not* taking risks. The size of these golden parachutes alone constitutes an insult to a system designed to reward honest risk. They violate the venerated utilitarian ethic of maximizing the greatest good for the greatest number. A golden parachute assigns top priority to a single constituent—the CEO (or a few top executives). Is this a message designed to inspire and assure other constituents? The free enterprise system thrives on leaders willing to take risks, leaders willing to risk their personal lives, if necessary. The challenge for CEOs today is to broker the legitimate interests of *all* of the corporation's constituents. Happily, many CEOs have caught a glimpse of this challenge.

The editors of *Fortune* magazine celebrated their sixtieth anniversary by interviewing scores of prominent citizens in the nation.[23] They were asked to state what Americans will *need* or *need to resolve* in order to deal effectively with the future. Many of the responses from business executives called for significant changes, either in personal attitudes or institutional performance. You can infer their diagnosis by their prescribed cure. A sampling:

John Welch, General Electric	Less bureaucracy
Lee Iacocca, Chrysler	Greater motivation
Ross Perot, EDS	More adversity
Thomas Watson, Jr., IBM	More fear of failure
Donald Ephlin, Colgate-Palmolive	Unions as partners
Walter Wriston, Citicorp	Intellectual capital
Frank Popoff, Dow Chemical	Solid waste disposal

Businesspeople were not the only interviewees. The mayor of Cleveland, Ohio, Michael White, states: "Our welfare system doesn't teach people to be independent or think for themselves." Harvard philosopher Robert Nozick cited a need for meaning and value beyond material acquisitions along with a humanizing of institutions. Yale psychologist Daniel Levinson envisioned a society wherein people helped each other more. He also called for less emphasis on materialistic values and more responsive institutions.

Business executives want to see attitude changes in people. Politicians want to see changes in the system or its institutions. A philosopher and a psychologist want to see changes in values and behavior. Questions of emphasis notwithstanding, these diverse perspectives share a common goal: change. They also share a common method: evolutionary and educational growth. So, where shall we start? With people, their institutions, or their values? Which came first? If people's attitudes change, will they create different institutions? Conversely, if institutions are changed will the people serviced by them change? Or should we start with values and behavior? The only answer, of course, is all three. Everyone must start wherever they are, whoever they are. *Fortune*'s visionaries are insisting, each in their own way, that our future prosperity requires change. CEOs can play a major role. Business ethics is the process of defining what constitutes the welfare of a corporation's constituents, paraphrasing Powers and Vogel. CEOs can launch that challenge.

Summary

Rockefeller, Carnegie, Morgan, and Stanford were four extraordinarily successful businessmen who managed to strike some sort of balance between self and society. They took personal risks. They became rich. They enriched society. They have their critics, then and now. Nevertheless, each demonstrated a respect for the free enterprise system and the larger community of which it is a part. We may question their ethics but not their integrity. They gave generously of what had been given to them.

CEOs today face a different challenge. Society is more diverse in every way. Simple intuition and impulse will not resolve the ethical dilemmas facing them. They need to know and acknowledge the ethical expectations of multitudes of constituents and provide the necessary leadership to unite them in functional harmony. Leaders inside and outside of business already perceive the need for change. CEOs can nurture it.

Footnotes

1. Donald Hill, "A Letter from Cicero," *Business Ethics Resource*, vol. 1, no. 3, August 1987, p. 2.
2. Matthew Josephson, *The Robber Barons" The Great American Capitalists*, Harcourt Brace Jovanovich, New York, 1934, p. 46.
3. Fortune, March 26, 1990, p. 26.
4. Andrew Carnegie, in Edward C. Kirkland (ed.), *Gospel of Wealth and Other Timely Essays*, Belknap Press of Harvard University, Cambridge, Mass., 1962, p. 25.

5. John Brooks, *The Autobiography of American Business*, Doubleday, Garden City, N.Y., 1974, p. 3.

6. Lincoln Steffens, *Autobiography of Lincoln Steffens*, Harcourt Brace Jovanovich, New York, 1930, p. 587.

7. N. S. B. Gras, *Business and Capitalism: An Introduction to Business History*, Crofts, New York, 1939, p. 247.

8. Frederick L. Allen, *The Great Pierpont Morgan*, Harper & Row, New York, 1949, p. 8.

9. Gustavus Myers, *History of the Great American Fortunes*, Modern Library, Random House, New York, 1936, p. 535.

10. Matthew Josephson, *The Robber Barons: The Great American Capitalists*, Harcourt Brace Jovanovich, New York, 1934, p. 299.

11. J. Irwin Miller was the guiding genius and CEO at Cummins Engine during its growth decades following World War II. He was an active member of his local church in Columbus, Indiana, and served for a time as lay president of the National Council of Churches. Miller preached to his colleagues that "Business has a war to win" in *Harvard Business Review*, March–April 1969.

12. Myers, op. cit., p. 517.

13. Myers, op. cit., p. 527.

14. Josephson, op. cit., p. 293.

15. C. Wright Mills, *The Power Elite*, Oxford University Press, New York, 1956, p. 344.

16. Herman E. Krooss and Charles Gilbert, *American Business History*, Prentice-Hall, Englewood Cliffs, N.J., 1972, p. 326.

17. *The Wall Street Journal*, Feb. 11, 1980, p. 1.

18. Rogene Buchholz, *Business Environment and Public Policy*, 3d ed., Prentice-Hall, Englewood Cliffs, N.J., 1989, pp. 14–16.

19. *Business Week*, Oct. 14, 1985, p. 63.

20. Ibid., p. 66.

21. Christopher Stone, *Where the Law Ends: The Social Control of Corporate Behavior*, Harper & Row, New York, 1975.

22. Warren Bennis, *The Unconscious Conspiracy: Why Leaders Can't Lead*, AMACOM, New York, 1976.

23. *Fortune*, March 26, 1990, p. 30.

5
Dilemmas Facing Directors

*"To close on an upbeat note, I'm happy to report we received twenty-two
per cent more in kickbacks than we paid out in bribes."*

Drawing by Dana Fradon; © 1976 The New Yorker Magazine, Inc.

A Double Dilemma

Directors of corporate boards face a double dilemma when it comes to questions of right and wrong. First, should they take action at all? Second, on whose behalf should they act? Their fiduciary role on the business side of enterprise is commonly enough understood: ensure a profit. What is their role on the ethical side? Here, board members often confront a classic dilemma. They are sure to be gored by one of the horns of this charging bull. Which should they choose: the horn of speaking up or the horn of remaining quiet; active participation or passive resignation?

Board members privately confess that a sense of uneasiness accompanies this dilemma. They rationalize that they are not fully informed or that they are not involved in the day-to-day operations of the firm. They prefer not to second-guess their CEO and other senior executives upon whom they are dependent for accurate information and leadership. Yet, some policies and decisions do strike them as plainly unethical. What is their role when ethical issues surface? Should they challenge or comfort management?

This chapter will suggest why and how directors can play a larger and more powerful role in creating decisions and policies that match the rising ethical expectations of corporate constituents. The ethical algorithm will help us analyze situations on three levels—the microethical (company or industrywide), macroethical (nationwide), and metaethical (worldwide)—to determine how actions by board members can create more desirable consequences. First, the whys and wherefores.

Not to Choose Is a Choice

Pick any recent corporate ethical misfortune and ask what role board members played, or didn't play, in producing the end result. General Electric and General Dynamics were only two of several defense industry firms that paid huge fines in the last decade rather than defend possible illegal accounting activity. Were their respective board members even aware of what was going on? Were they in agreement with management's decision to pay the sizable fines? Stockholders of Exxon displayed their displeasure with CEO Lawrence Rawl in the aftermath of the Alaskan oil spill, creating one of the longest corporate annual meetings on record. What role did board members play in this costly catastrophe? Did they foster trouble beforehand by inaction? Did they help in any way to resolve the problem after the event happened? How do board members figure into the bank failures and the savings and loan debacles that surfaced in the 1980s? Did these various board members make a conscious choice?

Many corporate constituents remain unsatisfied with the solutions that arose from these ethical dilemmas. The cost in dollars, ill will, distrust, and even consumer retaliation has not been calculated, let alone paid. Not to decide is not only a solitary decision with specific and usually costly consequences, it is defaulting on a responsibility that spawns its own descendants of disorder. Directors must choose.

Gresham's Law Applies to Ethics. The law named after Sir Thomas Gresham, financial adviser to Queen Elizabeth I, stipulates that bad money drives out good money. While Gresham's Law has several applications from the financial perspective, there is an ethical equivalent. Namely, bad ethics drives out good ethics. Or, phrased differently, ethical standards tend to be reduced to their lowest common denominator. This principle pops up in a variety of ways. Even the most expensive hotels now bolt their room radios to the furniture because a small percentage of their guests stole them. Businesses large and small now eschew cash payment by check because a minority of customers violated the privilege. After credit cards replaced bank checks, this newer financial instrument soon became a target of exploitation and major fraud. Other examples abound. Hitchhiking, so safe and popular after World War II, is now too dangerous because of its abuse by a few citizens. Airlines overbook their flights in part because "no-shows" fail to honor a verbal reservation. The bad ethics of a few eventually lower standards for the whole. Tremendous energy is required simply to avoid social chaos, let alone maintain reasonably high standards.

Gresham's law as applied to ethics is not the same as "one bad apple spoils the rest of the barrel." That's a passive, one-way action, contamination by proximity alone. In the world of ethics, the good apples "make allowances" for the bad apples and share in their self-putrefaction, if you will. The hotels bolt down their radios (or remove them entirely) instead of seeking more austere means or even legal recourse, for example. Unethical behavior is managed indirectly instead of confrontationally. Who wants to offend a potential customer? The next level of compromise might call for a small "gratuity" or favor in exchange for overtime or work speed-up. At a deeper level there's something that's both inevitable and perfectly natural about this process. It is the nature of a democratic, pluralistic culture to compromise on definitions of right and wrong. The goal is to get the work done. But compromising on the methods lends itself to an atmosphere of ethical uncertainty.

People respond differently to what they perceive as an ethical vacuum. When those with a short-term or self-centered perspective abuse the permissive climate, and are rarely confronted by naysayers, the result is *minimalist ethical standards*. Demand exceeds supply on the ethical front as well, creating ethical inflation. In practical terms, large corporations find it easier to "get along by going along." They may formally adopt higher ethical standards, but they essentially fail to weave them solidly into the fabric of their policies, decisions, and everyday practices. What we discovered in the 1980s is that minimalist ethics offends our idealism, increases litigation, destroys interpersonal trust, bankrupts companies, and polarizes society into factions.

Boards of directors can reverse this deep and debilitating erosion of corporate ethics. Just as retail clothiers have found it easier to tag their goods with antitheft devices rather than address the declining ethical standards of their customers, so firms within an industry find it easier to follow the practices of the least ethical company in their number. Management is inclined to believe that they can't afford to be more ethical than their competitors. Again, the result is minimalist corporate ethics.

There have been two prodigious examples of corporate efforts to raise the level of the ethical playing field. The creation of the Sullivan Principles in 1976 delineated standards for more than 300 United States firms doing business in South Africa. The Defense Industry Initiatives in the late 1980s produced an 18-point ethical code for about 25 participating North American companies. Neither of these efforts secured the complete and total participation of all their colleagues or critics. Nevertheless, efforts by corporations to raise their own standards represent a viable and visionary alternative. Boards of directors are crucial to the success of such an undertaking. Consider the alternative.

Governments Will If Boards Won't. If boards of directors have been unwilling or unable to resolve their double dilemma, governments have shown less reluctance. In the 1960s the federal government inaugurated a stream of social legislation unequaled in our history. These new laws and new agencies regulated many details of corporate activity.

Murray L. Weidenbaum, director of the Center for the Study of American Business at Washington University in St. Louis documented the case against government regulation.

> The costs arising from government regulation are basic: (1) the cost to the taxpayer for supporting a galaxy of government regulators, (2) the cost to the consumer in the form of higher prices to cover the added expense of producing goods and services under government regulations, (3) the cost to the worker in the form of jobs eliminated

by government regulation, (4) the cost to the economy resulting from the loss of smaller enterprises which cannot afford to meet the onerous burdens of government regulations, and (5) the cost to society as a whole as a result of a reduced flow of new and better products and a less rapid rise in the standard of living.[1]

It is a costly process from start to finish. After extensive and expensive investigations and the legislative process, dollar costs can be categorized as direct, indirect, and induced. In the late 1970s Chase Manhattan Bank estimated the aggregate cost of corporate compliance at more than $100 billion a year. Robert DeFina calculated the direct and indirect costs at 3.6 percent of the gross national product, which in 1979 amounted to $102.7 billion. He further calculated that indirect costs also came to approximately 20 times direct expenditures.[2]

Early in the eighties Robert B. Reich alerted business to the prospects of increased governmental regulation in a *New York Times* article provocatively titled "Business Is Asking for Trouble Again."[3] A 1983 Justice Department survey of retired *Fortune* 500 middle managers revealed that they "believe government regulation is needed to prevent misdeeds by business."[4] This was a particularly low blow. Managers themselves had apparently lost faith in self-governance. They saw themselves as small children who needed a spanking. Congress obliged, launching one investigation after another. This was not exactly new. Will Rogers wryly observed more than a half century earlier that "Congress opens with a prayer and ends with an investigation."

If directors fail to respond, it is clear that local and state governments and the federal government will legislate ethics at the expense of corporate freedom and common sense. If boards fail to become more active on ethical issues, it's possible the present system of corporate governance itself will be altered by an enraged public. The corporation might lose control of director selection. More than one academic has suggested that directors of large corporations be chosen like political representatives. In addition, the public is becoming increasingly aware and critical of the generous stipends paid to directors. What kind of advice does Henry Kissinger impart for the $50,000 a year he receives as a member of Atlantic Richfield's board? Stockholders are calling themselves *stakeholders* and demanding results more beneficial (or less harmful) to society at large. Fortunately, a growing number of sensitive board members understand that a more active role is essential:

1. They can help reduce the trend toward costly lawsuits filed by corporations against each other and by clients and consumers against the corporation.

2. They can stem the rising tide of criticism leveled against the system by consumer advocate groups.

3. They can slow the erosion of corporate autonomy and invasion of governmental regulation.

Board members can do a lot to foster a better climate for economic growth, human satisfaction, and cultural harmony. Corporate directors need to plan and manage the change that is overwhelming society.

Legislation or regulation simply reduces ethical compliance to obeying the laws. Obviously, that's not an insignificant achievement. But we live in an age when the ethical boundaries are shifting, changing, stretching. Complying with only the letter of the law is simply not enough. It is another kind of minimalist ethics. Organized labor, the financial markets, international trade, and the development of drugs for cancer, contraception, and abortion are just a few areas where regulatory legislation has created as many problems as it has solved. In addition, legislation narrows the discretionary authority of decision makers. Laws inhibit innovation and emphasize punishments rather than rewards. Directors face a need and opportunity to contribute more forcefully to corporate ethical standards. This will be a challenging task.

Choosing Sides

If a board member should opt for the horn of active participation, whose interests should he or she represent? There are any number of corporate constituents from whom to choose. Should board members unfailingly back the CEO, the one who probably had a hand in getting them on the board? Is their primary obligation to stockholders, customers, or some idealized concept? Responses vary widely. When Bill Agee, then CEO of Bendix Corporation, presented an unfriendly takeover plan of Martin Marietta to his board, three members quietly resigned without public explanation. Were their reasons financial or ethical? It was never clear. They did act, however.

Sometimes corporate disasters will reveal an underlying conflict of obligation which pits personal ambition against corporate well-being. Neil Bush, the President's son, recently achieved unenviable notoriety when he allegedly used his position as a director of the Denver Silverado Banking Savings and Loan Association to secure favorable action on a loan request of a colleague. Was he guilty of an unethical conflict of interest or was he a political scapegoat? Is it ethical for board members to press their own interests at the expense of other constituents? Is the situation involving Neil Bush only a well-publicized example or is it representative of a typical board member—namely, one more greedy, manipulating capitalist who is quietly exploiting the public trust? Choosing the right side is not easy.

Corporate directors do not have sharply defined roles, despite the best attempts of critics, scholars, and management experts to define them. The absence of clear roles and the complexity of ethical issues may explain this board leadership vacuum. Beginning in the early 1970s, directors in most major corporations were under pressure from a minority of their stockholders to cease doing business in South Africa. There are no sensational instances of boards responding positively to this pressure. Perhaps for this reason stockholders turned to annual meetings resolutions. A stockholder resolution presented at a Caterpillar Tractor annual meeting left little room for compromise. The dissident minority demanded that stockholders take a position inasmuch as the board of directors hadn't. The resolution called for total withdrawal of Caterpillar from South Africa.

> There is no neutrality; taking no position on apartheid [legalized racial discrimination] is helping it. For American companies pay taxes to the state, and their very presence lends a certain prestige and legitimacy to the system.[5]

The issue that failed to surface clearly in this controversy was that all stockholders may have shared a common goal. That goal, of course, was full and complete social and economic justice for blacks as well as whites. No stockholders were on record as supporting apartheid. The stockholders did disagree on methods. The minority wanted to withdraw. The majority voted to be a force for change from within as a signatory of the Sullivan Principles. This agreement on GOALS and disagreement on METHODS constituted a subtlety lost on all disputants. Directors and management, for their part, failed to point out that they shared the goal implicit in the resolution. The dissidents failed to acknowledge or take advantage of this point of agreement. Both sides, in other words, were probably too insecure in their ethical positions even to articulate them fully, let alone consider a compromise. Each apparently sought a quick win for their point of view rather than a victory for all constituents, which would have included the black population in South Africa. Up to that time no one had written a script for the role of either a stockholder or board member confronting an issue like South Africa. Both were ad-libbing their parts. Up to that time no one had assigned board members the role of corporate conscience. Since that time, ethically astute and diligent board members have begun to take on some new roles.

Can a Corporation Have a Conscience?

Should a corporation's conscience be the board of directors? Corporations are certainly being asked to take on something resembling a conscience, according to Irving S. Shapiro.

> With public expectations ratcheting upward, corporations are under pressure to behave more like governments and embrace a universe of problems. That would mean, of necessity, that private institutions would focus less on problems of their own choice.[6]

Shapiro does not suggest that corporate leaders should cave in to this pressure. While he concedes that competitive markets and governmental legislation have so far failed to fulfill rising public expectations, the solution is an expanded and clearer role for the board of directors. He specifically cites the board's role in setting ethical standards. Conceding the vital role played by the CEO, whether a corporation has a conscience eventually becomes an issue for each member of a board of directors. On the surface the choices are amazingly simple. You support senior managers when they are right, stimulate them when they are reluctant, challenge them when they are wrong. At another level, providing the corporation with a strong conscience becomes a subtle art. To have a conscience means to take action. Action is revealed in deeds done rather than a plaque on the wall or a formal code in a drawer. The corporate conscience shows up in a corporation's GOALS, METHODS, MOTIVES, and eventually any CONSEQUENCES of its actions. The corporate conscience involves everybody. It is created by the intentional and careful weaving of ethical sensitivities into the day-to-day corporate policies and practices. Shapiro implies that board members are being called to account for the minutia of corporate life. If so, then boards need to become more active in shaping corporate conduct.

What Is "Conduct Becoming a Corporation?"   Shapiro is not alone in calling for increased participation from corporate boards. Robert K. Mueller, former chairman of the board of the international consulting firm of Arthur D. Little, has counseled countless corporate boards around the world on governance issues. In an article entitled "Conduct Becoming a Corporation," he called upon chief executive officers to seek higher ethical standards. Ethics, Mueller observed, borrowing from English barrister Lord J. F. Moulton, is the domain of "obedience to the unenforceable." Obedience to the law, in contrast, is enforceable. The law serves as a baseline of constraint for corporate action. Its demands are relatively clear. Unfortunately, dynamic ethical issues are clearest in hindsight, he noted, and constitute a domain of uncertainty for boards of directors. They typically call for action which is not specifically required but proves to be highly desirable. We are in a period of transition, he acknowledges, wherein values and ethical expectations are in flux.

> A slow but inexorable wave of new directors attuned to social, political, and technological changes is upon us, but this generation still faces the challenge of reducing increasing uncertainties to a governable set of probable risks and clarifying some of the confusion. This requires reexamination of the concept of ethics and of individual values with respect to corporate governance and board culture.[7]

Ethics is unenforceable, then, in the sense that it is action undertaken by decision makers who are convinced of its mutual importance to all parties. These decision makers should not require external agents to goad them into action. Their own perceptions, visions, and convictions motivate and guide their decisions. Furthermore, an action is undertaken to reduce uncertainty on the ethical side of enterprise. It is not a gesture of goodwill. It is as vital as the financial bottom line. Directors are in a key position to inspire this obedience to the unenforceable.

Boards Have the Power.   Since the Civil War and the advent of industrial capitalism, there has been a growing concentration of corporate power. Adolph Berle and Gardiner Means completed the first major study of corporate structure and power in 1932. One of their most astounding discoveries was that approximately 50 percent of the country's manufacturing assets were controlled by only 200 firms.[8] Berle and Means concluded that corporate management was remarkably free from either market or government control. Naturally, this information was not greeted with equal enthusiasm by all citizens. The specter of unchallenged corporate power has been a constant source of academic irritation and research. Since the Berle and Means study, bold and far-reaching legislation, in the 1930s and 1960s especially, curtailed corporate freedom but not the concentration of power. A similar study of corporate power undertaken in 1971 revealed that 60 percent of the manufacturing assets were now in the hands of a mere 100 firms.[9] In the spring of 1978 the Senate Committee on Governmental Affairs confirmed the concentration of corporate power. It revealed direct and indirect interlocking directorships among the largest banks, insurance companies, airlines, oil companies, the automotive industry, and telecommunications. Two ancillary factors may account for part of this consolidation. Mergers have reduced the number of manufacturing firms. Service industries have overtaken manufacturing companies and now account for more than 50 percent of the GNP. Naturally, critics suspect abuse and conflicts of obligation if not interest. The numbers document a concentration of corporate power. Is this good or bad?

Corporate power is concentrated, according to the cited studies. But was power abused in the formation of this confederation? That is not an easy question to answer convincingly. Corporate scholars have been involved in a tug-of-war on that issue for decades, with neither side gaining any convincing ground. Less arguable is the failure of these boards and interlocking networks to establish high ethical standards to which all comers might aspire. Such a task constitutes an ethical frontier that has impatiently awaited exploration. The heroes of the "dirty decade" of the eighties have broken new ground in this frontier, convincingly proved to us that it's there, and given us some object lessons in what not to do. Despite some public handwringing, the situation has not inspired concerted corporate action.

This concentration of corporate power must be viewed as an underutilized resource. Despite the decades of governmental regulation, corporations still have the power and freedom to alter the ethical landscape of the nation. Jeremiah J. O'Connell, dean of the graduate school at Bentley College, had some interesting observations after his 10-year stint observing managers in Europe.

> Europeans frankly envy us in the States...particularly the fact...that the right to manage remains largely intact in the U.S. Beyond envy...the European observer is awed by the transformation during the past 10 years of the *Fortune* 500 boards of directors without one piece of national legislation.[10]

O'Connell identifies a unique characteristic of ethics and U.S. culture. Both rely on large doses of voluntary compliance, or going the second mile to achieve harmony. The boards of directors of the nation's major firms could play a larger and more pivotal role by exercising the power and freedom available to them. They could provide the impetus and critical mass necessary to keep business out of the courts and Congress off their backs. Were this to occur it would rank as an achievement of unprecedented magnitude. It would constitute the ethical equivalent of completion of the transcontinental railroad.

Resolve the Double Dilemma

Boards of Directors Need to Become More Active. It is rare that stockholders, let alone the general public, are privy to what really happens behind closed corporate doors. Those doors are now being pried open by the accelerating expectations, growing egalitarianism, and at least the *perception* that executives and boards are just plain unethical.

Sometimes it's more than a perception. *Fortune* magazine opined that "the directors woke up too late at Gulf."[11] The eighth-largest industrial company in America secretly funneled hundreds of thousands of dollars in corporate cash to Richard Nixon's 1972 presidential campaign. Board Chairman and CEO Robert Dorsey readily acknowledged this "peccadillo" before the board. What Dorsey did not reveal until a year and a half later was that he had personally authorized payments of more than $4 million to the political campaign of President Park Chung Hee of Korea. Finally, another year later and under a pressing investigation from the Securities and Exchange Commission, the board convened a day-long, soul-searching meeting. A vote was unnecessary for them to reach the conclusion that Dorsey and three other executives should resign. The process was painful, time-consuming, courageous, and necessary. Boards need to become more aggressive on the ethical side of enterprise.

Boards of Directors Need to Take Sides.   Taking sides is the only way to resolve ethical dilemmas. Not only do directors need to speak out more often and more clearly on ethical issues, they also need to choose the interests they represent very carefully. It's perfectly natural and understandable that directors should support the interests of management and stockholders. But as we look more closely at those interests, we see that the business environment has changed in recent years. The best interests of management and stockholders now perforce include everybody: employees, customers, communities, governments, vendors, professional associations, and religious institutions. It's a challenging list (see Figure 5-1). Opposite each constituent are examples of issues peculiar to that constituent.

Note that the terms *microethical, macroethical,* and *metaethical* divide the constituents into three groupings. Each set of constituents encompasses a wider circle of interests. Each introduces a greater level of uncertainty. Executives and board members may share decision-making powers at all three levels. It is readily apparent, however, that once we reach beyond the corporate walls the exercise of power becomes problematic. At the macro- and metaethical level there are some constituents whose influence or power may equal or exceed that of senior management—national and foreign governments, for instance. Each level presents board members with a new set of questions.

At the *micro*ethical level the emphasis falls on compliance with acknowledged standards. Board members should know whether those standards are formalized in a written code or an individual employee contract. How were the standards created? What mix of input from employees, managers, board members, and stockholders accompanied the

Microethical Level: Internal to Company or Industry	
Employees	Fairness___affirmative action___safety___ health___training___promotion___ privacy___compensation and benefits___
Vendors	Selection___compensation___ handling gifts to and from___
Customers	Product quality___price and safety___ packaging and labeling___product service___ gifts to and from___
Competitors	Pricing___marketing practices___ proprietary information___advertising___
Stockholders	Accounting___reporting___insider information___officers and directors roles, responsibilities, and perquisites___
Management	Compensation and perquisites___ pensions___loans to officers___ insider information___use of company name___promotions___expense accounts golden parachutes___
Directors	Compensation and perquisites___ insider information___conflicts of interest and obligation between firms, self, employees, or customers___ethical audits___stockholders' resolutions___
Professionals	Conflicts of interest and obligation between and among clients, employers, and professional standards or formal codes___
Macroethical Level: National Policies and Standards	
Government	Product safety, quality, and warranties___ relationships with elected officials___ political contributions___ bidding on contracts___
Society	Community citizenship___environment___ jobs___corporate benevolence___ resource consumption___

Figure 5-1. Checklist of constituents and issues by ethical levels.

Competitors	Interpretations of antitrust laws____ changes in light of emerging global economy____
Directors	Efforts to democratize boards____ change corporate governance____
Employees	Changes in laws regulating organized labor, pensions, health care____
Special interests	Religion____education____medicine____ professional organizations____

Metaethical Level: International Policies and Standards

Governments	Laws____regulations____relationships with elected officials in different nations____ political contributions____
Society	Community citizenship____environment____ resource consumption____cultural and religious differences____
Competitors	Treatment of domestic versus foreign firms regarding open market, access to scarce resources, financial markets____

Figure 5-1. (*Continued*)

formation of those standards? Are the rewards and punishments clearly stated? Who is responsible for enforcement? How are changes in standards introduced?

At the *macro*ethical level the focus shifts to the setting or the changing of standards. When was a national policy adopted, for instance, if at all? Are there specific laws dictating behavior? Are there recent new developments which support a policy change? Should boards aggressively pursue changes via lobbyists or a public relations campaign? Should they wait for the problem to come to them? Government regulation and consumer advocacy, high-growth areas since the 1960s, have altered this ethical landscape dramatically.

At the *meta*ethical level the scope broadens to complying, recognizing, or negotiating ethical differences among cultures or nations. Some large issues surface here if boards move beyond simple compliance with local customs. Can the firm dictate its own rules in countries without clear legal or ethical precedents? Should they use market power to coerce a change in another country's ethics? Should either a firm or a country act unilaterally in forcing change? To what degree might such actions become a violation of national sovereignty?

Board members are in an ideal position to exercise responsibility for this conglomerate collection of interests. Sometimes only board members are positioned to resolve ethical dilemmas that span all three levels of deliberation. They are not involved in the day-to-day operations. They can assume an objective and omniscient perspective on behalf of the company. They can bring insights from other parts of the business community. They can strengthen an interlocking network of firms and people committed to high ethical practices. Board members are in a unique position to negotiate on behalf of the best interests of all constituents for the long term. They are the torchbearers for the corporate future.

Cases and Commentary

How would you phrase the ethical responsibility of board members? Would you agree that board members will want to help anticipate and avoid unethical CONSEQUENCES? This is ideally accomplished by carefully selecting and monitoring the GOALS, METHODS, and MOTIVES of corporate decisions. However, in the following cases and commentary we will be examining action that has already occurred. We will be looking backward rather than forward. The ethical bottom line is the consequences. Who got hurt? Who benefited? What was the environmental impact? True, some constituents might be more concerned about motives of the decision makers. Were their intentions good or evil? Were they unlucky or just thoughtless? We'll review those aspects later. Let's review a few corporate stories to see what we can learn from corporate history. We'll begin by focusing on the CONSEQUENCES component of the algorithm and citing cases with micro-, macro-, and/or metaethical applications.

Anticipate the Consequences

Review the ethical algorithm outline in Figure 2-1 (page 56). Note the three ancillary considerations under CONSEQUENCES.

1. What is the likely long-term versus short-term impact of the decision under consideration?

2. Which constituents will be the most affected and what are their likely reactions?

3. Is there an exogenous factor looming on the horizon?

Exogenous factors are like Murphy's law: if anything can go wrong, what could it possibly be? Let's look at some real-life examples from the perspective of these three considerations. What went wrong and in the eyes of which constituent?

What Is the Long- versus Short-Term Impact?   Allied-Signal Corporation, as it was known in the 1970s, was found guilty of incredibly lax employee safety and hazardous materials disposal methods in its manufacture of Kepone. Employees suffered permanent damage to their respiratory systems. Contaminated chemicals polluted the James River. Visitors to the Kepone manufacturing plant in Hopewell, Virginia, were astounded by the visible pollutants in the air.[12] The community had long since abandoned swimming in the river. The long-term effects of Allied's poor methods were discernible but not yet documented. OSHA and EPA, the two federal agencies charged with safety standards and environmental issues, respectively, were only a few years old at the time. Nevertheless, their intervention was finally required to bring about the necessary changes. Why? Where was management? Where were the directors? Is common sense not so common? Are long-term considerations of employee welfare and environmental pollution so commonly overlooked?

Directors can lend greater emphasis to long-term considerations. One way to start is to get out of the boardroom and onto the floor of manufacturing plants. Directors could steal a page from Tom Peters' *In Search of Excellence* and start practicing DBWA—directing by walking around. Find out not only *what's* going on but *how long* employees and management can successfully continue present practices. Make these visits with senior managers. Your mere presence may open everyone's eyes to what's really going on. *Get out of the boardroom.* Don't wait for critics to develop a case against your firm. Tour the plant, see what's happening. It may be necessary to ask why some practices started, let alone continued.

Free enterprise dotes on short-term measures. Managers and investors alike are aware of the harmful effects. They realize both short- and long-term considerations should be treated equally. But like devoted parents with two children, to one they give their heart, the other their head. Directors can correct this imbalance. The free enterprise system is not forgiving. It relentlessly calculates both the short and long terms. It is biased toward short-term financial measurements. Stockholders, investment advisers, and Wall Street, in general, are geared to a "quarter mentality." Stock prices rise or fall in response to last quarter's performance. Stocks are purchased or sold in anticipation of next quarter's projections. The ethical bottom line, in contrast, is usually a long-term measurement. Let top management take the pressure for the financial short term. Directors are better positioned to keep an eye out for the ethical long term. The fable of the tortoise and the hare is not only a maxim about myopic overconfidence. It underscores the virtue of plodding persistence. The race is won over the long term.

The demise of International Harvester (IH) underscores the importance of short- versus long-term considerations and also the pivotal role of the board of directors.[13] IH, founded by Cyrus McCormick in the nineteenth century, was a company that supposedly knew how to survive. McCormick had invented the reaper and enjoyed exclusive patent and production rights for a number of years. Most of its plants were located in the farm belt states of the midwest.

The board of directors had been playing a larger major role in selecting the chief executive officer as early as the 1950s. Their most egregious decision was the choice of Archie McCardell in 1977. He inherited costly labor contracts, excess plant capacity, inefficient national and global operations, and nearly 100,000 cynical employees. IH had a long history of excellent employee relations. Workers remembered that no one had been laid off during the depression years of the 1930s. Times were different now. Competition was more intense. A recession raged. Employee loyalty had completely shifted from management to the union.

The board of directors picked McCardell to steer the ship in the mistaken belief that IH could return to profitability by slashing operations cost—a short-term solution. McCardell had a reputation as a cost-cutter. He did not sell his skills cheaply. His salary package was a focal point of concern at the outset. He received a base salary of about $0.5 million, a contract signing payment of $1.5 million, another $1.8 million in a conditional loan to buy company stock, plus annual bonuses which amounted to nearly a third of a million dollars in one year. When McCardell launched an all-out attack on the United Auto Workers union (UAW) two years later, it is hardly surprising that his compensation package became a significant issue. It telegraphed an attitude on the part of management and the board of directors. About this same time Lee Iacocca was busy jawboning Congress and saving Chrysler for a salary of $1 a year! The contrast between the two CEOs did not go unnoticed. The role of the directors did. The union strike that followed was the longest in UAW history.

McCardell was fired in 1982. IH was in advanced financial hemorrhage, selling assets far below book value, laying off veteran employees, and cutting executive salaries. A short-term mentality had apparently dominated IH for decades, if measured by the generous union contracts and high management salaries. IH had needed an executive with a long-term approach for some time. The responsibility to provide IH with such an executive rested with the board of directors. Corporate loyalty on the part of both labor and management seems not to have extended beyond financial considerations. It was all take and no give, from top to bottom. Few loved the company enough to make the requisite sacrifices to keep it alive. In the long term, everybody lost. IH eventually sold its name and logo to Tenneco and reorganized as Navistar.

Selling out the long term for the short term is a constant temptation for executives of multinational corporations. It is easy to adopt the convenient ethic of "when in Rome, do as the Romans." Board members need to be alert to the pressures exerted on their senior officers. Do they know how their CEO might be conducting business in some foreign country? The top two executives of Lockheed resigned under pressure as a result of the media coverage focused on huge contributions to politicians in Korea. How knowledgeable were Lockheed Corporation board members? Did the directors at Northrop know about the huge slush fund their top executives had secreted? Why was it left to a Northrop stockholder to bring suit which revealed untold millions in unlawful political contributions? It's not likely that the directors at United Brands were aware of the complicated payoff schemes to Honduran political figures. Senior executives calculated that a $5 million "contribution" to the politicians would save them $7.5 million in the first year. They paid it. Eventually they were found out. Just before the scandal became public, CEO and board chairman Eli Black, a former rabbi, smashed his office window with his briefcase and jumped to his death.

In contrast, an audit committee of outside directors at Grumman Corporation uncovered a series of questionable transactions which they eventually reported to the Securities and Exchange Commission. Moreover, these illegal political contributions were in violation of board policy. The Grumman case reveals the difficulty boards face in monitoring company policies but also proves that it can be done. The alternative is public indignation, destruction of stockholder confidence, and degradation of executives. In addition, such gross violations as those cited prompted enactment of a Foreign Corruption Practices Act (FCPA). Boards need to utilize every opportunity to see that their executives are not isolated and privately pressured into unethical methods to achieve their goals.

Let's turn now to another algorithmic consideration under CONSEQUENCES, namely, the impact on various constituents.

What Was the Impact on Constituents? Many ethical dilemmas arise from genuine conflicts of obligation between the corporation's constituents. How do you resolve the conflicting demands of employee safety or environmental pollution and company profits? Directors can play a significant role in settling these conflicts. The well-being of each constituent needs to be considered.

Allied-Signal faced both of these dilemmas. Its managers were caught in a double conflict of obligation between employee health plus environmental welfare and corporate profits. Initially, Allied placed a higher priority on corporate profits. Later, Allied changed its priorities and took decisive action on behalf of employees and the environment, prompted by OSHA and the EPA, respectively. As noted, the board could have played a role in this priority reversal simply by getting out of the boardroom and providing another perspective through which these decisions could be viewed. Who are the constituents to be considered and how are they affected? Boards are in an ideal position to run through the entire list of constituents and ask how each will be affected by corporate decisions. It's better to be asking questions early than to be answering them too late.

Top management at Lockheed, Northrup, United Brands, Grumman, and Allied assigned top priority to the corporation over the short term. The corporation, as they defined it, was the only constituent of significance. They ignored the long-term consequences. It would be unjust and misleading to write these people off as simply greedy, selfishly corrupt, or "bad apples." The situations are more complicated than that. Instead, board members might ask how they might have lifted the visions, strengthened the latent ethical resolve, or otherwise been a broadening influence in their role as overseers.

There are some advantages to separating the roles of CEO and board chair. Separate assignments could underscore the short- versus long-term perspective. The board chair, functioning as a facilitator, would elicit the participation of board members on behalf of long-term considerations. The chief executive would handle the short-term perspective. Boards might have a better chance of sharing fully the ethical responsibilities of corporate leadership if these distinctions between board chair and CEO were more sharply drawn.

What Are Possible Exogenous Factors?   Exogenous factors are people or events who enter the corporate environment with the suddenness of a squall at sea. The warnings may be there but they go unheeded. Boards should be continually asking themselves, "If something can go wrong, what's it likely to be?" What people or events cannot be controlled? What sources of risk and uncertainty are easily overlooked? Senior managers and board members might be tempted to consult a soothsayer or corporate fortune-teller, if they thought predictions would be reliable. Exogenous factors often give rise to that temptation.

Farah Manufacturing Company was a victim of an exogenous event called "the Chicano movement."[14] CEO William Farah completely misjudged its power and character. He employed lots of Chicanos in his textile manufacturing plant in El Paso, Texas. The movement grew out of the revolt of migrant farmworkers in the southwestern United States under the leadership of Caesar Chavez. Its objectives ranged from better wages to increased respect for Chicanos. Farah assumed that his modern plants and above-average benefits would satisfy both objectives. He neither understood nor accepted the workers' growing desire to exercise some control over their work life. As a result, he plunged his company into endless labor strife, expensive and inconclusive squabbles with the National Labor Relations Board, plus diminished market share, profits, and prestige. The Chicano movement was an exogenous factor which could have been anticipated by an informed and forceful board of directors.

A more forceful board of directors could have made a big difference at another textile manufacturing firm. CEO James D. Finley *was* the exogenous factor at J. P. Stevens. He was uncontrollable. He was also the first CEO in the firm's 160-year history who was not a member of the Stevens family. Acting unilaterally, he plunged the company into one crisis after another. The main issue was treatment of workers. When Whitney J. Stevens succeeded him in 1979, Finley left a legacy of lawsuits alleging unfair labor practices, charges of racial discrimination, intentional mispreparation of state income tax returns, price fixing on government contracts, and occupational health hazards for workers. *The Gallagher President's Report: A Confidential Letter to Chief Executives* listed him as one of the 10 worst chief executives in 1977.

The board of directors was unable to discipline Finley. His corporate colleagues were equally timid. Only pressure from the Amalgamated Clothing and Textile Workers Union effected his removal as an outside director on the board of Manufacturers Hanover Trust. Stockholders questioned him sharply an annual meetings, to little avail. He announced on one occasion that "This is my meeting, I'm running it." A stockholder asked whether he intended to follow Robert's rules of order. He answered, "No. No rules.... Now just be quiet and sit down and behave. I can overrule anything. It's the J. P. Stevens rule of order here. That's the way we've been doing it for over 160 years."[15]

Both William Farah and James Finley exemplify executives who had difficulty sharing authority, exacerbating the ethical crisis. Farah's board needed to find ways to expand its role. They exercised too little authority. Finley's board needed to find ways to retain its authority. They had it—150 years of it—and gave it away. The Farah Manufacturing and J. P. Stevens cases are glaring examples of a dilemma all boards face, namely, sharing control of the corporation. Boards unclear about their role and insecure about their authority constitute a power vacuum easily victimized by exogenous events or people, whether social upheavals or maverick chief executives.

The Tylenol scare presented Johnson & Johnson (J&J) with an exogenous event of frightening and costly proportions. This thoroughly publicized tragedy resulted in the death of several persons when some still-unknown person (or persons) laced the acetaminophen pain reliever capsules with cyanide. The issue was quickly and ably managed by CEO and board chairman James Burke, who was supported daily by an 11-member executive committee. Burke has been cited repeatedly for his exceptionally sensitive handling of a corporate nightmare and national crisis.

Burke faced a microethical dilemma. J&J was in full compliance with all relevant laws and procedures regarding preparation and packaging of its products. The dilemma surfaced in the misuse of those products by consumers. Did corporate responsibility end once the product reached the shelves of drugstores or did it extend to events clearly beyond its control? The company met legal demands. What did good ethics require? Burke opted for the most responsible and costly horn, based in part on a corporate credo that placed doctors, nurses, and patients at the very top of their constituent priority list. (Stockholders were last.) The J&J credo, dating back to the days of "General" Robert Wood Johnson, son of one of the founders, includes a written commitment to ethical goals. The ethical side of their algorithmic answer sheet is filled in. They simply followed it, albeit at considerable cost, effort, and anxiety. The product was recalled and new packaging techniques were developed.

Can boards of directors anticipate exogenous events? Not entirely, but they can be prepared for them. First, boards need to recognize that such ordeals are inevitable. Don't panic. Plan. Get ready for them. Second, part of the plan should be a code of ethics. List your goals, both financial and ethical. Prioritize your constituents. Do people or profits come first? Third, identify the most likely sources of trouble, places where the competition is intense and the need for secrecy or confidentiality is high. Intense competition puts pressure on the corporate ethic. Boards can anticipate problems wherever the competition is intense. The pressure to cut ethical corners increases along with competitive intensity. Directors can anticipate, and possibly avert, dilemmas emerging from these corners by sound policies, appropriate credos, and constant monitoring.

We've been reviewing the unethical or undesirable consequences some corporations have suffered when they failed to anticipate over the long term the impact of their decisions on one or more critical constituents. Sometimes it's a failure to anticipate the improbable. More specifically, we have been focusing on the peculiar challenges and opportunities which fall to the board of directors. We've been looking at corporate action from the vantage point of hindsight. In ethics, even hindsight is not 20/20.

The biggest challenge for boards, however, is to anticipate and satisfy the rising ethical expectations of corporate constituents anywhere in the world. Directors can help in this process by carefully selecting and shaping the goals and methods of the corporation and refining the motives of its principal decision makers. Let's explore this process utilizing examples from the micro-, macro-, and metaethical levels. We start with goals.

Develop Solid Goals

It's become commonplace for firms to ask the strategic question, "What business are we in?" The ethical counterpart is, "Why are we in business?" Both of these questions are answered as corporate leaders begin to list their goals. On the business side the answer is obvious and inevitable: survive; make some money; increase market share or even dominate the market. But what about the ethical side? Is that also obvious and inevitable: good intentions and stay legal? Selecting an ethical goal is neither obvious nor inevitable.

Be Specific. Every firm can benefit by articulating a special ethical goal. Some managers and boards believe they have attended to this matter when they create policies or codes based on prevailing laws. That's certainly a good beginning. It's a commitment to function legally. But is it a commitment to function ethically, to be obedient to the unenforceable? Some written policies or codes may do little more than establish constraints. They set limits or boundaries for employees. Outlining constraints and setting ethical goals are not the same. A constraint is passive. It marks something you struggle to avoid. A goal is active. It identifies something you strive to reach. A sound ethical goal is dynamic. It can be as exciting and powerful an incentive as making lots of money. In times of crisis it serves as a reminder of why you're in business. The Tylenol calamity proved how important a clearly articulated ethical goal was to J&J.

Few corporations have been as vocal and as successful in defining "conduct becoming a corporation" as Minneapolis-based Dayton Hudson. A key figure has been Kenneth Dayton, former CEO and chairman of the board. During his years as board chairman he introduced an unorthodox view of corporate priorities. He took every opportunity to challenge boards of directors to examine theirs.

I maintain that business must change its priorities. We are not in
business to make maximum profit for our shareholders. We are in
business for only one reason—to serve society. Profit is our reward
for doing it well. If business does not serve society, society will not
long tolerate our profits or even our existence.[16]

Kenneth Dayton spoke from experience. He was not only a former
CEO but son of the company's founder. He believed that board members share the responsibility of goal setting with top management. Directors are in the best position to argue for corporate goals with an ethical component. They have the least interest in a specific constituent
and the most interest in all of them. They do not have to function like
whistle-blowers. It might mean going public with a private controversy.
H. Ross Perot, the maverick board member of General Motors, openly
challenged CEO Roger Smith on his leadership of the company generally. The resignation of Louis Cabot from the Penn Central Transportation Company in 1963 is one of the few published stories of a board
member challenging a CEO on what later proved to be ethical grounds.
Confrontation is probably not the method of choice for most board
members, however. The place to start is to establish a climate of shared
responsibility. If boards of directors are increasingly being held accountable for corporate outcomes, it behooves them to assume greater
responsibility in goal setting. Take a look at the different kinds of goals
various corporations have set for themselves in recent years.

International Business Machines has long been guided by a clear set
of ethical goals. Thomas J. Watson, Jr., committed them to writing in
1963 when he was chairman of the board.[17] They are, in brief: respect
for the individual, the best customer service, superior performance
from its people. For decades, IBM was the most profitable corporation
in the world. Their ethical goals accounted for achievement of their
business goals, according to more than one IBM employee.

Firms like J&J, IBM, and Ross Labs, among others, have sharply articulated the ethical dimension of their goal structure. They have multiple goals. There is a financial side and an ethical side. IBM's goals, we
noted, were especially interrelated; they nourished and strengthened
each other. Unfortunately, this is not always the case. Companies with
multiple goals will be under greater pressure to ensure goal compatibility. Can they achieve all goals?

Check Goals for Compatibility.   Companies always face the prospect
of incompatible goals. It's become increasingly difficult in the modern
world to make lots of money and maintain the appearance of doing it
ethically.

The most common goal incompatibility dilemma occurs between the business goals of making money and the ethical goal of treating employees fairly. The issue is far larger than salary and benefits. Sometimes it's a matter of race, gender, or age discrimination. Sears, Roebuck and AT&T were involved in lengthy litigation on the gender issue. Setting racial quotas or adopting affirmative action programs are major microethical questions with complicated nuances. Directors can help launch such efforts, perhaps, and monitor progress. But successful implementation usually falls on middle managers. In the last decade in particular, however, board intervention was most needed (and not always provided) on behalf of hundreds of thousands of otherwise competent senior executives who lost their jobs in corporate mergers, hostile takeovers, or corporation downsizing and restructuring. While many firms set ethical goals for vulnerable executives, golden parachutes for the favored few received the most attention. Since the dominant issue in these cases was corporate survival, the business side simply overpowered ethical considerations. Many careers suffered permanent injury. Directors need to ask whether multiple goals of survival and employee welfare are truly as incompatible as they seem.

Donald Burr, the guiding genius of People Express, aspired to create an airline that gave the top priorities to less affluent passengers and its employees rather than corporate passengers and stockholders. Passengers handled their own luggage and brought on board whatever refreshments they wanted. Employees were encouraged to think of themselves as managers. For a time it appeared that these goals might prove to be compatible. Unfortunately, the abused constituent in this case turned out to be the customer. The experiment failed. Frank Lorenzo added the airline to his growing empire at Texas Air.

Dow Chemical faced a macroethical dilemma as the manufacturer of napalm B for the United States government during the Vietnam war. Management argued that the money earned was insignificant. The financial goal was not the determining factor, in other words. Dow believed it was serving a patriotic (and therefore ethical) goal. Unfortunately, such a reasonable perspective was lost on those who opposed the war in Vietnam. Dow became a target of their moral indignation. In a curious twist of logic, Dow ended up defending its ethics rather than its business.

Chemical firms manufacturing herbicides or pesticides also face potential goal incompatibility on the macroethical level when their products threaten the environment or humans with harmful side effects. In such instances the source of the incompatibility is due to the harmful side effects rather than the goals themselves. It sets up a conflict of obligation between two constituents, the farmer and the consumer, or the intermediary user and the end-product user. Conflicts of obligation permit compromise, as a rule. Directors can encourage and help management to find appropriate points of compromise. What's the documentation on the harmful side effects, for instance? Is there contradictory evidence? Are the effects short-term or long-term? Is there likely to be legislative action? Directors can help maintain an atmosphere of balanced inquiry rather than panicky reaction. When goals are truly incompatible, of course, no compromise is possible and one goal or the other will have to be sacrificed.

The tobacco industry itself represents goal incompatibility on the macroethical scale. The business side of the operation is very strong. Tobacco companies have consumers aplenty. Tobacco stocks are popular on Wall Street because they're such great money makers. However, the product is believed to cause lung cancer. Ethically, tobacco companies are vulnerable in the extreme. If the product is clearly unethical, i.e., harmful to users, why isn't it declared illegal as well as "unethical"? Good question. There is no unambiguous answer. Consequently, the lion's share of the industry's considerable marketing talent has been directed at the ethical side of their enterprise while the business side hauls in mountains of cash. The public pressure to justify their operations continues to increase, mandating new efforts aimed at sustaining an ethical foundation for smoking. An early tactic was questioning the evidence of probability in the absence of scientific proof. Another stratagem has been research on a "smokeless," or nonnicotine, cigarette. A recent promotional ploy developed by Philip Morris virtually wrapped the company in the U.S. Constitution. Respondents to their ads were given free copies of the Declaration of Independence. The message was unmistakable: Citizens have a constitutional right to smoke. It seems very unlikely that tobacco companies will be categorized as Quadrant IV enterprises, unethical and illegal. More likely, as with IBM in South Africa, the smoking issue will finally be resolved by financial considerations rather than ethical ones. Manufacturing cigarettes will become profitless and smoking too expensive.

Check the Priority Ranking of Your Constituents. Once goals have been set and checked for compatibility, directors can assign rankings to their many constituents. (Review the potential list of constituents in Figure 5-1 on page 146.) Which constituents are most favored by the goals chosen? Which might be unintentionally excluded? Clearly, a firm's constituents today are no longer just stockholders. The fact that the list is so long is evidence that the American dream of democratic equality is coming true. Everybody counts! It may not be possible to please all of them all of the time, but if too many are displeased, unwanted troubles lie ahead. There are a few corporate stories where boards have radically altered constituent priority.

The board of directors at Pan Am, unlike Bill Agee's at Bendix, openly challenged their CEO's strategy and leadership. They fired their CEO in what appeared to be an effort to appease organized labor. The current spate of golden parachutes notwithstanding, even some CEOs are no longer indispensable.

How unusual was the dilemma confronting the board of directors at Pam American World Airways? This story hit the newspapers in mid-January of 1988. The previous year the airline had lost $150 million, blamed on strikes, rising fuel costs, and foreign exchange rates. Pan Am was in big trouble. Labor costs had to be cut. The unions were pressured for sizable wage givebacks. They responded with a demand that the CEO be fired. In time, three of the five unions at Pan Am backed a plan to secure CEO Edward Acker's resignation as part of a labor-cost concessions deal. The unions became more important constituents than the CEO. The determining criterion was survival rather than ethics.

The meltdown of a nuclear oven at Three Mile Island (TMI) depicts a macroethical example of the failure to assign sufficient priority to an important constituent — the surrounding community.[18] The plant near Harrisburg, Pennsylvania, was one of 72 in operation in the United States in 1979. It was one of the pioneering efforts in the use of nuclear power to generate electricity. In addition to providing cheaper electricity, the nuclear plants held promise of decreasing the country's dependence on oil imports. Then President Carter, among others, repeatedly stressed the inevitability and promise of an all-nuclear age. Confidence in nuclear energy was high.

The meltdown at TMI was a simple accident. It's difficult to fault the management team at Metropolitan Edison Company. They had taken normal precautions. Safety measures were deployed. The reaction of the community, indeed the entire nation, was what they had not anticipated. It was more than 10 years before the plant was back in service, owing in part to fears rather than facts. The hysteria of some citizens was beyond reason. Otherwise well-intentioned executives and their boards simply did not accurately calculate the impact of this latent terror. It was and is a costly mistake. Community opposition to placement of plants still plagues the industry nationwide. Board members need to don the hats of Mr. and Mrs. Average Citizen when innovative products or projects are launched. Try to imagine how each and every constituent will respond to your company's goals.

How Ethical Are Your Methods?

Once the goals have been selected, checked for multiplicity, compatibility, and constituent priority, decision makers can turn their attention to

METHODS, the second major series of questions in the ethical algorithm. Boards can help senior management sort through the various options and select those which lead to the successful and ethical implementation of their goals.

METHODS in the algorithm are just that. They include manufacturing, sales techniques, marketing, financing, employee compensation and benefit plans, and even corporate charity. They constitute the various and specific means by which firms survive and make money. On the business side they might include questions such as financing through debt versus stock issuance, setting up your own manufacturing plant versus buying parts through vendors, paying sales personnel a set salary versus a percentage of sales. Those sundry business methods need to pass through three checkpoints, discussed in the next three sections, in order to satisfy the ethical side of enterprise.

Which Constituents Are Unhappy?   It's reasonable to assume that decision makers will try to select methods that meet with the acceptance of their constituents. If boards phrase the constituency acceptance question in the negative, they can get quickly to the root of possible unethical consequences. Who's happy and who's not, presuming the goals are already implemented?

Allied-Signal has already been cited as an example of a firm that chose methods that proved to create unethical consequences. Employee health and the environment both suffered. Were alternative methods available to them? Were there protective devices that could have been added to the manufacturing processes, for instance? Did the emphasis on profitability preclude consideration of alternative methods? Were the methods chosen at the whim of a manager, for example, without solid relevance to the context? Will new technology, environmental study, or medical research uncover hazards which demand a change in methods?

The Manville Corporation was a catastrophic victim of advancing medical research. The carcinogenic qualities associated with the manufacture and use of asbestos clearly emerged only after years of damage had been done. In contrast, stockholders were very happy with the dividends and capital gains the company churned out. Board members were not alone in failing to foresee that the health and long-term happiness of employees and consumers were being sacrificed.

In somewhat the same manner, bondholders, brokerage houses, and commercial bankers were elated with the profits pouring from the so-called junk bond frenzy of the eighties. Few perceived the long-term damage accruing to both the financial markets and the general economy. This microethical issue of noncompliance with the spirit of our regulatory laws created a macroethical dilemma. The abuse of good judgment, business as well as ethical, raised the specter of reregulation.

The deregulation which began in the late 1970s appeared to provide more freedom than the financial community could handle. Radical shifts in the business environment created new concepts of debt, risk, property ownership, employee and client rights, to name a few. Decision makers sailed into uncharted ethical waters. They made mistakes. The ethical failures of the 1980s conveniently created sufficient moral outrage to justify numerous legislative crusades. Boards of directors were confronted with a new dilemma. How should they respond? Should they passively await the next spate of legislative action that transforms the unenforceable into the enforceable? Or should they make an effort to set some higher standards among themselves and forestall further erosion of their discretionary authority? Aside from the fact that the Sherman and Clayton antitrust laws draw an indistinct line between collaboration and collusion, corporations have generally resisted rising to such lofty aspirations in the past.

The Nestle Company, like the Ross division of Abbott Laboratories, was also the target of unhappy consumer advocates who believed they represented the best interests of citizens in developing nations. This metaethical controversy focused on the advertising methods utilized in marketing their infant formula (see Chapter 3, page 95). Again, who but an alert board of directors was in a better position to broaden the constituency horizon of the company?

Is Your Firm Maximizing Profits or Popularity?   It costs to be ethical, at least in the short term. Profits suffer when firms develop the ethical dimension of their operations. New standards of product safety, job security, environmental care, and social usefulness introduce countless dilemmas for firms today. Boards of directors have an important role to play in helping to strike an acceptable balance between profits and popularity.

Robert Townsend addressed the microethical issue of fairness in executive compensation. When he was CEO of Avis he insisted that salary differentials follow modest, proportionate increments. Executives who felt underpaid left. Surprisingly, few did. Townsend's standard prevailed throughout his tenure at Avis. The role of his board of directors on this matter is not recorded. Townsend's example was not widely followed by other firms. The issue is alive, nonetheless. Nowhere in the world are salary disparities greater than in the United States. Firms are now required to report the compensation packages of the topmost executives. The news media highlight this information. The public is becoming better informed. Directors have to be concerned about the long-term impact of the public's growing disenchantment with business. Either they need to provide ethical foundations for the huge salaries paid to top managers or work together across industry lines to achieve a more defensible balance.

At the macroethical level, more and more companies have embraced the concept of *corporate responsibility* to justify their existence. The definition of the term has been as controversial as some of the practices. At one level corporate responsibility is a minimal "do no harm." This is essentially the position enunciated by Milton Friedman.

> There is one and only one social responsibility of business—to use its resources and engage in activities designed to increase its profits so long as it stays within the rules of the games, which is to say, engages in open and free competition without deception or fraud.[19]

At another level, corporate responsibility means using corporate profits to contribute generously to society at large. (Exxon, Mobil, ARCO, IBM, General Motors, and AT&T consistently give multimillions from their corporate coffers to community projects and organizations.) At still another level, corporate responsibility is viewed as the deeper dimension of such ordinary business goals as providing excellent products or services at fair prices. The emphasis is not on *what* you do but *how* you do it. At the extreme, there are those who view corporate responsibility as a means of income redistribution. As with so many business issues, we can trace a spectrum of ethicality along which corporations are arrayed. There have been some interesting experiments.

Aetna Life & Casualty Company pledged millions of dollars to rebuild some of the decaying neighborhoods around Chicago, Illinois, in the late 1970s. Their efforts loosened storms of protest from one constituent or another, lengthening the time frame of their commitment and lessening their hoped-for impact. Union Carbide underwent a similar disenchantment in efforts to remodel the slums of East Harlem in New York City. Directors will want to investigate the experiences of other corporations and plan such interventions very carefully before recommending the investment of corporate talents and profits in untested ways. Most firms have found it easier to give money.

Corporate giving has never constituted the lion's share of eleemosynary effort in the United States. On average, of the approximately $100 billion donated annually for charitable purposes, only about 5 percent comes from corporate coffers. Over 60 percent is given by individuals. The rest comes from foundations, most of which are or were company-sponsored; AT&T, General Motors, Amoco, Ford, and Exxon were the top five givers in 1988. Forty percent of corporate foundation giving is funneled into education, partly through matching gift programs. These are the least controversial corporate efforts to discharge their "responsibility." Corporate philanthropy is controversial.

The Internal Revenue Service limits tax-exempt corporate charity to 5 percent of pretax profits. The Business Roundtable issued a major statement on corporate responsibility in the early eighties. Corporate philanthropy was listed as one of a half dozen "policy instruments" to help implement corporate responsibility. No percentage goals were recommended, however.[20] Economist Milton Friedman has long insisted that corporate profits accrue to stockholders.

> The claim that business should contribute to the support of charitable activities...is an inappropriate use of corporate funds in a free enterprise society.[21]

Perhaps Friedman took his cue from Evelyn Y. Davis. She has long advocated higher dividends to stockholders so that they can give to charities of their choice instead of the director's choice. She allegedly admonished CEO Melvin W. Allredge at an annual stockholders' meeting of A&P grocery stores not to "make any charitable contributions....Give us higher cash dividends so we can make contributions to whoever we want."[22] Despite these objections, direct corporate charity is a rising trend with lots of variations. A few examples follow.

1. *Cause-related marketing.* American Express was an early and strong advocate of relating corporate giving to a particular cause that marketed the company's products or services as well. The inside story there was that the board of directors was sharply divided on the issue of corporate charity. Some were intensely in favor of giving away corporate profits. Others resisted. Cause-related marketing (CRM) was the compromise. The most highly publicized example of CRM was the $1.7 million American Express contributed to refurbishing the Statue of Liberty. In the calendar year of 1985 American Express donated a single penny for every charge card transaction and every new account. While no precise tabulation was kept, Amex estimated that revenues increased about 10 percent. Both the cause and the company benefited. Amex reported even better results with CRM in San Jose, California, and Atlanta, Georgia.

2. *The stockholder-designated alternative.* Warren Buffett, founder of the highly successful investment firm of Berkshire Hathaway, found another way to silence the dissent of both stockholders and board members. Each year the board determined that a certain dollar amount be set aside for corporate charity. The unusual wrinkle in Buffett's plan allowed individual stock owners to designate their favorite charity. The nominees were then awarded a proportionate amount of the total corporate figure, based on the number of shares held by that stockholder.

Minimum and maximum contributions were set, naturally. Monies not designated by individual stockholders went to donees selected by a committee of the board. Buffett's plan had the added value of educating stockholders in the art of beneficence.

3. *Charity is good public-employee relations.* Joyce Clyde Hall, founder of Hallmark Cards, made no bones about it. Despite the frequent attempts of the kindly disposed to dub his sponsorship of *The Hallmark Hall of Fame* as a gesture in corporate responsibility, "Mr. J. C." specifically denied such high-minded motives.

> I do not have a philanthropic attitude toward culture.... The simple truth is that good television is good business.[23]

Hall never went public with his company, passing up the opportunity to capitalize his wealth. When he died in 1982, his employees owned 25 percent of the company through an employee stock ownership plan.

4. *The 5 Percent Club.* Dayton Hudson, a diversified retail company operating in nearly 40 states from Massachusetts to California from headquarters in Minneapolis, Minnesota, is a founding member of the 5 Percent Club. Annually it donates the maximum allowable 5 percent of its pretax income to community activities of various sorts, ranging from the Minneapolis Symphony Orchestra to Head Start. This practice dates back to the founders of the once separate firms. Dayton Hudson later formulated a four-point policy of corporate citizenship. It included:

- A continued commitment to the 5 percent pretax giving
- Authorization of employee time and talent of behalf of community activities
- A strengthened commitment to the highest ethical standards in all business transactions
- Full disclosure of charitable giving

Kenneth Dayton himself developed a rather innovative scheme to encourage long-term investment.[24] Those who retain company stock for longer periods will be progressively taxed less on dividends and capital gains. For instance, if you hold a stock for less than a year, you are taxed 100 percent. If you retain ownership more than a year, your tax rate drops an additional 10 percent for each year you hang onto it. The idea has interesting ethical implications. It would counter the "get rich quick and quit" syndrome. It would strengthen stockholder loyalty, participation, and managerial accountability over a longer term. It might encourage more employee stock ownership. It might lessen the pressures on top management from the "quarter mentality."

These four different styles of corporate benevolence should inspire boards of directors to develop their own innovative approaches. In the free enterprise system, incredible wealth and power are placed at the disposal of a fortunate few. Today, citizens everywhere are better informed and more critical of how the fortunate few use their power and wealth. Maintaining the system requires sensitive and continuous consideration of the relatively less fortunate many.

Are Your Methods Absolutely Essential?   Boards can help scrutinize the methods senior executives select to achieve announced goals. Their methods may be only incidental or even extraneous. Other choices may be available and more desirable. If, for example, the obvious methods might threaten employee health and safety or damage the environment, are there alternatives? Methods are sometimes selected by default rather than thoughtful calculation. Allied-Signal's manufacturing process for Kepone, for example, was not intentionally harmful. The initial challenge, probably, was to solve the scientific part of the process. It hardly seems likely that E. F. Hutton deliberately set out to plan a check kiting scheme. Their goal, apparently, was to motivate the sales force. The method was given less attention: base commissions on good cash management. Boards may not be included in discussions of such methods. But they can sensitize managers to the need to examine methods carefully.

If the chosen methods appear to be incidental — i.e., selected as an afterthought — it means there *are* some alternatives. What are they? What are the pros and cons of each? Explore these alternatives from the perspective of both the business and ethical sides and the key constituents. International Harvester confronted determined unionized employees seemingly bent on a strike. What method should management have picked in response? Senior executives had a choice. Was the eventual decision to resist further negotiations and encourage the strike absolutely essential or only incidental? In hindsight, would they be likely to make the same choice? Was the choice ethical, that is, reasonably beneficial to all constituents?

If the methods can be classified as extraneous, it means that the reason they have been chosen may be unknown or may be an executive's whim. Examples of extraneous methods are rare because the real reasons for the choice of methods are often unknown or hidden. Imputing reasons may be either unfair or risky.

Ralph Cordiner's decision to decentralize General Electric might serve as an example of an extraneous method. When he assumed the helm of General Electric in the 1950s, he was determined to make some changes.[25] His intentions were the best. He'd served time as an underutilized subordinate. He remembered what it was like to be a cog in a giant wheel where vital decisions were handed down from above.

He set up profit centers. Managers inexperienced in making big decisions on their own were suddenly given new powers and a bundle of money. Some handled it very well. Others did not. The result was a six-company price-fixing scandal that landed several of GE's senior executives in jail. Was decentralization absolutely necessary? Was it the only method available? What were Cordiner's goals? Were they only personal—and therefore extraneous—or corporate—and at least incidental? Was decentralization, or the hasty way it was done, a contributing cause of the price fixing? The case of General Electric does raise the question, even if a yes answer is impossible to prove.

What Motivates Top Management?

Peter Drucker remarked that profit is not a motive. It is a measure. Greed and fear are motives. Profits measure the dollars accruing to corporate coffers, gathered by executives motivated perhaps by greed and fear. The new age, however, invites a more inclusive constellation of motives. In the context of the ethical algorithm, the MOTIVES component involves exploring the personalities and values of the key decision makers. As unbusinesslike as it sounds, what characterizes the attitudes and feelings of these important individuals? Corporate values will be rooted in its senior managers. What feelings accompany their choices of action? What drives them to succeed? The board of directors needs to know what kind of people fill the major leadership spots. Obviously, if the decision-making power is centered in a single person, his or her values will likely prevail, unless that person can be influenced. If power is shared with the board members, there will be more opportunities for directors to shape the values of the corporate elite. The most difficult challenge board members face is that of converting their personal values into corporate policy.

We must leave the selection of specific values to each board member, manager, and employee—and even each stockholder and/or stakeholder, for that matter. This is the spirit of free enterprise and democracy. In that same spirit, however, we can ask some evaluative questions about motives and values. Namely, are they out in the open for others to see and discuss? Are they the kind of motives and values that can be widely shared by others? What is their basic orientation? Let's address those three questions briefly.

Are Personal Motives Out in the Open?   Do employees up and down the corporate ladder understand what drives their leaders? Do board members know? Reflect upon the MOTIVES element with special care. Focus on just the key employees first. What are their personal goals? Why do they work here rather than somewhere else? Is it possible for all of them to be equally motivated to achieve the announced goals? Are some senior executives so driven by powerful personal motives that they either inspire a matching selfishness in some or diminish entirely the enthusiasm of others? Are employees proud of their work? What's their work ethic? A nine-to-five mentality? These are just a few of the general questions directors can ask about their people. If a corporation is to have a conscience, it will enter by this door.

Michael Maccoby studied several hundred corporate managers in a major effort to understand their motives and values.[26] We can't do full justice to that study here, but Maccoby's four managerial types might inspire board members to look closely at the kind of executives who occupy the top offices. Despite the dangers of oversimplification, the four types can be summed up as follows.

The *craftsmen* (or *craftspersons*) are work-oriented technicians. Their motive is to create or build. Their goal is to perfect. The *companymen* (or *companypersons*) are motivated by loyalty. Their goal is to protect the company at all costs. The *junglefighters* are driven by a lust for power. Their goal is to achieve that power for themselves. The *gamesmen* (or *gamespersons*) are motivated by a desire to win. Their goal is to achieve prestige or fame in the eyes of their peers. Board members should look critically at the personal motives and goals of their CEOs, particularly. Their first aim is understanding.

Craftspersons abound in the chief executive's suite. Their technical skills often turn them into entrepreneurs. If they are not actually the company founders, their knowledge of the product earns them successive promotions. Maccoby describes their values as traditional. Their understanding of interpersonal and group dynamics may be underdeveloped. They may miss the subtleties of individual differences and ethical dilemmas. Willie Farah, we can speculate, was a craftsman. He was probably more motivated by the pure techniques of modern textile manufacturing than he was in the workers' health, safety, and self-esteem, for example. The competitive intensity of the industry provided ethical justification for shortchanging employee well-being. Profit margins were low. Labor was unskilled. Employee turnover was high. Farah Manufacturing may well have become a target for union organizing because the CEO's motives and values were so clearly displayed. It was easy to make the case that he cared more about machines than people.

The companyperson is likely to build a constellation of shared values that are passed on to successive corporate generations. Levi Strauss, "the jeans people," is a company with a long tradition of unusual sensitivity to issues other than a bottom line measured only in dollars and dividends. Their commitment to their employees during the lean years of the 1930s is still remembered and recalled, according to David Freudberg.[27] Rather than lay off any workers, management first cut back on everyone's hours. When work further slackened, workers were assigned odd jobs around the plants totally unrelated to their routine production jobs. The company's dedication to its employees cost a bundle of money. The company spent working capital—retained earnings. Profits were nonexistent. The spirit of this decades-old business ethic on the part of Levi Strauss is still alive. Companypersons nourish such traditions.

Junglefighter executives, in contrast, constitute a real hazard for corporations. They may be highly motivated, capable of tough decisions, and able to get quick results, but their goals, in Maccoby's taxonomy, are too self-centered. The long-term interests of the company are likely to suffer. Junglefighters, as the name implies, are the most likely to break the rules and be laws unto themselves. They create ethical dilemmas.

Lee Iacocca is a gamesperson. His motives and values are visible to the whole nation. He is very open in sharing his values and opinions. His goal to turn Chrysler into a viable company was widely but not totally shared. He fought the battle on behalf of the Chrysler Corporation against great odds. He won in a manner that created few enemies and many friends. Later, his name kept cropping up as a presidential candidate. His open, selfless style had made him very popular. The same might be said for D. J. De Pree, founder of the Herman Miller furniture company in Zeeland, Michigan. In response to the proliferation of golden parachutes for beleaguered chief executives confronting possible hostile takeovers, De Pree created "tin parachutes" to cover all his employees. He guaranteed severance pay for every employee with at least a year's work record. That decision reveals something about the man's values and motives. It's hardly the kind of action employees could demand. The gamespersons do not wait for the demand to develop. They anticipate the need.

Board members enjoy a unique personal relationship denied many others inside and outside the firm. They are in an excellent position to make some inferences about the motives and values of their senior managers. They can evaluate the ambiguities and discrepancies between reality and perception. For instance, are the actual motives and values of the CEO being communicated accurately? If an ethical dilemma were to surface—like the Tylenol tragedy or the Alaskan oil spill—are the senior officers ready and able to respond publicly? Might they be convicted of greed, for example, before they have a chance to explain? Openness builds a bridge of trust to carry the heavy freight of crisis or disaster.

Are Motives Shared by Other Constituents?   Again, board members are ideally situated to evaluate how widely and deeply the motives of the key decision makers are shared. Is the CEO driven by powerful personal feelings that turn subordinates into virtual corporate captives? Do other employees down the corporate ladder imitate this autocratic style? Or is there a team spirit that encourages cooperation and innovation? Of course, team spirit alone may be nothing more than a partnership in crime. Corporate loyalty is deepened and broadened when motives are shared. The corporate work ethic described by William H. Whyte in *The Organization Man* revealed the extreme to which this factor could swing. Loyalty becomes the only criterion for employment and promotion. Directors can help ensure a productive, ethical balance.

Texas Instruments (TI), under the leadership of James Hagerty, achieved a fine balance between corporate loyalty on the part of employees to each other, to the firm itself, and to the marketplace. Their company's success is measured in part by its early dominance of the hand-held calculator market. Success was achieved in part by the matrix restructuring mandated by Hagerty. Employees were organized into teams that required cooperation and trust. Here, the matrixing method was at least incidental if not absolutely essential to their eventual success. TI gained a reputation as an ethical company, equally attuned to its employees, the consumer, and its stockholders.

Hewlett Packard (HP) is another microethical example of shared motives and values. Employees work in teams which encourage high levels of trust and sharing across management levels. David Freudberg's description of the open work space, task rather than time-clock orientation, and quality control commitment earned HP an ethical five-star rating in Freudberg's lexicon.[28] The director's challenge at HP is to maintain this high standard.

Corporate boards might find innovative opportunities at the macroethical level. Large corporations, especially, are not universally trusted, in part because of their sheer size. Consequently, the credibility of the free enterprise system is under constant evaluation and even attack by a variety of constituents. The general public appears not to share the motives and values of corporate leaders. Directors could "take to the stump" in political fashion and invite greater public participation in shaping at least the ethical goals of their corporations. One avenue readily available is the annual corporate report.

The annual corporate report is an underutilized instrument. The Borden Company initiated this venerable ethical innovation in 1854 as a gesture of trust. Gail Borden simply opened his financial records to public scrutiny. He started a tradition that was gradually adopted by other firms. The New York Stock Exchange first requested (1866) and then required (1900) listed companies to provide annual reports to stockholders. Despite the requirement, only 50 percent of the companies were actually doing so by 1926.[29] It proved necessary to legislate financial disclosure, which the Securities and Exchange Commission

(SEC) finally did in 1974. In light of changing ethical expectations, directors could encourage innovation appropriate to this new age. The annual report itself could achieve a higher degree of integrity. In the first place, as an accounting document it represents only a single day in the yearly life cycle of a firm. It is misleading to the general public to pretend otherwise. Second, the current ethic of corporate accounting entitles management to present the facts in their most favorable perspective, which they do. The *true* story becomes the province of insiders and brokers who make it their business to find out what's really happening. Third, the cost of an elaborate annual report often exceeds the annual dividend. Some stockholders might prefer a higher dividend than an expensive booklet of dubious value. Others might prefer a fuller accounting of the ethical side of a firm's life.

There have been quite a few innovations in the corporate annual report in recent years. Some appear aimed at broadening the scope of constituent acceptance and accountability. Pictures of rank-and-file employees at their jobs have replaced posed portraits of senior executives. Stockholder resolutions questioning corporate policy have been extensive and balanced. Immoderate costs had been curtailed and financial accounting abbreviated with a simple reference to the mandated 10-K filing with the SEC. More recently, with the rise in environmental anxieties, some reports now include supplemental statements on the firm's performance in this area. Innovations on the ethical side are in an experimental stage.

Some companies are voluntarily doing more to meet the rising ethical expectations of their constituents, according to Jonathan B. Schiff of Fairleigh Dickinson University. His study indicates that 20 of the largest 22 companies are adding a section called the "management report" to their annual reports. Schiff notes that 91 percent of the time management acknowledges responsibility for financial reporting, discusses internal controls, and addresses the role of outside auditors and audit committees; 73 percent of the time they add the signatures of top management; 32 percent of the time they cite company ethics policy.[30] Those who fear some future age of legislated conformity can take heart in the voluntary character of these reports. That's business ethics in action.

What Is the Value Orientation of Your Firm?   Few subjects are as controversial or elusive as values, whether personal, corporate, or cultural. One person's necessities are another person's luxuries. Values are states of mind, body, or spirit to which we assign relatively greater worth through the expenditure of our life's energies in securing or achieving. There is no easy or quick way to do full justice to the issue of corporate values. What follows is intended to inspire the reader's creative imagination and evaluative reflection.

Task	Process
Profits	People
Capital accumulation	Contribution to society
Short term	Long term
Deplete	Conserve
Extravagance	Frugality
Exploit	Employ
Consolidate	Share
Ends	Means
Destination	Journey

Figure 5-2. Value orientation polarities.

The Managerial Grid is a product of the creative efforts of Robert Blake and Jane Mouton.[31] They perceived that managers distinguish themselves by the relative emphasis each placed on task versus process, on *what* gets done versus *how* it gets done. A manager with a high score on the task side—labeled 1 to 9 on a 10-point scale—creates the proverbial sweatshop. People may be unhappy but the job is completed on time. In contrast, a manager with a high process score—9 to 1 on the grid—creates a country club atmosphere. Getting the work done is less important than keeping the members happy. Blake and Mouton argued that it was possible and desirable to strike a happy balance between the two polarities. Moreover, it was also possible and desirable to achieve maximum scores on both sides as well for a 9–9 rating.

The same grid concept can be used to distinguish the value orientation of a company. Figure 5-2 lists some of the polarities to be balanced *and* maximized, as impossible as it appears. Board members can assign numerical values to each of these qualities to determine the relative emphasis given to each in their company. What scores high? What low? How can maximum scores be achieved? Would employees have to be treated differently, for example? Consumers? Investors? Management? Next, how would the firm's constituents—from employees to severest critics—rank your firm? What other competing values should be added to the list? The value orientation of the corporation sets the ethical climate for daily decisions and dilemmas. Boards could schedule a meeting each year devoted exclusively to the company's orientation.

Summary

Boards of directors face new challenges and opportunities for leadership as the twenty-first century approaches. Their challenge is to resolve their double dilemma by speaking out on ethical issues. Boards are uniquely positioned to balance the competing interests of the corporation's constituents. They can help ensure corporate compliance with established laws and ethical expectations at the microethical level. They have the opportunity at the macroethical level to shape new national policies that redefine what it means to be ethical. The same opportunity prevails at the global or metaethical level. The ethical algorithm can help directors anticipate and avoid undesirable or unethical consequences through careful selection and open shaping of corporate *goals, methods,* and *motives.* Cooperative efforts at all levels among all constituents are desirable in this new age. Boards of directors can take the lead. Boards might begin by scheduling annual meetings with ethical issues as the only items on the agenda. A means of sharing these corporate discussions and any decisions would eventually emerge. The entire world, as well as its future, would be the beneficiary.

Footnotes

1. Murray L. Weidenbaum, *The Future of Business Regulation: Private Action and Public Demand,* AMACOM, a Division of American Management Associations, New York, 1979, p. 6. Weidenbaum is a former assistant secretary of the Treasury and former chairman of the President's Council of Economic Advisers.

2. Ibid., p. 22.

3. *The New York Times,* Nov. 22, 1981, Sec. 3, p. 2.

4. *The Wall Street Journal,* May 16, 1983, p. 12.

5. *Report of Annual Meeting of Shareholders,* San Francisco, Calif., Apr. 11, 1979, p. 9.

6. Irving S. Shapiro, "Power and Accountability: The Changing Role of the Corporate Board of Directors," paper presented in the *Fairness Lecture Series,* Carnegie-Mellon University, Oct. 24, 1979, in W. Michael Hoffman and Jennifer Mills Moore (eds.), *Business Ethics: Readings and Cases in Corporate Morality,* 2d ed., McGraw-Hill, 1990, p. 221.

7. Robert K. Mueller, "Conduct Becoming a Corporation: A Value-Calibrated Board Culture," paper delivered at *Corporate Governance: Institutionalizing Ethical Responsibilities, Fifth National Conference on Business Ethics,* Bentley College, Waltham, Mass., Oct. 13, 1983. *Proceedings* reprinted by Lexington Books, D. C. Heath, Lexington, Mass., 1984, p. 11.

8. Adolph A. Berle and Gardiner C. Means, *The Modern Corporation and Private Property,* Medallion, New York, 1932.

9. Betty Bock and Jack Farkas, *Relative Growth of the Largest Manufacturing Corporations, 1947–1971,* Conference Board, New York, 1973.

10. Jeremiah L. O'Connell, "Corporate Governance—The European Challenge," speech delivered at *Corporate Governance: Institutionalizing Ethical Responsibilities, Fifth National Conference on Business Ethics,* Bentley College, Oct. 13, 1983. *Proceedings* reprinted by Lexington Books, D. C. Heath, Lexington, Mass., 1984, p. 3.

11. Wyndham Robertson, "The Directors Woke Up Too Late at Gulf," *Fortune,* June 1986, vol. 93, no. 6, p. 121.

12. Frederick D. Sturdivant and James E. Stacey, *The Corporate Social Challenge: Cases and Commentaries,* 4th ed., Irwin, Homewood, Ill., 1990, p. 628.

13. Ibid., p. 161.

14. Ibid., p. 5.

15. Ibid., p. 381.

16. Kenneth Dayton, "Seegal-Macy Lecture," University of Michigan, Ann Arbor, Oct. 30, 1975.

17. Thomas J. Watson, Jr., *A Business and Its Beliefs,* McGraw-Hill, New York, 1963, pp. 13, 29, 34.

18. Sturdivant and Stacey, op. cit., p. 606.

19. Milton Friedman, "The Social Responsibility of Business Is to Increase Its Profits," *The New York Times Magazine,* Sept. 13, 1970, p. 32.

20. Thomas G. Marx, *Business and Society: Economic, Moral, and Political Foundations,* Prentice-Hall, Englewood Cliffs, N.J., 1985. *Statement on Corporate Responsibility,* The Business Roundtable, p. 151.

21. Milton Friedman, *Capitalism and Freedom,* Chicago University Press, Chicago, 1962, p. 135.

22. Evelyn Y. Davis is editor of *Highlights and Lowlights,* headquartered in Washington, D.C. She monitors corporate governance issues and regularly attends the annual meetings of many companies.

23. *The New York Times,* Oct. 30, 1982, p. B16.

24. Kenneth Dayton, "Corporate Governance: The Other Side of the Coin," *Harvard Business Review,* January–February, 1984, vol. 62, no. 1, p. 34.

25. Richard Austin Smith, "The Incredible Electrical Conspiracy," *Fortune,* April 1961, p. 32.

26. Michael Maccoby, *The Gamesman,* Simon and Schuster, New York, 1976.

27. David Freudberg, *The Corporate Conscience,* AMACOM, New York, 1986, p. 207.

28. Ibid., p. 153.

29. Frederick D. Sturdivant, *Business and Society: A Managerial Approach,* Irwin, Homewood, Ill., 1981, p. 373.

30. Alison Leigh Cowan, "More Mea Culpas for the Annual Report," *The New York Times,* May 27, 1990, p. 15.
31. Robert R. Blake and Jane S. Mouton, *The Managerial Grid,* Gulf Publishing Company, Houston, 1961.

6

Dilemmas Facing the Corporation

"All along I thought our level of corruption fell well within community standards."

Drawing by Bernard Schoenbaum; © 1988 The New Yorker Magazine, Inc.

Changing the Corporate Ethic

Every corporation has a culture. It's created by the workers in response to each other, the nature of the work, and the design and direction imparted by management. The frequency and degree of interaction with the world beyond the corporate walls also contribute to that culture. Edgar Schein describes the formation of corporate culture in this way.

> Organization culture is the pattern of basic assumptions that a given group has invented, discovered, or developed in learning to cope with its problems of external adaption and internal integration, and that have worked well enough to be considered valid, and therefore, to be taught to new members as the correct way to perceive, think, and feel in relation to those problems.[1]

Note, particularly, that the assumptions are "invented, discovered, or developed." They change and evolve in response to internal or external needs. So it is with business ethics.

Business ethics is the depth dimension of corporate culture. It is best described as a pattern of mutual expectations, formally or informally mandated to settle a broad variety of questions such as fairness, truthfulness, justice, and lawfulness. A corporation is considered ethical when it reasonably satisfies the expressed and latent expectations of all of its constituents. That's a tough assignment.

In this chapter we will study a couple of corporate stories in some depth. We will identify some of the primary constituents. What kind of dilemmas did they face? Were mutual expectations surreptitiously changed or violated in some way? Which constituents were satisfied and which were not, for example? What explains the breakdown in the mutual fulfillment of expectations? Is it flawed character? Simple greed? Undue survival pressures? These questions will lead to a consideration of how business ethics is taught and learned. This, in turn, will create some insights and observations on how corporations can better satisfy the ethical expectations of all their constituents and thus avoid unethical consequences. A good business ethic doesn't just happen. It has to be planned.

The Horns of a Dilemma

Imagine for the moment that you're the founder and owner of a small manufacturing firm in the midwest. You specialize in customized, batch-process metal fabrications for a variety of medium-sized companies. They create the end-user products. Business has turned very bad in the last year. The possibility of losing all you've sacrificed for the past 4½ years is frighteningly real. Sales are down. Cash flow is negative. Operating reserves will be exhausted in about a month or so at the rate things are going. Taking on additional debt is out of the question. You can't sleep. You lie awake most of the night wondering what to do. A plan begins to evolve in your mind. Among all the ideas you've considered and rejected, this emerging plan appears to be the only solution, even though there are things about it that make you uncomfortable. But, it's either take some risks or go broke.

Your perilous plan calls for a lot of cooperation from three key officers. First, you'll have to convince the treasurer to delay some accounts payable. You'll advise him to pick a few of the smaller vendors rather than a couple of big accounts, even though the latter would be quicker. He'll have more leverage with the smaller firms. They need your business. Second, you'll have to talk your operations managers into making some deals with a couple of clients who owe her a favor or two. She'll have to persuade these select customers to accept delayed delivery on goods for which they've already paid. Then, you could use materials intended for their jobs on several others which would bring in some quick cash. Your third stratagem involves your sales manager and offers two opportunities. You'll have to sit down with him and go over the accounts receivable very carefully and target the ones that will respond quickest to a little arm twisting. Next, you'll ask him whether your competitors have a couple of big customers that he could seduce with some deep price cuts or kickbacks. Naturally, such offers would have to be handled very secretively. Some small success on this final point is necessary, however much you dislike the idea, if the whole plan is to work.

Which Horn Do You Choose?   There are just a couple of problems. Until now your business ethics have not required pressure tactics or secrecy. It won't take long for your clients to sense that a different ethical wind is blowing. But times have changed. You're being pinched. Even when you review your plan in the cold light of day, cutting a few ethical corners seems the only way. Your competitors, you strongly suspect, have been doing similar things right along. You may be bending the rules a bit, but think of the consequences if you don't. It's not just your investment that will be lost. There are your employees, the venture capitalists who helped you get started, the big debt you have with your local bank, even your customers. Surely this is one of those times when the end justifies the means.

The second problem is an even greater challenge. You've got to bring your three key officers around to your point of view. You can admit to them that the plan is ethically flawed, but insist it's the only alternative. It wouldn't be a good idea to get them together in your office and discuss it. It would be best to talk to each of them separately and convince them that your approach is only a temporary solution, a few months at the most. You're the boss. You've got to make the decision; you can't hold them responsible for this kind of plan.

How Do You Get Your Employees to Cheat?   It's not easy to talk your subordinates into cutting a few ethical corners, even when the pressures to do so are powerful. It's easier to slide into unethical behavior as though unaware of what's happening. But you've never been one to run from the facts. You're not going to start now. You anticipate that each of your three officers will resist your plan for the same reason you're uneasy about it. It's not up to your usual ethical standards. You're going to change the rules. You've been forced into a new point of view. Now, how are you going to persuade them to change their minds? Appeal to their friendship? Point out that their jobs and future are on the line, too? Might you intimate that one of the reasons the business is in trouble is that your competitors have been cheating all along? What arguments might you use to convince them? Could you do it? Why or why not?

Turning the Tables.   Suppose now that the situation above is reversed. You accidentally discover that those same three key employees are already cutting ethical corners behind your back. You're not sure why. Maybe their motives are the best—stay competitive and keep the company going. Nevertheless, you see your company threatened by possible scandal and lawsuits that could destroy your efforts of nearly five years. What arguments might you use to convince them that they are in error? Could you do it? Why or why not?

In this second scenario you face the same challenge as before. You want to change the ethical behavior of your employees. It's the same mountain peak approached from the reverse side. Your three key employees have secretly and unilaterally changed the corporate ethic in response to external pressures. Their changes conflict with your expectations. What are you going to do? The dilemma is *whether* to intervene, as well as *how*.

An Ethical Paradox

Strange, isn't it? It's no easier to talk your employees into doing wrong than doing right. Lots of firms do both by accident. They don't always plan it. It just happens. Plans or no plans, it's tough to face ethical issues openly. Something there is that doesn't love business ethics, that doesn't want us to face the ethical issues squarely. Why? Because we consider ethics an intrusion into our personal life, an unwelcome restriction placed on our behavior? Does it remind us of an overbearing parent harping at us to be home from the movies by 10 p.m., ruining the evening before it's started? Or are we all just too greedy for our own good? Is our personal or corporate survival really at risk?

Ethical dilemmas are inevitable in the pursuit of survival. Life is filled with choices. The good news about dilemmas is that they are evidence we are taking life seriously. We are trying. We are pursuing a vision of some sort at least. Dilemmas do not force themselves onto lazy people.

Dilemmas force us to choose. They raise questions about the nature of our goals and visions. How big are they? Are we pursuing them with full intentionality and awareness? Are we so wrapped up in our vision that we close off options, ignore other people and parties who have an equal right to shape that vision? In the modern world of rapid change, increasingly complex technology, urbanization, and egalitarianism, business ethics must be talked about more openly, more intentionally, more forcefully. We can no longer hide.

A Tale of Two Corporations

Charles Dickens opened his tale of two cities with a memorable and evocative line: "It was the best of times, it was the worst of times." So it seems in the world of business ethics today. The cynics remark that business ethics has become the acme of oxymorons, topping such well-known contradictions in terms as "military intelligence," "giant shrimp," and "constructive criticism." Both friend and foe debate whether ethical standards have risen or compliance fallen. Less arguably, *concern* about ethics is at an all-time high, whether individual, institutional, or societal. The focus of concern runs the gamut from sports figures taking bribes and drugs, through faked medical research and congressional conflicts of obligation, to the much publicized scandals on Wall Street. These competitors typically confront once-in-a-lifetime opportunities. The corporate arena provides immense incentives to corruption, whether for riches, prestige, or both. But why do some cheat? Why do some violate the ethical expectations that have been built up over the years? Are their actions planned or unplanned? How do they explain what happened? It may be tough to talk about business ethics. But it can be very costly not to talk about them. Let's look at a couple of corporate stories.

Bonuses That Backfire: E. F. Hutton

"When E. F. Hutton talks, people lose interest." This biting parody of Hutton's once popular advertising slogan — "when E. F. Hutton talks, people listen" — reflects a profound change in public confidence and respect. Senior managers at Hutton, relying in part on their highly regarded Wall Street name, allegedly pressured banks into accepting extended floats on large checks and utilizing transcontinental time differences to earn a few extra days' interest. Check kiting, the practice of writing a check for an amount greater than the balance on deposit to take advantage of the time lag between credit and collection, is easier to define than to prove. Hutton money managers wrote checks so large and numerous that they virtually created "an unnegotiated line of credit," to put the best face on it. Securing a line of credit was not the objective, as everyone later learned.

Eventually, complaints from banks arrived at the desk of the vice president and money manager. It wasn't long before the media picked up the story. Top management was embarrassed. They had no ready explanation. No contingency plan was in place. As the full tale unfolded, these executives debated whether the problem was internal or external. Defensive doubting gave way to aggressive anger. Had they actually done something drastically wrong or only pushed a common but dubious practice too far?

The Search for the Guilty.   Hutton top management hired former Attorney General Griffin Bell, Jr., to investigate their overdraft practices. He discovered that branch managers received a percentage of any interest earned from the overdrafting. The accounting practice failed to distinguish between the interest earned from cash management and commissions earned from brokerage transactions. This minor discrepancy was enough to inspire a new and easy way to hit the gross revenue targets. Branch managers alleged this executive money manager actually instructed them in overdrafting procedures. The executive sales manager considered it his unspoken assignment to stimulate branch managers to increase their earnings through commissions on sales and interest earned from smart cash management, although Bell did not hold this officer to blame, interestingly enough. The senior vice president and money manager bore the brunt of the blame for failing to monitor the draft-down system installed by his predecessor.

The executive money manager claimed that his boss rejected his request for changes in the system. Griffin Bell agreed that the chief financial officer at the time should have been more responsive to these requests and exercised proper responsibility. The Hutton culture evidently provided supervisory slippage at all three levels, from branch manager to executive money manager to the chief financial officer. Officers and company personnel either failed to grasp the implications of their system or simply took liberties with what was becoming a clearly enunciated corporate ethic.

Hutton concluded that their officers were not basically at fault. They were just overzealous. They reasoned that their real ethical problem was now external—that is, how they were perceived by clients. Thus, they decided against an in-house ethical "cleanup" program which could have created a tighter organization with articulated ethical standards. Instead, they retained the services of Bill Cosby at a cost in excess of $1 million to polish their tarnished image. Admittedly, there is a fine line between good ethics and good public relations. Hutton executives failed to find it. As one IBM executive puts it, it's the difference between doing good and just looking good. You can look good without being good, but you can't be good without looking good.

Good Intentions Are Not Enough.   Mr. Bell, it appears, confused motives with consequences: if you mean well, that's all that matters. You can't be held responsible for what happens if your intentions are good. That's ethically naive. Giving full credit for fine motives works well with small children where the consequences are usually less significant. Bell's magnanimity poses a basic question in business ethics. Does it make any difference whether your sin was one of omission rather than commission? Does it make any difference whether it was committed in innocence rather than cold-blooded calculation? Not much as far as the victims are concerned. Many victims will be indifferent to the motives of their swindlers. It is not very significant in the Hutton case whether the transgressors were driven by personal greed and ambition or corporate survival. Who can be sure what the motives were? Was the firm's existence under threat? Again, Bell appears to give the officers the benefit of the doubt. Others are not likely to be so generous. When motives are unclear, victims and critics will assume the worst. Fanatics will project their own self-righteousness or petty moralisms onto this unusually large canvas of corporate corruption. They are predisposed to believe that all Wall Street types are confirmed crooks. Any evidence, however inconclusive, becomes proof positive. They forget that fairness in judging motives requires that they be documented form observable behavior.

Facing the Consequences.   E. F. Hutton eventually pleaded guilty to more than 2000 counts of fraud through checking account overdrafts. Hutton executives were not entitled to be surprised. A year earlier, in May 1984, the equally venerable accounting firm of Arthur Anderson reported that E. F. Hutton was second to Dean Witter in use of this questionable practice. Prudential Bache and Merrill Lynch were close behind. Why, then, was Hutton singled out? Perhaps Arthur Anderson was surprised at the size and frequency of the overdrafts. In a 1982 memo, Arthur Anderson cited an $8 million check drawn against the E. F. Hutton account at a small upstate New York bank, creating an overdraft considerably in excess of a "normal" float. As far back as 1980 Arthur Anderson had questioned the ethicality of Hutton's check writing practices. They were assured by Hutton's general counsel at the time that the practice presented "no legal problem." Whether the banks initially approved of the practice and were silent, albeit unwilling, partners in modest extortion is not clear. Not surprisingly, Hutton paid their fines.

The Punishment of the Innocent.   The firm failed to survive the market crash of October 1987. Shortly thereafter Hutton's financial losses forced it to accept a buyout by Shearson Lehman. The careers of hundreds of executives and support staff were radically and permanently changed. Many of these were not directly involved in the controversial procedure. Client confidence in E. F. Hutton, which once approached religious awe, was shattered. The ill-conceived practice victimized more than 2000 banks. The name of a once-prestigious Wall Street firm now evokes bitter memories from clients and ridicule from industry colleagues.

What Really Went Wrong?   Was this a carefully calculated, unethical scheme or just innocent and imaginative cash management? What motivated these executives? If we could be certain that their motives were relatively innocent, would it make any difference in our assessment of the practice? Put yourself in their places. What would you have done if you had been CEO at Hutton? Would you have pleaded guilty to fraudulent overdrafting? Would you have argued with your local banker that having your corporate account was of sufficient prestige value to justify occasional overdrafts? Since we can't turn the clock back on these decisions, how might you anticipate these developments and perhaps avoid them in the future?

Ethical issues in business are situational. Each must be evaluated in its own context. They emerge here at several levels. First, what were the motives of executives in question? Do we have any clues? What distinguished their methods? Was Hutton a unique organization in some sense? At another level, we must ask about the financial industry itself, the marketplace. Legally, every bank account holder must be notified in writing of various rules and procedures, such as overdrafts. Nevertheless, are certain customers, such as brokerage houses, entitled to operate by special rules because of the size of their accounts and their reputation? Is this an informal understanding that is commonly accepted? Is such an informal agreement discussed at all or is quietly noted in passing, like an unwritten agreement or a bribe? Or are the parties to this behavior each guided by a separate ethic and therefore harboring a different expectation of the other? How do they articulate mutual expectations, if at all? Finally, who should be held responsible for misadventures of this nature? Bell exonerated the sales executive, the chairman of the board, and the chief executive officer. Who within the firm determines what's ethical and who is responsible for its enforcement?

Telltale Motives and Aggressive Methods.   Greed and ambition are commonplace among stockbrokers. They are not the attributes likely to surprise or anger clients. Something else bothered the victims. Comments from victims of the Hutton caper indicate that they were most offended at the arrogance of the executives who expected special favors. They weren't just cheated. They were demeaned. They treated their banking colleagues as slaves rather than equals. The Hutton money managers seemed unmindful or unaware of any possible cost or inconvenience to others. They were imperialistic. Little, if any, consideration was extended to clients. Someone powerfully offended by such insensitive arrogance probably blew the whistle on the perpetrators of this gargantuan scam.

Hutton executives abused a fine reputation. They expected to be treated differently. Alas, they were – in a manner they did not anticipate. The overdrafts were neither casual nor occasional. They were planned. Hutton was distinguished by these motives and methods.

The Organization.   The organizational design and culture of Hutton also provides some valuable clues about why things happened as they did. Organizational design resides within the power of top management. It constitutes part of management's methods. While the Hutton name is vintage, it is not a closely knit family of brokers and money managers with a long history of close working relationships. It is a loose collection of small firms, each with a distinct and separate past. Firm loyalties were local, not national. Executives at headquarters had little experience in mobilizing and motivating a nationwide sales staff. They had not built the company brick by brick, so to speak, office by office.

The decision to pay bonuses for good cash management bears the mark of managerial naiveté. We can well imagine that the decision seemed ingenious at the time. Brokerage sales were slow; commissions were down. Managers probably asked, "How can we boost the morale of our local offices? How can we put money in their pockets during this current market downturn?" Since corporate loyalty was weak, or at best untested, financial inducements were the only instrument available to keep brokers and branches from jumping ship, reverting to their former, independent ways. The bonus idea was implemented. It worked, too well. Cash management achieved new heights of creative aggression. The inventiveness of the avaricious human mind authors a new chapter in money management, sanctioned by a flaccid organizational structure and a laissez-faire ethical environment.

The Industry. Organizational experts have remarked that colossal corporations like General Electric and IBM are run with the discipline of an army at war and the zeal of a missionary among cannibals. They are also like battleships: large, ponderous, and highly structured, requiring a lot of time and space to turn around. In contrast, the brokerage industry is the business equivalent of guerrilla warfare. There is an enemy but no general. Warriors share a common goal, but discipline is loose and methods used to achieve the goal vary considerably. Some brokers are inclined to see themselves as the lone rangers of free enterprise: They work in isolated secrecy behind masks which conceal their true identity; they often feel misunderstood; only a driving passion or private provocation keeps them going; they believe that they are equipped with the equivalent of silver bullets—a unique and infallible approach to the market; they are friendly with all but friends with only a few, and those are outside the business. It can be a glamorous and financially rewarding job. It can also be lonely and emotionally crippling.

This is not to suggest that the lone ranger style is a necessary condition for success on Wall Street, but it certainly is sufficient if all you're looking for is money. Competition is intense both within and among the prominent firms. Little wonder that the most incredible ethical scandals in the past decade have come from Wall Street. Ethically, it remains an untamed wilderness, retaining features resembling the popular mythology of our western frontier: lone ranger brokers, gunslinger traders, easily spooked or stampeded clients, crusading media coverage, and a "no law west of the Pecos" legal vacuum that might curb the likes of a Michael Milken comfortably ensconced in Beverly Hills, California.

Are the Financial Markets a Vanishing Frontier? The financial markets in the free world constitute one of the last frontiers. They are uniquely capitalistic and generally held in awe. Legislators are fearful that too many laws will kill the goose that lays the golden eggs. The scandals on Wall Street, the nation's savings and loan associations, and the free world's banks all provide ample evidence that this industry retains considerable discretionary power. The businesspeople who populate this huge market make and break many of the rules which regulate their activity. In that sense it's an ethical frontier. They have the free-dom to do wrong, and some have taken advantage of it. The absence of rigid regulation has lent itself to an "anything goes" ethic. Will this fron-tier vanish as a result of both the abuse of freedom and global changes?

If freedom in the financial markets is nothing less than a cover for unmitigated greed, government regulation looms on the near horizon. Discretionary authority will disappear unless individuals as well as in-vestment houses broaden their goals. This is hardly a new idea. Bernard Baruch, a venerated and envied Wall Streeter, took note of this need several decades ago. "The greatest blessing of our democracy is free-dom. But in the last analysis, our only freedom is the freedom to disci-pline ourselves." At the microethical level such discipline calls upon in-dividuals and institutions to take increased cognizance of the greater social good they serve. Hutton apparently never caught a glimpse of this larger picture. It is no longer enough to ask, "What business are we in?" The key question in this new ethical age, is "Why are we in busi-ness?" This leads to a macroethical issue.

What about the secondary markets in options and market indexing? What about program trading? Are they parasitic or symbiotic? Do they just feed the greed of a few or do they make a vital contribution to the capital markets? Are they ethical? Do they contribute to the greater eco-nomic good of the world? The underlying ethical justification for finan-cial markets is to provide capital for businesses. Is there any ethical jus-tification for secondary markets? In some parts of the world, notably the United States, there is another ethic that states that anything not clearly harmful should be permitted. Thus, we have the secondary mar-kets. However much they're questioned, they remain in place. Recent activity by the SEC and Congress represents the latest moves to bring civilization to this urban jungle. The authorities have been more suc-cessful in taking action on the microethical issues rather than the macroethical, the small picture rather than the large. That may change.

Is the Business Environment to Blame?   Excuses for Hutton's behav-ior are easy to concoct. The increased competition among brokerage firms and signals from Washington provided impetus for "ethical inno-vation," to put it politely. Increased pressure on the financial bottom line always puts pressure on the ethical bottom line. Something's got to give. You take your choice. The mounting deficits in Washington along with its probusiness attitude gave birth to an "anything goes" mentality. Couple that with the independence of brokers in general and Hutton in particular, and it's easy to understand, although not necessarily con-done, the Hutton caper. Survival and competitive pressures beget be-haviors that eventually prove to be unethical.

Wall Street outsiders have trouble appreciating the seductive sense of urgency which often accompanies questionable practices and procedures. Personal or corporate survival is felt to be at stake. Therefore, unusual and perhaps unethical means are believed to be a necessary and, of course, only temporarily evil. This shallow rationale is utilized repeatedly in stories of corporate corruption: if we don't do something drastic, we're dead!

Wall Street insiders have difficulty appreciating the long-term consequences of their unethical actions. The situation may not actually be as desperate as it seems. Moreover, unethical solutions invariably only delay an inevitable demise, not circumvent it. In the heat of corporate battle such cool reflections are difficult to contemplate.

Long-term measurements really count. While stockbrokers insist they resist the temptation to overdramatize the significance of a particular day's gains or losses, the thrill of the hunt and the pain of loss can anesthetize one's perspective on the future. Hutton executives did not anticipate the long-term consequences of unrestrained motives and ill-conceived methods. If they possessed an articulated ethical side to their business, it remained locked away in some file. It was not visible in their behavior or public relations.

Thinking Ahead

Can business executives anticipate the long-term consequences of their decisions? Undoubtedly, even if rarely to perfection. If they spend time making a solid effort, and it's clear they've tried, they may at least get credit for trying.

Every executive and employee can use the ethical algorithm to pose what-if questions. What if we manufacture, package, or market this particular product this particular way? Who will benefit? Who will be harmed? What if others do not share our objectives willingly? What if others do not know or accept our motives? The major decision makers face a longer list of constituents. Will constituents each view our decisions as fair or considerate? Will they be able to understand any compromises we've made? It will be impossible to please everyone every time. In this regard the ethical side of enterprise is like the financial side: you can't guarantee maximum profits every quarter. Nevertheless, achieving your ethical goals must become just as satisfying and significant as a good financial bottom line. Moreover, increasingly it will be the ethical bottom line that sinks the corporate ship. Fewer excuses are accepted these days for failure to chart and sail a smooth ethical course.

Innocents Abroad: H. J. Heinz

Founder Henry J. Heinz proclaimed that his goal was "to bring home-cooking standards into canned foods, making them so altogether wholesome and delicious and at the same time so reasonable that people everywhere will enjoy them in abundance."[2] He succeeded beyond his wildest dreams. In 1979, 110 years later, H. J. Heinz operated in more than 30 countries with its products available in about 150. Sales revenues exceeded $2 billion; net income was almost $100 million. Over the years Heinz has maintained an enviable reputation for fine products. If we can call this an ethical goal, Heinz reached it.

Motivated to Manipulate.   Growth in annual revenues has also been a corporate goal. In the early 1970s it was pegged at a rigid 15 percent. Those were the years of President Nixon's mandated wage and price controls. Hitting an annual 15 percent growth on the nose was both a necessary and elusive target. World headquarters, facing potential profits exceeding those guidelines in Heinz USA in 1974, arranged to transfer income to other cost-revenue centers and effectively prepay approximately $2 million in advertising expenses. There was no solid evidence to suggest that these accounting aberrations were undertaken solely to violate either the wage and price laws or avoid taxes. Nevertheless, a seemingly innocent accounting anomaly was established at the highest corporate level. It did not go unnoticed. Later, some divisions would follow this example, but not because of pressure from wage and price controls. The incentive now as inspired by a new bonus system.

The Plan.   H. J. Heinz, acting upon a recommendation from a prominent management consulting firm, adopted an aggressive motivational scheme. The plan assigned management incentive points (MIPs) to those few superior performing executives who achieved exceptional sales growth. Reactions from the divisions were mixed. One division, for instance, could conceivably get all the bonus points. It appears that the MIP plan had the strongest appeal for the most aggressive and ambitious sales and marketing executives. That's certainly not unethical by itself. The undesirable consequences were a by-product of MIP in the context of the Heinz organizational climate.

The Organization.   The organizational chart of Heinz reveals a highly decentralized company. A very small cadre of senior executives headquartered in the United States provided worldwide coordination of the divisions. Each of the various divisions enjoyed considerable freedom. They had complete autonomy in local decisions and limited financial accounting to headquarters. The key officers of each division — president, managing director, and chief financial officer — signed a representation letter each year which, among other things, confirmed their compliance with Heinz's code of ethics.

The MIPs were awarded on a worldwide basis, rather than as equal shares to each division. Some employees felt this was unfair. The scheme was also criticized because it awarded huge bonuses to a few top performers and almost nothing to those who came in second or third, creating an intensely competitive atmosphere. This incentive system, coupled with the company's commitment to a steady, 15 percent annual growth rate, created an interesting dilemma. Sales executives were simultaneously stimulated to be top dog but restrained by that 15 percent growth rate. It was not unlike point shaving in college basketball: win, but keep the margin of victory within a prearranged spread. What seems obvious from hindsight, happened. In order to hit those exacting numbers executives began to record sales and expenditures not when they occurred but when their entry on the book would be most advantageous to their MIPs.

Accidental Discovery.   The whistle-blowing role fell to Heinz's perennial rival, Campbell Soup. The disturbing accounting procedures came to light, interestingly enough, when Heinz and Campbell filed monopoly lawsuits against each other. That action alone raises a macroethical question. Namely, do expensive and ambiguous legal actions against competitors fundamentally enhance the welfare of stockholders and consumers? In Heinz's case, the risky strategy backfired. In the customary exchange and perusal of each other's documents, the Campbell Soup lawyers stumbled on Heinz's years of "creative accounting." The legal spotlight came to rest on whether Heinz had paid the correct amount of taxes in each of those years. Recalculating the corporate tax owed the IRS based on "proper accounting" of sales and expenditures yielded a measurable but negligible deficit in taxes paid. It might easily have been the reverse. The legal consequences were measurable but hardly significant. The methods utilized by Heinz, however — both the MIP plan and the lawsuits — disquieted employees, stockholders, and corporate critics.

So why all the excitement over a few accounting irregularities at Heinz? Isn't this just an innocently crafted misdemeanor motivated by modest greed? Hey, it wasn't even their idea to begin with. A highly respected (and probably highly paid) management consulting firm came up with this scheme. Senior Heinz executives simply asked for a workable plan. It did work, maybe a little too well. The impact on stockholder equity and working capital by improper recognition of revenue and expenses was less than 2 percent. And if we're looking for someone else to blame, let's call a foul on government interference.

Was President Nixon to Blame?   Someone might make a good case for Nixon's wage and price controls as the culprit in crime. Can't you hear the argument: "It's another straightforward case of what happens when the government interferes with business. Nixon's unilateral freeze laid the foundation for this problem. You can't set arbitrary limits to wages, prices, and profits. Markets have to be free." Ironically, senior management also interfered with the free market, first by setting an arbitrary and idealistic 15 percent growth figure and then manipulating the allocation of sales and revenues so they could "hit their numbers." At the most, Nixon's wage and price freeze was an exogenous factor in the Heinz case. Governmental action—an outside force beyond the control of the company—changed the rules of the marketplace. Management responded with a particular plan that benefited their financial bottom line. Other options were available to both parties. The decision makers were left to suffer the consequences of their choices.

Was the FSAB at Fault?   Anyone familiar with corporate policy knows that accounting practices vary widely. The Financial Standards Accounting Board (FSAB), which creates the uniformity that exists, is a private agency. The rules and recommendations it issues are not binding on companies. The Internal Revenue Service (IRS) and the Securities and Exchange Commission (SEC) become the critical regulators. Amazingly enough, the federal government has resisted further intrusions into corporate accounting procedures. The Heinz case is only one of many that raises the question whether the FSAB ought to be tougher on firms or whether federal legislation is necessary. Blaming the system only delays and obscures examination of more fundamental causes, namely, the underlying attitudes of corporate executives.

What attitude does top management bring to the matter of publicly accounting for their actions and achievements? Corporate annual reports to stockholders, for example, originally a voluntary act of accountability started by the Borden Company in 1854, are now masterpieces of business euphoria. In the mid-eighties, Heinz took the prize for the most expensive annual report at about $9 a copy. Expensive photographs sang the praises of the tomato. The prevailing ethic encourages a chief financial officer to present the company in the best possible light. As long as you pay the proper tax and avoid outright falsehoods that might mislead a stockholder, the sky's the limit on annual report schmaltz. The corporation's internal accounting is the last bastion of managerial control still relatively free from government regulation.

Is there less here than meets the eye? You be the judge. What would you think if you were a stockholder? Would you be pleased? What's your perspective as a taxpayer? How would you feel as one of the benefactors of the MIP plan? Or one who played the game but didn't win? How unethical a practice is this, really? Is it wrong only in principle or are there truly harmful consequences?

Counting the Costs.   Heinz shareholders were shortchanged in both equity and dividends as management spent millions of dollars to determine whether any wrong had been done. The IRS insisted that Heinz recalculate earnings to determine whether any additional tax was due; again, more wasted resources. Very few employees benefited substantially from the MIP program. The majority were indifferent or displeased. Wall Street and *Fortune* were their kindest critics, making little fuss over a relatively minor incident. At the other extreme, new ammunition was handed to critics of corporate affluence and power to launch at the impregnable walls of corporate indifference. Customers could complain that management's attention was drawn to bonuses and promotions rather than providing "canned foods...so altogether wholesome and delicious and at the same time so reasonable that people everywhere will enjoy them in abundance."

A Clear Case of Goal Subversion.   This reminder of Henry Heinz's original goal brings us full circle. The MIP plan symbolizes a typical example of goal subversion. A skewed incentive program tied to a rigid and arbitrary annual percentage growth rate subverts the founder's goal. A goal of wholesome products at reasonable prices has been pushed into the background by unwholesome and unreasonable methods. Henry Heinz's original mission statement put the emphasis on the value he sought to bring to the marketplace. The MIP plan places the emphasis on the value accruing to a few employees. To be sure, founder Heinz intended to make money, which he did. He articulated the ethical rather than the financial side of his enterprise in stating his goals. It was a different age. H. J. may have presumed that the financial side would take care of itself. Today, apparently, corporate management assumes the reverse—that the ethical side will take care of itself. The Heinz case provides abundant evidence that such assumptions are unwarranted.

Who Sets the Firm's Values?

Who is responsible for setting and monitoring a firm's values? In theory, every employee and board member bears some responsibility, in what they either do or fail to do. In practice, that responsibility falls upon top management, the chief executive in particular.

Managers in today's largest firms receive a rich inheritance. Plants and markets are established. A work force has been assembled and reasonably well trained. Managers step into big titles, lots of prestige, and large salaries. They also inherit the responsibility for managing a firm's goals, and that includes setting the firm's values. The CEO's own values are a determining factor. If the CEO values only dollar profits, that message will permeate the organization. If he or she values some of those qualities which fall on the ethical side of enterprise, that will show up too. In fact, the imparting of values is inevitable. It's only a question of what they will be. The CEO can delegate many duties and responsibilities. Setting the firm's values is the single exception. The CEO's years at the corporate helm will eventually be judged by how well those values are managed. The CEO strikes the first note, but a full harmonious chord of ethical behavior requires the concerted cooperation of all players. Each plays a vital and unique role.

The CEO as Chief Ethical Officer

In the spring of 1990, CEO and board chairman James Robinson of American Express asked his directors to change the company bylaws to give him a third title, namely chief quality officer. That proved to be a newsworthy and imaginative request. Boards of directors could just as easily pass a resolution declaring that the title CEO also stands for "chief ethical officer." Such a declaration would reassure the public as well as send a message to employees and competitors. It would not require a change in the bylaws. Actually, the most vital change might occur within the CEOs themselves. The new title would call for some soul-searching among CEOs. Some might discover they need more heart, others more courage. They could begin with that strategic ethical question, "Why are we in business?" Senior managers and board members could extend the process with day-long seminars devoted exclusively to that question. Personal responses would eventually blend into a corporate statement. It should be made public. Private responses can too easily slip into a narrow self-interest that excludes critical corporate constituents, as with Hutton and Heinz. Again, not all constituents will be equally satisfied, but the commitment to a corporate ethic is established.

Developing Ethical Employees

Eventually, all employees need to address some basic ethical questions — not only "why are we in business" but "why do I work?" Money is not the only measure of human effort. In fact, it may be a poor one. Ethics aside, there is excellent management psychology research which states that money is at best only a negative motivator. It can create dissatisfaction but not satisfaction, according to Frederick Herzberg.[3] Salaries and bonuses do not motivate. They can only demotivate or keep employees from becoming unhappy. Management psychology notwithstanding, placing so much emphasis on monetary rewards crowds out consideration of other measures. It diminishes the human spirit. It pushes aside values such as personal trust, corporate and customer loyalty, job satisfaction for all employees, enduring customer relations, a sense of teamwork, job tenure, and the long-term health of the entire economy. These considerations should not be sacrificed on the altar of higher salaries and bonuses.

Business Ethics Can Be Learned

The hypothetical case that opened this chapter, along with the Hutton and Heinz stories, raises the question of whether ethics can be taught. A more pointed question is whether ethics can be learned. The answer should be obvious. If we can learn bad ethics without hardly trying, we can learn good ethics with a little effort. As noted at the outset of the chapter, ethics is the depth dimension of a corporation's culture. It is created by the employees, particularly the senior officers, on the basis of their values in the context of the marketplace. Like Schein's corporate culture, ethics is also "invented, discovered, developed" in response to particular situations. If unethical behavior is learned, it can be unlearned. It's not clear that this truism is sufficiently appreciated until it's too late. Paul Thayer, former CEO of LTV and deputy defense secretary, remarked, after being sentenced to four years in prison for stock fraud, that "Most of us have a child's notion of ethics and a graduate-school notion of finance, marketing, and management." Where do we get such insight before it's too late? In good business fashion, a plan helps. Here are some points to ponder.

Beware of Unwarranted Assumptions

Hutton and Heinz assumed that the ethical side of the business would take care of itself. Heinz further assumed that signed statements annually from senior executives would forestall unethical behavior. Both sets of assumptions proved to be wrong.

Similar unwarranted assumptions afflicted Drexel Burnham Lambert (DBL). It was never clear how much CEO Fred Joseph knew about

Michael Milken's activities. The outcome indicates that he was ethically naive. There are no media accounts which suggest that Joseph tried to set the ethical tone in his firm.

Fred Joseph accepted an invitation from Dean Lester Thurow of MIT's Sloan School of Management to sit in on an ethics panel convened at MIT in 1988. The scandal that virtually destroyed the company was still embryonic. At this little-publicized event, Fred Joseph supported training in ethics on the one hand but fell victim to a questionable assumption on the other. He spoke candidly about the investment banking business. "There are opportunities every day to act unethically many times. I favor special training in ethics for investment bankers along with tough, clear standards." These words did not carry the ring of deep conviction. Joseph pointed out that Dennis Levine and Martin Siegel, both convicted of insider trading while employed by DBL, were not trained by DBL. Joseph did not describe any ethics seminars or workshops as an integral part of the training at DBL. He replied during the panel discussion, instead, that "people will be ethical if you expect it of them." He did not say how top management communicates that expectation. Was he a victim of an unwarranted assumption? Clearly. He is not alone. Many business leaders share the assumption that ethics is something you shouldn't have to talk about. You suspect that some are too embarrassed to talk about ethics. They prefer to just expect people to behave properly. Unfortunately, Fred Joseph's star pupil, Michael Milken, completely shattered his assumption, his company, his professional life. The training in investment banking was obviously sufficient. The training in the ethics of investment banking was obviously *not* sufficient. Beware of unwarranted assumptions. Every workplace develops its own ethic. Whose and what kind do you want it to be? Ethics will be learned.

Develop a Positive Attitude

In the hypothetical case that opened this chapter, we reviewed the dilemma of a young entrepreneur who discovered that the reasons for teaching good ethics is not much different than that for teaching bad ethics. It's a question of perceived need and an appropriate strategy. It is also a matter of believing you can do it.

Business schools and the larger companies both believe in the effectiveness of management training at all levels. Why do they have so little faith in ethics training? Dean Lester Thurow, presiding at that aforementioned ethics panel at MIT in 1988, sounded as naive as Fred Joseph. He doubted whether business ethics could be taught and averred that it was something you got before you were five years old or not at all. It was a bit breathtaking to hear a fine teacher and exemplary business school dean voice such an incredibly antipedagogical statement. It suggests gross misunderstanding of what happens in those first five years of life as well as what causes either ethical or unethical behavior in adults.

Alas, Thurow is not alone in his confusion about either what's ethical or whether it can be taught. The reaction of public figures to disclosures of unethical behavior is unpredictable and variable. *The Wall Street Journal* (April 25, 1990) asked a number of prominent business and political leaders, including several of Drexel Burnham Lambert's clients, for their reactions to Michael Milken's guilty plea to six felony counts. Charles Keating, chairman of American Continental, a DBL client and under governmental fire himself for savings and loan fraud, compared Milken to Michelangelo or da Vinci. John Dingle, chairman of the House Energy and Commerce Committee in Congress, wondered why the government isn't doing more and whether "the punishment fits the crime." Rabbi Arnold Wolf of the KAM Isaiah Israel Congregation in Chicago was strongly critical: "He's a terrible person. He's a symptom of the worst in America." Studs Terkel sympathized with the rabbi: "The whole thing depresses me....We live in a corrupt, amoral moment....There are a million Milkens....People have lost their sense of outrage." Former Philadelphia Mayor Frank Rizzo hasn't lost his: "I hope he gets a lot of time....He'll be viewed as a crook." Financier H. Ross Perot opined that there is "A lesson for young businessmen: Don't govern your life by what's legal or illegal, govern it by what's right or wrong." These reactions from Milken's peers and clients underscore the absence of a clear and strong national ethical consensus. They reveal how badly the nation's business leaders have neglected the depth dimension of enterprise. Society will increasingly hold them responsible for both the ethical and financial bottom lines. We look to them to begin teaching ethics, to the nation as well as to their employees.

Those who believe that ethics can only be caught, not taught, are a throwback to an era that extolled vocational skill specialization and the compartmentalization of human existence. To such a mind, religion is little more than a special section of *Time* magazine. Thomas Merton, American priest, essayist, poet, and Trappist monk, lamented the superficiality of modern existence and the tendency of Americans to overemphasize the practicality of everything, even nature.

> Let me say this before rain becomes a utility that they can plan and distribute for money. By "they" I mean the people who cannot understand that rain is a festival, who do not appreciate its gratuity, who think that what has no price has no value, that what cannot be sold is not real, so that the only way to make something actual is to place it on the market. The time will come when they will sell you

even your rain. At the moment it is still free, and I am in it....One would think that urban man in a rainstorm would have to take account of nature in its wetness and freshness, its baptism and its renewal. But the rain brings no renewal to the city, only to tomorrow's weather.[4]

Corporate leaders—whether at headquarters or in the classroom—need to develop their own positive attitude toward business ethics. This may involve nurturing their own minds and souls in what Merton called "The unspeakable." They cannot fully rely on others to explain or defend their actions. In any event, independent spirits that they tend to be, they would not tolerate answers or principles determined by others. Business ethics will be taught; it is only a question of how and by whom.

Share the Leadership Responsibility

Evidence of corporate wrongdoing in the past argues for stronger leadership from top management—the CEO, board chair, and directors in particular. Looking to the future, the evidence suggests that top management personnel will need to share their leadership role with their various constituents, from employees to stakeholders.

Edgar Schein believes we stand on the threshold of a major organizational revolution. It cannot proceed until managers surrender what they perceive as "their divine right to manage."[5] Future managers are likely to be less dependent on hierarchical authority and more dependent on group support. The management function, for instance, will be distributed to networks and teams rather than individuals. We already see this happening on a small scale in the sphere of business ethics. Business leaders have given up their "divine right" to determine what's ethical with a host of constituents. It is not yet a process that has been fully embraced or smoothly organized. Business leaders can take the lead in developing the structures and opportunities to continue what progress has been achieved.

In a similar vein, Murray Weidenbaum compassionately calls upon corporate executives "to curtail and perhaps dismantle what can be called the imperial presidency." While Weidenbaum addresses the specific abuse of executive perquisites, he is also questioning the imperialistic attitude of senior corporate officers. Executives ought not to think of themselves as royalty and demand concomitant loyalty and deference.

> What is at stake...in the issue of the private imperial presidency is that excessive and at times ludicrous uses of perks are harmful to business themselves. Moreover, the perks are altogether likely to generate sanctions in the form of broad government regulations

which restrict not merely the blatantly improper perks but perks in *any* form....Clearly, then, what is needed within business itself is conscious self-restraint—and, we might add, the sort of professional and ethical integrity in the use of perquisites that should be expected of any responsible official, public or private.[6]

Both Schein and Weidenbaum point to the need for business leaders with an egalitarian spirit about them. Such leaders would not look upon their powers and privileges as things to be grasped but rather used on behalf of many others. Our times call for a new kind of leadership, poignantly noted by business school professor and management consultant Warren Bennis.

> The passing of years has...given the coup de grace to another force that retarded democratization—the "great man," who with brilliance and farsightedness could preside with dictatorial powers at the head of a growing organization and keep it at the vanguard of American business. In the past he was usually a man with a single idea, or a constellation of related ideas, which he developed brilliantly. *This is no longer enough.*[7] [Emphasis added.]

Bennis calls for changes in managerial behavior which will match up with a new concept of human nature, a new concept of power, and a new concept of organizational values. Managers and executives need to spend more time trying to understand these changes. Until they do, their leadership will be marginal and superficial.

Managers at every corporate level face some tough questions if they take the challenge of shared leadership seriously. How might this challenge alter the approach of the young entrepreneur whose ethical dilemma opened this chapter? Would the young entrepreneur already have had some communication bridges built to carry the heavier freight of crisis? Would it have been possible to discuss the problem with senior colleagues rather than manipulate a solution? If you are a manager with supervisory responsibility, ask yourself what human versus organizational values you represent to your employees and colleagues. Are these two sets of values the same? Do your people see you as a human being with human needs or as a boss who wants something from them? Do you carry your authority easily? In their eyes is your stature as a person larger than your job description?

The nations of the world hunger for leaders who are human first and politically able second. They are willing to accept gross weaknesses in other skills to get them. Technical competence means little unless accompanied by personal warmth, whether in politicians, academicians, clergy, or doctors. We have technicians and experts galore. People hunger for leaders who will make them feel good about themselves and life.

These hungers are a by-product of our economic successes. They should be welcomed as a happy consequence of our labors and affluence. We have changed the world. Now the world is changing us, including how we lead the world and continue the push for change.

Summary

The corporate stories in this chapter reveal how easily and quickly unethical consequences emerge from decisions taken with relatively good intentions. The decision makers are often surprised by the outcome and mystified by the judgments of the public. Decision makers can learn to anticipate unwanted consequences. They begin by carefully reviewing the possible reactions of all their constituents before taking the action. This chapter also stressed the importance of articulating an ethical goal that is as significant as the financial one. The ethical side of enterprise must also be managed. Senior executives, especially the CEO, play an important role in this effort. In order to achieve their ethical goals, business leaders must become committed to teaching ethics and even changing their understanding of what it means to be a leader. Good ethics doesn't just happen. It has to be planned.

Footnotes

1. Edgar H. Schein, "Coming to a New Awareness of Organizational Culture," *Sloan Management Review,* vol. 25, no. 2, Winter 1984, p. 3.

2. Richard J. H. Post and Kenneth E. Goodpaster, "H. J. Heinz Company: The Administration of Policy," A, B, Case Study 382-034, Harvard Business School, Cambridge, Mass., 1981.

3. Frederick Herzberg, "One More Time: How Do You Motivate Employees?" *Harvard Business Review,* January–February 1968, vol. 46, no. 1, p. 53.

4. Thomas Merton, *Raids on the Unspeakable,* New Directions, New York, 1964, pp. 9, 11.

5. Edgar H. Schein, "The 'Divine Rights' of Managers," *MIT Management,* Fall 1989, p. 2.

6. Murray L. Weidenbaum, *The Future of Business Regulation,* AMACOM, New York, p. 100.

7. Warren Bennis, *Changing Organizations,* McGraw-Hill, New York, 1966, p. 23.

7
Creating an Ethical Corporate Climate

"Miss Johnson will now pass out the moral blinders."

Drawing by Richter; © 1988 The New Yorker Magazine, Inc.

The Work Ethic Is Changing

To declare that the work ethic is changing introduces a broader meaning to the term *ethics*. In this chapter the word *ethic* will refer to an *attitude* people acquire, in or out of the workplace, that either creates or explains many of their specific actions on the job. People generate attitudes about their work that determine the amount of effort they expend, whether they're cooperative or competitive, whether they're team players or loners, whether they'll stay with the job until it's done or just "give it a lick and a promise." Ethics, in this context, describes a set of mutual expectations that develop between and among employers and employees. That ethic is in flux. Despite an established tradition of explicit job descriptions — or possibly because of them — it is often not precisely clear what employers expect of employees, employees of employers, and even employees of each other. Look at it from a worker's point of view.

Who's Responsible?

Once upon a time you knew the precise contours of your job. The agrarian-based economy which assigned a single farmer to a single piece of land, once the norm in capitalist countries, simplified an important question in the human struggle for survival. Namely, who's responsible for your successful survival? Farmers would answer, often with considerable pride and satisfaction, by pointing to themselves. Each farmer was responsible for his or her own plot of land. They bought or rented the plot, the seed, and the farm implements and bent their own backs to generate its prosperous yield. They may have joined with other farmers to raise a barn, harvest the big crops like wheat and corn, or round up a herd for market. But there was never really any question who was responsible, who "owned" the work. If a farmer misjudged, goofed around on the job, or was an innocent victim of nature's vicissitudes, his family went without food and shoes. It was that simple.

An industrial economy dilutes and diffuses the lines of responsibility. A boss, a manager, has been interposed between the work and the worker. The boss knows and creates the work that is supposed to be done. On a small family farm, in contrast, the farmer is accountable to the work itself. The work is the boss. There is no supervisor, no one to lay out the work, no one to give orders. You have to know and do it all or face the painful reality of failure alone. It's different on an automobile assembly line. The worker is accountable to a boss who supposedly knows and directs the work. The worker knows and does only a small piece of the total. Who's to blame if something goes wrong? Did the boss give the wrong instructions or did the worker fail to hear them correctly? It's usually easier to figure out who's boss than it is to figure out who's responsible. The industrialization of an economy introduces a subtle element of uncertainty. That element is the ownership of work. Who owns the job, mistakes, misfortunes, and all? It is not a small problem.

The Old Work Ethic Is Dying

Many of our social and economic problems today, from the homeless wandering through the streets of our cities to the destruction of our global environment, stem from our collective confusion about who's responsible for what. The old work ethic was very clear on this point: the individual is responsible. That ethic, it should be noted, was not created by business or for business. But businesspeople used it. Jobs were defined in terms of individual responsibility. That work ethic in all of its richness has changed. Work was redesigned by the industrial revolution. On the assembly line, for example, the manager was interposed between the individual and the work. For first-generation workers still guided by some variant of the work ethic all went well. For second and third generations it changed. Just as firms sought incorporation in order to limit personal liability, workers and citizens sought to limit their responsibility on the job. This ethic eventually infected society at large. It didn't claim everyone as its victim, fortunately, or infect each in the same way. Irving Berlin was one of the exceptions. He astonished the nation by saying that he loved to pay his taxes and instructed his accountant to be generous. Despite the exceptions like Irving Berlin, and there were many, the dominant ethic that surfaced with such viciousness in the 1980s especially was one of limited responsibility. "Take care of number 1." People who started out inspired to work hard were often discouraged by those who did not. Those who tried to be fair and honest were overwhelmed by those who didn't. We have now reached the point where everyone, from CEO to newly hired, needs some guidance from a work ethic that encourages or inspires them to be more responsible.

Who, then, is to be held accountable for success or failure in today's workplace? There are a couple of standard answers. Idealistically, both boss and worker, or everyone, really. That does not pinpoint responsibility, however. Practically speaking, the answer to who's responsible is, it depends. It depends on the people and the situation. It depends on what's at stake. It depends on what it costs in time or dollars to find the right answer. Oftentimes it's not clear. Lack of clarity has led corporations to spend billions of dollars on quality circles and total quality management programs to pin down responsibility and build up morale. This same need and challenge exist in the ethical sphere. Who's responsible for unethical behavior? Remember how often that question surfaced in the 1980s? Who is ultimately responsible for what happened at E. F. Hutton, Drexel Burnham Lambert, for example?

Responsibility Shared Is Responsibility Diluted

Shared responsibility introduces several elements of uncertainty for both bosses and subordinates. Suppose the boss delegates the work rather than assigns it. Discretionary authority to complete that piece of work is passed along too. Subordinates accept the responsibility and complete the work. However, the workers, having been delegated discretionary authority, do it their way. They might finish it late, with apparent good reason, for instance. Or they might use a questionable method. Let's say it's legal but unethical in the eyes of the boss. Who's responsible? Should the boss have anticipated and prohibited the method in question? Or should the worker have known better without being told? This pattern of uncertainty in ethical matters accounts for a large portion of the so-called corporate crimes in recent decades. There is so much more to anticipate and prohibit. Ethical uncertainty is at an all-time high.

There are many faces of uncertainty. Workers assigned to menial tasks face a sense of uncertainty about the relative urgency or importance of what they do. If the job doesn't require the full range of their capabilities, they may question their own importance. Unemployment is a permanent feature of a capitalist economy. A small percentage of the work force is not needed at all. For these and similar reasons, it's all too easy for individuals to become insulated or divorced from questions of responsibility. If the economic system gives individuals the message that they are marginal, only partially needed or needed only part of the time, they are less likely to feel a strong sense of responsibility for their actions. Now comes the big question: Who's fundamentally responsible for this diminishing sense of responsibility in the workplace? The boss or the worker? The corporation or the individual? Let's look at these questions from an employer's point of view.

Large corporations, particularly, have demonstrated an amazing willingness and ability to accept responsibility for the performance of their workers. Formally, corporate efforts to train and develop the kind of workers they need started at the turn of the century with Frederick Taylor's scientific management. Corporate history of funding training programs and business schools is well documented. Corporations have spent billions and billions of dollars in this century. They have trained workers. They have developed managers. They have educated executives. They have educated potential employees. They have accepted an incredible amount of responsibility for the work force, ranging from the unskilled to the disgruntled or the unmotivated worker. To a degree it's been in the corporation's self-interest to do so. It increases profits. The scope of that self-interest has grown larger in recent decades. Corporations are now being pressed to assume even greater responsibility for the handicapped, victims of discrimination, drug addicts, AIDS carriers, and society generally. In the short term at least, these newer responsibilities do not increase profits. The financial justification for these diminished profits is long-term. Society will benefit. Corporations will thrive. The humanitarian justification is obvious. Corporations are wrestling with these accumulating responsibilities, each in their own way and in their own time. Critics say it's not enough or not fast enough. Nevertheless, hundreds of corporations have earned some praise for their achievements in these areas. The question facing society today in the aftermath of the seventies and eighties is who will accept responsibility for the work ethic itself. Who will address that obscure bundle of attitudes or expectations residing within the hearts and minds of white-collar and blue-collar worker alike? Will it be corporate management?

Business Needs to Take the Lead

It is certainly in the corporation's best interests to put this challenge at the top of its list of corporate responsibilities. There are six good reasons why corporate executives, rather than some other group, should take on the responsibility for developing a new work ethic for this new age.

1. Business is result-oriented. It sets realistic goals, regularly measures progress toward them, makes necessary adjustments. It keeps its visions and illusions well in hand. Business can do the most practical job.

2. Work consumes the largest percentage of our waking hours in life. It is the major contributor to our happiness and well-being, on and off the job. Efforts to enhance the quality of work life through a better ethic should start in the workplace.

3. In a pluralistic society, business is the one place where different cultures and personal values are forced to cooperate and compromise. It is the one place where a single and unifying ethic is essential.

4. Work has an intrinsic value. Aside from products and profits, work provides a pleasure of its own. That pleasure cannot be injected from the outside. It can be spotlighted and nurtured from the inside.

5. Business has the most to gain over the long term from a work ethic that enhances respect, increases profits, and reduces human suffering and humiliation at work.

6. A good work ethic will do more to forestall unethical behavior than a simple code of ethics. The strength of a code is punishment after the fact. The strength of a good work ethic is prevention before the fact.

Senior executives are best situated to bring about this new work ethic. The frontier for businesses in the new age is building a viable corporate work ethic. Let's explore how that might be done.

Defining the Work Ethic

The work ethic is a process of defining what employers and employees expect of each other. It is a process, as is business ethics generally. It is dynamic rather than static, changing rather than rigid. The work ethic is a bundle of expectations. These expectations are not articulated as clearly as job descriptions or job benefits. They are less tangible. The work ethic can be compared to a marriage. Job descriptions and job benefits are the equivalent of the marriage ceremony, the "I do" part. The full spectrum of expectations evolves in the subsequent days, weeks, years. Some wit remarked that marriage is the process of discovering what sort of husband his wife would have preferred. So it is in the workplace. Both employer and employee often discover over time what they really wanted in each other. Employees have their expectations of each other as well.

Work ethic expectations are virtually numberless. They vary with the firm and the individual. For instance, some workers need more praise than others. If they don't get it, they hunt for another job. Similarly, some workers carry the expectation that bosses should be fair in distributing praise, even though, again, it's not written into the work contract. If these workers are disappointed in their expectations, they may stay on the job but not work as hard. These latent expectations we carry of boss and colleagues typically surface when their absence gives rise to pain or discomfort. We can think of these vocational intangibles as bearing a marked resemblance to what marketing expert Theodore Levitt calls "intangible products and product intangibles."

> The most important thing to know about intangible products is that the *customers usually don't know what they're getting until they don't get it.*[1]

These less tangible qualities run the gamut from elusive values such as honesty and fairness to personal needs for power and self-esteem. They are as important to employees as safe and serviceable products are to customers.

This bundle of personal expectations constitutes a vital part of the work ethic. These intangible expectations require special handling. Warren Bennis noted a change more than a decade ago.

> [There is] an irreversible shift in our society from tradition-directed policies and practices to knowledge-based policies and from unconscious historical selection of viable patterns and forms of living to deliberate human choice, invention, and evaluation of such patterns and forms.[2]

Corporate managers, from personnel officers to CEOs, will need to have a solid understanding of the psychological and sociological factors which shape latent employee expectations. Proper management of expectations not only determines employee satisfaction, it is a key element in fostering good ethics. Employee expectations that are handled badly will create some very costly ethical problems. The cost of these failures to business is mounting. The need to create a work climate conducive to good ethics and employee satisfaction has never been greater. A new work ethic is needed. Constituents inside and outside the workplace are demanding management action. There are some misapprehensions about human behavior that need to be addressed.

Unethical Behavior Is No Accident.   Human behavior is caused. This statement is not intended to assert an observable fact. It is presented as a prerequisite attitude for managers of people. Unethical behavior has an explanation if we can find it. Managers can often find the subtle incentives to unethical behavior and remove them. The best way is to build incentives for ethical behavior. We may not be able to find the cause or inducement for some behavior. We may not be able to change either the causes or the people motivated by them. Believing that behavior is caused, however, starts us off on the right foot in remedying causes of unethical behavior.

The Rule of the Hammer.   This rule states that when you give a small child a hammer, everything looks like a nail. Managers have a lot of sophisticated tools for measuring the business side of enterprise these days: linear programming, exponential smoothing, macroeconomic computer models, decision trees, multiple regressions, market pretesting, what-if economic forecasting. Our burgeoning business schools are enormously skillful at teaching young MBAs to use these tools. They dump approximately 70,000 newly taught practitioners on the market each year. Those skills are extremely seductive. You indeed learn how to "crunch your numbers" but little or nothing about the overriding purpose which they are to serve. There are not enough tools to measure the ethical side of enterprise. Measuring something makes it important even if it wasn't before. In the army the saying goes "don't expect what you don't inspect." The corporate equivalent is, "what the boss watches well gets done well." The same principle applies to the ethical side of enterprise. It only becomes important if and when it's measured. A firm cannot simply pay lip service to either the financial or the ethical bottom line and expect to survive. We need new tools to measure what's ethical in the workplace and to satisfy the growing expectations of business constituents.

Building a New Work Ethic

Four Critical Ingredients

There are four areas where expectations are particularly acute. The configuration of these key expectations tends to determine whether the human relationships at work will thrive, merely survive, or die altogether. These areas will be labeled *ingredients* of an ethical corporate climate inasmuch as each makes a major contribution to an acceptable mix. These ingredients are *predictability, control, shared values,* and *self-esteem.* (See Figure 7-1.) Note that within each ingredient the pendulum of satisfaction swings from one extreme to another. Less predictability moves the work ethic toward chaos. More control from management pushes the pendulum toward slavery. These polarities represent the balances struck by employers and employees in the design of work and the informal culture which grows out of the design. All four ingredients interact with each other. Greater control by management, for example, also increases the predictability of employees, at least formally.

PREDICTABILITY	CONTROL
Chaos - - - - - - - - Boredom	Anarchy - - - - - - - - Slavery
SHARED VALUES	SELF ESTEEM
Pluralism - - - - - - - - Tribalism	Despair - - - - - - - - Conceit

Figure 7-1. Four critical ingredients for an ethical corporate environment.

The boxes as presented in the figure are all the same size. In real life their size, or their relative importance, varies. Companies in which shared values are a large factor, for example, may use less of one or more of the other three ingredients. Predictability and control will be less problematic. Self-esteem will be achieved through value sharing. In a world of ethical relativity these ingredients can serve as checkpoints in the search for the kind of employer and employee satisfaction which builds a good work ethic and good ethics into the enterprise.

Successful work relationships are distinguished by a proper mixture of the four key ingredients. A viable work setting must mix these four ingredients to the mutual satisfaction of those involved. The precise mixture of those ingredients, whatever it is, determines the depth and breadth of satisfaction that each participant experiences. For example, mutual respect is a quality usually cherished by both boss and worker. (Self-esteem.) How that respect is communicated in words, deeds, and nonverbal messages varies according to person, company, and nation or cultural tradition. How much respect each individual or company requires determines where it falls on the despair-conceit scale. Take a couple more quick examples. Are you a stickler for rules? (Predictability.) Are you the kind of boss who feels a need to watch employees closely? Are you the kind of worker who feels intimidated by close supervision? (Control.) How easily is your sense of fairness awakened by salary differentials, overtime work, other employees who are habitually late? Are you happier working with people who think the way you do, share the same interests and hobbies? (Shared values.)

The principle underlying use of these four ingredients is that all social relationships, whether involving two persons or many, whether at home or at work, can be distinguished by the particular mix of each. At work, for example, the boss needs *predictable* employees who show up on time, do their work, and leave as expected. The boss needs to be able to *control* employee behavior during this interval to some extent. Work is facilitated, furthermore, when boss and workers share core *values* (e.g., family, philosophy). Finally, the boss is rewarded with an enhanced sense of *self-esteem* when the work assigned is completed. Workers have these same needs in corresponding fashion. It's a two-way street.

Employees and work situations will vary considerably, of course. Some people have a high tolerance for ambiguity. Their predictability need, therefore, is low. The relationship among a group of like-minded people may approach chaos, but they still finish their work. Computer software programmers fit this category. The nature of the work attracts technicians with a high tolerance for ambiguity in the work ethic because the work itself has no tolerance for ambiguity. So it goes with each of the four ingredients. The "right" mix will be determined by the participants, each vying for their own interests. The relationship between employees and employers will thrive or decay on the basis of how much satisfaction both achieve. A high degree of dissatisfaction with regard to any one of the four ingredients may lead to severance of the relationship, if that option is available. An employee who falls outside the acceptable limits of predictability or controllability is likely to be fired. A boss who exerts excessive control or abuses employee self-esteem will likely lose those workers to other employers. Mismanaging any of these four key ingredients opens the door to a variety of undesirable consequences: employees will leave; one or more may blow the whistle; work becomes inefficient; unethical behavior becomes rampant. Again, managing the ingredients well creates an ethical corporate climate.

The Protestant work ethic was distinguished by a high degree of predictability from all parties. The bureaucratic model outlined by Max Weber evokes an aura of monotonous repetition of tasks approaching boredom. Control was one-sided; the boss had it all. We can infer that the degree of shared values was also high, approaching tribal conformity. This ingredient eventually spawned the WASP acronym — white Angle-Saxon Protestant. Self-esteem, on a group basis, bordered on conceit. God had destined WASPs to succeed. On an individual basis, self-esteem was satisfied by "bettering yourself" in comparison with your background or others less fortunate than yourself. It was not acceptable for "true believers" to challenge their position in life. The challenge came from nonbelievers.

Challenges to the Protestant work ethic grew slowly and steadily. Henry Ford's automotive assembly line, for example, gathered workers who did not share the same language, let alone values. As novelty paled, the monotony of the assembly line forced workers to collect their self-esteem in the paycheck. The total control by the boss was eventually challenged by labor unions. Uncertainty now characterized the workplace. A new work ethic was emerging.

The new work ethic developed without benefit of a master plan or a master builder. Organized religion played a less dominant role. Money and the marketplace were critical arbitrators: Could you make a profit? Could you get agreement from the relevant parties (with the help of a lawyer)? The result was a high degree of ambiguity, uncertainty, and change in the workplace. This is the situation today. Executives and managers at every corporate level are constantly troubleshooting issues that trace their roots to these four ingredients. Society itself is victimized by unethical behavior, ranging from bait-and-switch advertising to major fraud at the highest management levels. These are the by-products of the prevailing ambiguity, uncertainty, and change in the work ethic.

Executives and managers face a dilemma. They can sit around and wait for a miracle or a corporate messiah. Or they can take action themselves. Specifically, they can assume increased responsibility for the work ethic. Fortunately, some business leaders and corporations are already taking action. Let's look at each of these four ingredients more closely and link each with some corporate examples.

Key Ingredient 1: Predictability

Employee and employer need to know what to expect of each other. Van Maanen asserts that "People will not accept uncertainty. Regardless of how rich or poor the material at hand, people will make an effort to structure, interpret, and define the magnificently commonplace world of their experience."[3] If the company doesn't provide some clear direction, the workers will create their own, which they will do to some extent anyway. Throughout this century, the major goal of professional managers, aided by business schools, has been to reduce uncertainty, or manage risk, whichever emphasis you prefer. Managers developed some sophisticated tools in the process. Only now, at the end of the century, are we clearly seeing the need for tools which serve the ethical needs of corporations and society.

Corporate management may accept high levels of uncertainty in the marketplace, but they like certainty on the job. The tedious time card and storied work breakdown structure created abundant predictability on assembly-line jobs. They eliminated a lot of guesswork as to who did what and when. Little was left to chance. Rules built up around rules, some formal, some informal. Formal predictability needs were satisfied through negotiated compromise. Control needs between management and labor were regularly contested, never fully resolved by contract. There were always questions of interpretations, exceptions to the rules, and eventual negotiation of new contracts. Self-esteem was always problematic, catch as catch can. A strike by employees pushes the pendulum toward chaos. Once the strike is settled, however, the pendulum swings back toward boredom.

Chaos in the workplace is not determined solely by the nature of the work, however. When workers can't stand the boredom of their jobs, some may deliberately look for ways to break up the monotony. Their methods range from the silly to the serious, from practical jokes to wildcat strikes. In other words, managers have to attend to personal as well as group needs.

These changes in the work ethic are more than cosmetic because the nature of work itself is changing. More than 50 percent of our work force in the United States is now employed by the service sector rather than manufacturing. John Naisbitt argues that information is now the world's most valuable raw material.[4] Peter Drucker characterizes the knowledge worker as an employee who requires different handling. Expectations about work are changing: more people are seeking pleasure and fulfillment in their jobs. Attitudes toward authority are changing: subordinates insist that the boss must have more experience and knowledge, not just a higher position on the organization chart. The work itself is changing: it is less routine and predictable. Knowledge workers and service personnel cannot be so closely supervised. They also need more discretionary authority. This means their behavior will be less predictable when dilemmas surface. Management needs to instill a work ethic that provides some guidance for handling unanticipated events. Some young corporations have discovered this the hard way.

Working for the Fun of It at Lotus. Mitch Kapor had had some experience managing knowledge workers—the computer software programmer. He was one before he founded the Lotus Development Company in Cambridge, Massachusetts, in 1983. His background also included some time as a Transcendental Meditation instructor. He sounded like an evangelist as he prophesied "new world" developments in computer technology from "a small band setting out on a great adventure." According to an interview in *PC World,* Kapor proclaimed that his primary goal was to create a playful work atmosphere.

> ..."You have to have people who are happy."...it is the intangibles—trust, self-respect, feeling useful and appreciated—that keep people going and motivated to stretch to their limits. Creating an atmosphere that promotes individual well-being is a priority at Lotus. Achieving this starts with a humanistic code of ethics. "Fairness and openness should characterize how people deal with each other, regardless of where they are in the organization or how long they've been here."[5]

The *User's Guide to Lotus* recommends that employees cultivate a sense of humor and "not take themselves too seriously, as they may be the only ones that do so."

There were no time cards to punch at Lotus in the early days. Employee predictability was sacrificed to shared values and self-esteem. Employees enjoyed unlimited freedom. Working hours were irregular. Many had their own keys to the offices and worked when they felt "inspired." While the experiment was not entirely successful—it didn't last—it represents a significant effort to instill a new work ethic based on the requirements of the task and the needs of the workers. When Mitch Kapor resigned his management responsibilities and left the com-

pany entirely, many of his devoted followers described their feelings as
the grief that accompanies the death of a loved one.

Everybody Was a Manager at People Express.   Founder Donald Burr
was considered a motivational genius. Deregulation changed the airline
business by opening it up to many new start-up companies. People Express was one of them. Few anticipated the changes Burr introduced.
His management style was unique. Employees were called managers, no
matter how insignificant their assignment. Productivity, job satisfaction,
and initial customer enthusiasm reached new highs for an airline company. Every employee became a shareholder with stock value which
grew in most cases to equal one's annual salary in less than four years.
His achievement was remarkable, considering the kind of change he introduced. Employees didn't own the company but they owned the work,
which turned out to be the most critical determinant. Burr's experiment, like Kapor's at Lotus, did not last. People Express was bought out
by Frank Lorenzo as part of his Texas Air empire. Nevertheless, Burr's
effort elicited a new work ethic from his employees. It was long on
shared values and self-esteem. It was low on predictability and control
for top management. Employees had the lion's share of everything.

It would be wrong to imply the People Express failed because of its
work ethic. It is true, however, that its work ethic stood in stark contrast
to the industry generally. The airlines have traditionally been headed by
autocratic and adventurous CEOs. Not surprising. Their founders were
pilots, captains of the air. Some had been war heroes or barnstormers.
But even as professional managers took over, a strong, authoritarian
management style remained. Donald Burr challenged this deeply ingrained pattern. He succeeded over the short run, in part, by hiring
people new to the industry who were free from the fetters of tradition.
Their inexperience may have been the source of their demise, an inability to manage the bottom financial line. While People Express failed to
convert the rest of the industry to its management style and work ethic,
it solidified the conviction in many young managers that work could be
exciting when the sense of purpose and team spirit was strong.

This is other evidence that a new work ethic is emerging in America.
Xerox won the coveted Baldridge award for service quality in 1990 by
using the team concept. Employees carry more sophisticated expectations into the workplace today. As Herzberg noted in a salient *Harvard
Business Review* article, insufficient monetary rewards may drive employees away but money alone will not keep them on the job.[6] These
younger workers, enjoying the fruits of affluence, do not place corporate loyalty or job security as a top priority. They change jobs fre-
quently. They are looking for contentment rather than compensation,

deeper satisfaction in the present rather than a broader commitment in the future.

Both bosses and subordinates strive for some level of predictability about their work and the web of human relationships surrounding it. But where the pendulum eventually tends to rest and how far it swings will vary, depending on the people and the work. If work on the assembly line is characterized by high degrees of predictability, computer software programming, public relations, advertising, and medical research are at the other extreme. Working in these latter jobs calls for high thresholds of ambiguity all around. The right balance will be determined by employer and employees, either by management fiat and employee acquiescence or management-employee negotiation.

Key Ingredient 2: Control

Employers and employees will strike some sort of balance of power in their relationship. Employers understandably seek to maintain the formal upper hand. They believe that management's role is to give orders, direct the work. Employees will seek to control issues that are important to them. Sometimes control itself is an issue because exercising it affects self-esteem. Some employees are sensitive to whether work is delegated rather than merely assigned, whether supervision is close, how much discretionary authority goes with a given task, if any. The mix in this ingredient varies from industry to industry, among organizational levels, and from person to person. The conceptual extremes range from anarchy to slavery, or from anything goes to virtual bondage. In Figure 7-1, control is above self-esteem. If management expands its control downward, it may impinge upon the respect and dignity required by subordinates. Subordinates may push back, forcing a realignment of control factors. It is a dynamic process, always in flux and subject to greater change in recent decades. The changing status of minorities and women is reflected in this ingredient. The scope of change is even larger than that, however.

Frederick Herzberg presented convincing evidence of evolution in the work ethic by comparing and contrasting the changing nature of employee needs and values over a span of four shortened generations.[7] (See Table 7-1.) He made no explicit effort to tie these new needs and values to the changing nature of work. Instead, he selected 20 characteristics which trace escalating employee expectations in each generation. While there are many stimulating comparisons and contrasts in Herzberg's chart, two are especially noteworthy in the present context. First, these changing expectations have been occurring rapidly in the latter half of the twentieth century. Every decade since World War II

Table 7-1. Manifest Needs and Values

External immigrants (before World War II)	"Organization man" immigrants (1950s)	Internal immigrants (1960s)	Confused mixture (1970s)
1. Outside the social and organizational system	1. Created system	1. Lived in kitchens of the system	1. Captives of larger conglomerate and multinational "organization man" system
2. Accepted American myths	2. Expanded on myths	2. Saw weaknesses in myths	2. Confused about myths
3. Models were people of competence	3. Models were appurtenances of offices	3. Models were ideologists	3. Confused about models
4. Worked to gain rights and privileges	4. Gobbled up rights and privileges	4. Demanded stolen rights and privileges	4. Feel cheated
5. Time at work taken up with work	5. Time at work taken up with "looking good"	5. Time taken up with protest	5. Time taken up with special interests
6. Work perceived as directly related to technology	6. Work perceived as related to efficient organizations	6. Work perceived as related to society	6. Work perceived as indirectly related to technology, organizations, and society
7. Jacks-of-all-trades	7. Narrow occupational specialists	7. Deficient capabilities	7. Obsolete talents
8. Required monotonous jobs	8. Required experience rotation	8. Required remedial help	8. Require continuing education
9. Suffered physical pain in dark satanic mills and offices	9. Suffered social pain in bright satanic factories and offices	9. Suffered psychological pain at home and in all social institutions	9. Suffer existential pain from lost surroundings
10. Central meaning of work: career	10. Central meaning of work: career	10. Central meaning of work: personal significance	10. Central meaning of work: security
11. Life values already determined (tradition)	11. Life values multi-other-directed (no personal values)	11. Life values innovated (attempt at clarification)	11. Life values confused (externals of tradition)
12. Preached individualism but practiced collectivism	12. Didn't preach	12. Preached collectivism but practiced individualism	12. Confused preaching
13. Thrift-oriented	13. Growth would take care of debt	13. Debt-oriented	13. Confusion-oriented
14. Past-future-oriented	14. Future-oriented	14. Now-oriented	14. Time disorientation
15. Self-blame	15. No blame	15. Projected blame	15. Vacillating blame
16. Public expression of feelings: repressed	16. Public expression of feelings: abstract	16. Public expression of feelings: concrete	16. Public expression of feelings: cynical
17. Personal morality confused with ethics	17. Organizational morality confused with personal ethics	17. Morality distinguished from ethics	17. Morality confused with ethics
18. Believed in inequality	18. Believed in one-upmanship	18. Believed in automatic equality	18. Believe in injustice of equality
19. Believed in a hierarchy within organizations	19. Believed in open hierarchy of organization	19. Believed in participative organizations	19. Have lost trust in organizations
20. Believed in service to family and ethic groups	20. Believed in service to employer	20. Believed in service to social justice	20. Have lost belief in service

SOURCE: Frederick Herzberg, "Herzberg on Motivation for the '80s: Piecing Together Generations of Values," *Industry Week*, Oct. 1, 1979.

has ushered in a new set. Second, Herzberg sees a steep decline in ethical sensitivities in the generation in the 1970s (see item 17). He dubs members of this generation a "confused mixture." They have little sense of historical time — no past, present, or future (item 14). It's almost as if they exist in a social vacuum. Those with a weaker sense of the past and the future have fewer incentives to act ethically in the present. You might say they have nothing to live up to, nothing to look forward to, so it's eat, drink, and make merry. They may eventually be those with much to live down. On control issues, they would be content with anarchy. They know how to survive, to take care of themselves, but not how to build or nurture a system. If this sort of reasoning bears any resemblance to reality, the explanations for corporate ethical indifference are all there. Actually, ethical indifference is everywhere. The scandals on Wall Street and the financial institutions probably attract the most attention because they involve the most money.

Herzberg's chart further suggests that early twentieth-century workers (before World War II) had a higher tolerance for inequality and organizational hierarchy (items 19 and 20). Organized labor was once the symbol of a power struggle in the workplace. Even in those earlier days, however, labor accepted a measure of inequality and the inevitability of a hierarchy. In fact, they built their own. That has changed. Today, what often appears to be a personality clash between a 55-year-old traditionalist and a 35-year-old fast-tracker is in reality an intergenerational power struggle. Control over work and the associated sense of worth each person derives from it are related. Control issues are central and eternal to human relationships. Power struggles in the workplace today are no less intense. They are only more subtle. Some are more interesting.

Every Worker's a Stockholder.   Four thousand employees (of a total twelve thousand) purchased the Chicago & Northwestern railroad in 1972. Service to customers improved immediately and dramatically, quickly followed by increased productivity and financial strength. Within a decade your investment would have increased 10 times! This dramatic change in the work ethic underscores the importance of control factors. What must the work ethic have been like before the employee takeover? Employees claimed that management was rigid and uncaring. Management claimed the unions were power-hungry and the employees were lazy. Neither party was willing to accept control conditions the other brought to the workplace. Some of these conditions, of course, were measurable and monetary: productivity, salaries, profits. Others were more difficult to measure and resolve, such as self-esteem, the distribution of power and profits, the purpose of work. These less tangible considerations are becoming paramount in the workplace today. The Chicago & Northwestern railroad is one instance where the employees successfully assumed full control. Almost overnight, employees changed their attitudes about work. Control issues are important. One way or another, employees need to experience ownership of their work. Ownership of the company itself is no guarantee that this critical bonding will occur. Nor is it always necessary.

Fortune touted a work team at a General Mills plant in California where the sense of ownership was so strong the workers didn't need a manager. *Fortune* calls them "superteams" and suggests that they are the wave of the future, even though their numbers are still low. Employees testified they worked harder, took more responsibility, and were more productive, 40 percent more productive, at Lodi, California.[8]

Quality circles represent a similar innovation in the work ethic. They utilize the team concept to increase sensitivity inward to the role of other members of the team and sensitivity outward to customer needs. Management delegates control to the team. The team becomes responsible. They learn to care about other members on the team as well as the customer. Employee competition is converted to employer cooperation. Individual expectations are fulfilled by the circle's success. Everyone benefits. A sound work ethic does not have to coerce ethical behavior with a legalistic code. It inspires it with a clear and strong sense of purpose.

Resolution of Control Issues. Unresolved control issues can create tragic incidents with dire ethical consequences. One of the most dramatic occurred at the Union Carbide plant in Bhopal, India. It was never clear who was responsible for this disastrous pesticide spill, resulting in thousands dead and thousands more permanently disabled. Control was divided about equally among managers at the plant, executives at Union Carbide headquarters in the United States, and officials of the Indian government. There was more to this case than was stressed in the mass media. The plant was a joint venture of Union Carbide of America and Union Carbide of India. Ownership was split 51-49. Union Carbide of America was fighting a hostile takeover. Senior management had control issues of its own at home. Plant managers in Bhopal faced a recession, increased competition in the pesticide market, impoverished farmers unable to pay for the product, an Indian government unable to provide the leadership and subsidies the plant and farmers both needed. Finally, there was an unsubstantiated rumor that the accident was an act of sabotage by a disgruntled manager. To this day it is not clear who was specifically responsible *for* the accident. The courts merely settled who was responsible *after* the accident. Union Carbide of America has never publicized the full cost of this tragedy to employees and stockholders. Respect for the dead and the incurably disabled in India preclude such an announcement. Nevertheless, that cost is part of the legacy of mishandling control issues.

Control issues in cross-culture joint ventures are very complex. The number of constituents to consider doubles. Legal and ethical questions are equally numerous. Executive must devote even greater portions of time and money to their resolution if they wish to avoid undesirable or unethical consequences. Resolving control issues to the satisfaction of all relevant constituents and ensuring ethical soundness as well is a huge challenge in any marketplace, domestic or international.

Key Ingredient 3: Shared Values

Note in Figure 7-1 that the value polarities swing from pluralistic to tribal, from a work climate that permits or encourages differences to one that demands total conformity.

The image of tribal culture evokes an integrated sharing of values. Such a culture was harmonious because dissident behavior was suppressed or absorbed. Survival dictated conformity. The tribe was threatened if you failed to show proper respect for your parents or your elders. A loyal tribal member repressed such feelings. Social deviation was severely limited. Deviants were immediately disciplined if not ostracized. There is an appealing wholeness and simplicity to tribal culture, nevertheless. (See Figure 7-2.) Personal values, work values, and social

Figure 7-2. A harmonious culture.

values are neatly nestled in harmonious symmetry.

Employers and employees who hold many values in common reduce the sources of potential conflict, personal dissatisfaction, and production inefficiency. When basic values conflict, communication, camaraderie, and teamwork suffer. Personal values are deeply rooted and not easily changed. Corporate values have typically devolved from those of the founders or their successors and are interwoven with a company's goals and methods. In mature corporations, especially, corporate values are not easily changed. Value conflicts are extremely difficult to resolve; witness the number of corporate mergers and acquisitions that report unproductive degrees of incompatibility. Value conflicts between brokerage firm Kidder Peabody and industrial conglomerate General Electric were often cited in the press in the aftermath of GE's takeover. Similar stories emerged when General Motors bought out H. Ross Perot at EDS (Electronic Data Systems). Shearson-Lehman experienced tensions over corporate values with parent American Express. These mergers and buyouts were occurring, moreover, as society was undergoing *Future Shock,* according to Alvin Toffler.

> Value turnover is now faster than ever before in history. While in the past a man growing up in a society could expect that its public value system would remain largely unchanged in his lifetime, no such assumption is warranted today....We are witnessing the crackup of consensus.[9]

Employees' Needs and Values Are Changing.   Study Herzberg's chart again (Table 7-1). Item 17 in the right-hand column suggests that those building their careers on Wall Street in the 1970s and 1980s did indeed confuse morality with ethics. It would be reassuring to believe that they were only confused rather than clever, conniving crooks. It's easy to see that Herzberg's ethically "confused mixture" played a dominant role throughout the 1980s, contributing to what *The New York Times* called "the dirty decade."[10] Wall Street, the big banks, and lesser-known savings and loan institutions were the scenes of incredibly lax management and unbridled personal greed. Many critics were quick to blame this sad state on ill-conceived government deregulation. It can be blamed as easily on the preceding decades of debilitating government regulation that protected executives from full exposure to competitive markets. Whichever explanation you prefer, two developments are now uncontested. First, the unethical behavior and crimes of the last dozen years have been perpetrated by those in positions of highest trust and responsibility. They have had access to billions and billions of private and public monies. Second, the men and women were confused. They never revealed in public any real comprehension of the magnitude of their sins. It's not that their confessions—when they were made in public—were hollow or insincere. Their perspective was so limited. It was personal. They viewed their behavior as an excusable moral lapse. As Herzberg implies, they didn't understand the difference between private morals and public ethics.

Why do we have an ethically confused mixture in society today? One way of putting it is that they have been ethically deregulated. Our culture has encouraged pluralism, many values. It has encouraged individual differences, along with community respect and acceptance of those differences. That's not all bad. It's the democratic way. Still, little wonder that we have spawned a great number of individualists who are forever pushing back the ethical frontiers, always testing, always probing the soft underbelly of society. Toffler said it very well. "We are witnessing the crackup of consensus." While the consequences may present new challenges to managers, we should acknowledge that society's intentions were the best. Those intentions, or motives, ranged from an innate confidence in personal freedom to a belief that human beings are basically good. Trust them. Society did.

Management has been struggling with the challenges of pluralism for a long time. This is not a recent development. One of management's early experiments was the company town. It resembled a feudal village. Companies literally owned the town—the homes, the stores, and the places of amusement or pleasure. It shaped the lifestyles of employees as well as economic factors for citizens not on its payroll. Companies even tried to capture the souls of their employees, according to Liston Pope.[11] Management's goal was a harmonious blending of personal, corporate, and societal values. Neither the individual nor the corporation subscribed to values that were not shared by society generally. Some persons or corporations may have been off center, either left or right, but they still remained within society's circle of acceptability. In the nineteenth century, socioeconomic experiments such as the self-contained community of New Harmony, Indiana, sought to create their own versions of a harmonious culture. They were a culture within a culture. Most of these were not successful in the long run. The Amish communities are an exception, explained in part by their religious roots. The point to note here is that control is achieved through shared values.

A more subtle form of employee domination, the "organization man"—documented by William H. Whyte, Jr.,[12] and dramatized by Sloan Wilson[13]—is described in the second column from the left in Table 7-1. While that phenomenon has not disappeared, it is more disparaged than glamorized as the new century approaches. Some business schools offer courses which teach young MBAs how to avoid corporate brainwashing. A typical contemporary configuration is shown in Figure 7-3. Employees share some values with the company and society, but deviation is becoming the rule rather than the exception. The circles are dynamic rather than static. Each corporation—or even work team—can reposition the circles to reflect the degree of value overlap between them.

The contemporary configuration helps explain the so-called double or even triple standard phenomenon. There is indeed one ethic for the office, another for home, maybe a third for society. Albert Z. Carr addressed this issue in a *Harvard Business Review* article provocatively entitled "Is Business Bluffing Ethical?"[14] Carr neither condoned nor condemned business bluffing. He simply pointed out that the double standard exists. Letters in response to the article indicated that readers were distressed with any implied acceptance of a double standard, one for work, one for home. The distress suggests that many business people are blithely unaware of the pluralistic nature of American culture and its roots in history.

There's a Double Standard in Business.   The double standard has been around a long time. Both the ancient Egyptians and Hebrews had laws requiring fair treatment of the foreigner or alien, but it was not the same respect accorded one of their own. Mercantilism got its bad name because it openly exploited other nations. "Trade imbalance" is today's

Figure 7-3. A contemporary culture.

euphemism for mercantilism. Ethical standards do vary, from company to company, industry to industry, nation to nation. This complicates the manager's task. The alternative would be tribal conformity, a genie that can't be put back in the bottle.

Every employer today needs to identify and articulate that peculiar set of core values that employees must share on the job if the work is going to get done and the product or service marketed successfully in an increasingly competitive world, and if employees are to feel ethically comfortable about their work. Corporations who fail to understand this need get trapped in ethical dilemmas. Furthermore, managers can expect that the ethical standards ascribed to by some employees might be measurably "higher" than the company's. In that case you have a potential whistle-blower. The ethical aspirations of other employees might be exceedingly "lower" than company standards. In that case you have the potential for unethical behavior or even crime. The constellation of key values that absolutely must be shared by all employees needs to be clearly articulated.

Total conformity is neither necessary nor desirable, let alone probable. Harvard sociologist David Riesman coined a phrase to describe effective cooperation in a pluralistic society. He calls it *procedural consensus.*

> I believe it to be a fallacy to assume that people can cooperate only if they understand each other, or if they like each other, or if they share certain preconceptions. The glory of modern, large scale democratically-tended society is that it allows us to put forward in a given situation only part of ourselves.[15]

From a strictly practical perspective the "part of ourselves" we put forward at work in the form of shared values is critical to all parties. Again, it is in management's best interests to raise the issue and clear the record on values.

Key Ingredient 4: Self-Esteem

Few qualities are more elusive than self-esteem. It's impossible to measure objectively. It's a personal feeling, rising and falling in response to events and experiences. It is inconstant. In the context of the four critical ingredients, self-esteem is a subjective evaluation arising from either a single incident or an accumulation of events that provides individuals with some indication of their relative worth in the workplace. That sense of worth is neither absolute nor only monetary, although for some people the link between their self-esteem and money is quite strong. The polarities in this ingredient of an ethical work culture swing from despair to conceit, from unjustifiably low self-esteem to unjustifiably high.

Self-esteem is the most personal of the four ingredients. Many individuals reveal very little of what they really feel about work. Silence is easily misread. Chester I. Barnard noted as long ago as 1938 that the entire person comes to work even though the corporation hires them only for certain skills or activities.[16] In short, managers are compelled to see their employees as human beings rather than simply a bundle of skills. Proper attention to the self-esteem ingredient can determine whether those skills are efficiently utilized. Employees who feel good about themselves usually contribute more to their work.

Self-esteem is an intriguing ingredient. Individuals vary considerably in their need for self-esteem. Some need constant praise. Others are suspicious of a compliment. Some like their self-esteem fed privately rather than publicly, or vice versa. Despite such individual differences, self-esteem has a single reference point in the workplace, namely, the threshold of alienation. Employees can work without praise. However, few will accept constant criticism. Workers may be tolerant of a boss who contributes little or nothing to their sense of self-worth. But these same workers will quit, or at least want to quit, when work or the boss pushes them past that threshold of alienation. To an amazing degree, employees themselves will find food for a hungry self-esteem. Ideally, managers need to be aware of the threshold of alienation for every employee. If they push beyond it, employees may rebel, give less than they are capable, leave for another job, or engage in unethical behavior. Employees may stay with a job that does little for their self-esteem. They are sure to leave the job if their threshold of alienation is continually violated.

The Threshold of Alienation Has Many Faces.   Many managers already appreciate this phenomenon. Some respond more or less intuitively to it. Thomas Peters noticed in his research of companies searching for excellence that the most effective managers communicated a strong sense of personal worth to each employee. They accomplished this simply by abandoning their desks and paperwork and circulating among their workers. Peters called it "managing by walking around," or MBWA.[17] He took special note of managers who could communicate warmth and enthusiasm up and down the corporate ladder, conquering the alienation often created by rank. These managers pushed their companies to the peak of excellence. MBWA is a form of preventive medicine. It is an antidote which takes many shapes.

Tara Vanderveer, who coached Stanford University's women's basketball team to a national championship in 1990, developed her own way of managing alienation. Every team has its star performers, its varsity squad. How do you retain the enthusiasm and active participation of the second team? Vanderveer had an answer.

> Judge me on how well I relate to the last person on the bench. A good team is one in which everyone appreciates the contributions made by all members.[18]

For her, how the lowest-string team member responds serves as the ultimate measure of how the entire team will perform. Those who watched the finals on television that year were treated to an unusual sight when a Stanford team member went to the free throw line. Team members on the bench silently raised their arms in unison. The effect was electrifying. The fans were silenced, especially the first few times. The target, however, was not the fans. It was the team members themselves, all of them. This simple demonstration of support and solidarity by the nonparticipants on the bench gave everyone a role in and relationship to what was transpiring on the battlefield. Thoroughness in nurturing the participation of the least important individual helps create the super team that is stronger than any of its separate stars. One corporate executive has discovered this himself.

Third-Wave Managers at Apple Computer. John Sculley, CEO of Apple Computer, provides an unusually candid view of corporate dynamics in his book *Odyssey*.[19] Sculley was led to believe that Stephen Jobs, cofounder of Apple, ostensibly recruited him for his marketing skills. He was a very successful president at Pepsico and heir-apparent to the top job. Sculley writes that he was reluctant to leave the security and predictability of an established east coast firm. California was so far away. Traveling there seemed like a trip to a foreign country. As it turned out, Sculley's marketing skills were of secondary consideration. Apple had some serious problems. The entire work force suffered from one sort of alienation or another. Two divisions were competing viciously. There was a leadership vacuum. One cofounder had already departed. Apple Computer did not resemble a typical east coast firm on the threshold of success. Unusual measures seemed called for.

Sculley's book documents his personal transformation from a traditional, formal eastern manager to a low-profile, egalitarian team leader more in character with the Silicon Valley of California. Sculley puts his mind and heart on the line with a compelling tale of Jobs's ouster from Apple and the strengths and limitations of entrepreneurial geniuses like Steve Jobs. Sculley's story is not a primer on how and when to get rid of your founder and board chairman. Rather, it stimulates deep reflection on what the future might bring in management styles.

Sculley uses the phrase "third-wave" managers to reflect the difference in style. Study Table 7-2 carefully. Note particularly the transition to "networks," "individuals," "interdependencies," and "inspiration" in the third-wave column. Sculley insists that the new style is dictated by the speed and degree of change.

> Third wave companies are the emerging form, not only for high-tech companies, but for all institutions...the source of their strength lies in *change*.[20]

The marketplace is changing rapidly on a global scale. Old-style management is too slow, too inefficient, and too wasteful of human resources. Third-wave management unlocks the potential of each and every employee.

The Individual Is Accorded Greater Respect.   The radical new style of management reflects altered values. The shift in values is plainly visible. For instance, as an organizational style, the third-wave network is far more egalitarian than the second-wave hierarchy. The individual takes precedence over the institution. The team takes precedence over the individual. Sculley maintains that third-wave managers are willing to function as team leaders who are not necessarily the dominant voice at every meeting. The power relationship is altered, requiring less assertiveness from the boss and assumption of greater responsibility for outcomes by the subordinate. Respect for the

Table 7-2. Contrasting Management Paradigms

Characteristic	Second wave	Third wave
Organization	Hierarchy	Network
Output	Market share	Market creation
Focus	Institution	Individual
Style	Structured	Flexible
Source of strength	Stability	Change
Structure	Self-sufficiency	Interdependency
Culture	Traditional	Genetic code
Mission	Goals and strategic plans	Identity, direction, and values
Leadership	Dogmatic	Inspirational
Quality	Affordable best	No compromise
Expectations	Security	Personal growth
Status	Title and rank	Making a difference
Resource	Cash	Information
Advantage	Better sameness	Meaningful differences
Motivation	To complete	To build

SOURCE: John Sculley, *Odyssey: Pepsi to Apple,* Harper & Row, New York, 1987, p. 95.

individual is the key to these emerging new values. Like Peters and Vanderveer, Sculley averts the threshold of alienation with preventive measures. Feed everyone's self-esteem. Corporate survival today requires more creativity and initiative from employees, Sculley argues. Since the future will bring more change more rapidly, innovation becomes a neccssity. The key to innovation is respect for the individual, according to Sculley. He speculates, for example, that the reason the Soviet Union failed to experience a renaissance, the only developed country for which that's true, is a lack of respect for the individual. To be sure, in communist ideology sublimation of the individual was a matter of principle as well as practice. It appears that *glasnost* and *perestroika* will change this fundamental perspective. If so, it means that respect for the individual is rising through the entire world, from South Africa to the North Pole. Managing these rising expectations in the workplace alone represents an awesome challenge.

The managerial act of nurturing the self-esteem of members of the work force is hardly a new idea. Some managers have always taken this challenge seriously. What's new is the breadth and depth of this challenge. It's a key issue in this new age. To paraphrase Winston Churchill, never have so many expected so much from so few in so short a time. These are times of high expectations, some will say unreasonably high. Nevertheless, managing these expectations is the new ethical frontier.

Employees today are more aware of what they feel and more open about what they value. Managers must contend with both stronger and a greater variety of opinions among employees. It's no longer enough to check out people's feelings by simply talking with a couple of workers at the water cooler. Cooperation needs to be orchestrated through committees or task forces that alert everyone's attention and engage everyone's participation. Managers need to create two-way bridges of communication that can carry the heavy freight of deep feelings and value differences. This is the new ethic ascending in the workplace, that dominant time frame in everyone's life. Individualism has always been a distinguishing characteristic of life in America. Today there is new depth and breadth to its thrust. It's the spirit of capitalism and democracy in action. It's the unfolding realization of dreams which are centuries old. Our forebears risked and sacrificed to achieve these dreams. Indeed, some gave their very lives. Corporate constituents are demanding that managers sacrifice outdated attitudes and prerogatives that no longer serve the common good. Managers have an opportunity to lead the nation, indeed the world, toward greater fulfillment of those timeless dreams.

Summary

The theme of this book is the ethical side to enterprise. Business, like a sheet of paper, is a single entity with two sides. There is a financial side and an ethical side. Business decisions and performance can be evaluated from both perspectives. The financial side is usually measured in money. The ethical side is measured in people. What's ethical in business depends on which people become the focus of measuring, on the situation in which those people are analyzed, and on the long-term consequences of their actions. The book introduces an ethical algorithm to help decision makers sort through their GOALS, METHODS, and MOTIVES in order to avoid CONSEQUENCES that are unethical.

In this chapter the focus is on building an ethical climate or a work ethic that, much like preventive medicine, can satisfy all constituents and keep the corporation ethically healthy. The careful blending and balancing of four critical ingredients can help managers build a better work ethic. Those ingredients are a sense of predictability, a sense of control, a sharing of core values, and a growing sense of self-esteem. Every constituent from stockholder or stakeholder to lowliest employee looks for some measure of satisfaction in each of the four ingredients. Satisfying that multitude of expectations creates an ethical climate in which business will thrive.

Footnotes

1. Theodore Levitt, "Marketing Intangible Products and Product Intangibles," *Harvard Business Review*, vol. 59, no. 3, May–June 1981, p. 100.

2. Warren Bennis, *Changing Organizations*. McGraw-Hill, New York, 1966, p. 12.

3. John E. Van Maanen, "Experiencing Organization: Notes on the Meaning of Careers and Socialization," in J. E. Van Maanen, (ed.), *Organizational Careers: Some New Perspectives*, Wiley, New York, 1977, p. 15.

4. John Naisbitt, *Megatrends: Ten New Directions Transforming Our Lives*, Warner Books, New York, 1982.

5. Anita Micossi, "The Lotus Position," *PC World*, June 1984, p. 262.

6. Frederick Herzberg, "One More Time: How Do You Motivate Employees?" *Harvard Business Review*, vol. 46, no. 1, January–February 1968, p. 53.

7. Frederick Herzberg, "Herzberg on Motivation for the '80s: Piecing Together Generations of Values," *Industry Week*, Oct. 1, 1979, p. 58.

8. "Who Needs A Boss?" *Fortune*, May 7, 1990, p. 52.

9. Alvin Toffler, *Future Shock*, Random House, New York, 1970, p. 304.

10. Diana B. Henriques, "A Blue-Chip Name is Not Enough," *The New York Times*, Jan. 14, 1990, p. 15.

11. Liston Pope, *Millhand and Preachers: A Study of Gastonia*, Yale University Press, New Haven, 1942.

12. William H. Whyte, Jr., *The Organization Man*, Doubleday Anchor Books, Garden City, N.Y., 1957.

13. Sloan Wilson, *The Man in the Gray Flannel Suit*, Simon and Schuster, New York, 1955.

14. Albert Z. Carr, "Is Business Bluffing Ethical?" *Harvard Business Review*, vol. 46, no. 1, January–February 1968, p. 143.

15. David Riesman, "Values in Context," *The American Scholar*, vol. 22, no. 1, Winter 1952–1953.

16. Chester I. Barnard, *The Function of the Executive*, Harvard University Press, Cambridge, Mass., 1938.

17. Thomas Peters and Robert H. Waterman, Jr., *In Search of Excellence*, Warner, New York, 1982.

18. Donald Hill, "Directors Massage," *PD Currents*, vol. 2, no. 1, Fall 1989.

19. John Sculley, *Odyssey: Pepsi to Apple*, Harper & Row, New York, 1987.

20. Ibid., p. 92.

Index

About the Author

Verne E. Henderson is founder and president of Revehen
Consultants, which specializes in business ethics, consensus
development, conflict management, and career counseling.
He serves as a personal consultant to many major
corporations, and also teaches at the Arthur D. Little
Management Education Institute.